From Garvey to Marley

The History of African-American Religions Series

Florida A&M University, Tallahassee
Florida Atlantic University, Boca Raton
Florida Gulf Coast University, Ft. Myers
Florida International University, Miami
Florida State University, Tallahassee
University of Central Florida, Orlando
University of Florida, Gainesville
University of North Florida, Jacksonville
University of South Florida, Tampa
University of West Florida, Pensacola

The History of African-American Religions Series
Edited by Stephen W. Angell and Anthony B. Pinn

This series will further historical investigations into African religions in the Americas, encourage the development of new paradigms and methodologies, and explore cultural influences upon African-American religious institutions, including the roles of gender, race, leadership, regionalism, and folkways.

Laborers in the Vineyard of the Lord: The Beginnings of the AME Church in Florida, 1865–1895, by Larry Eugene Rivers and Canter Brown Jr. (2001)

Between Cross and Crescent: Christian and Muslim Perspectives on Malcolm and Martin, by Lewis V. Baldwin and Amiri YaSin Al-Hadid (2002)

The Quest for the Cuban Christ: A Historical Search, by Miguel A. De La Torre (2002)

For a Great and Grand Purpose: The Beginnings of the AME Church in Florida, 1864–1905, by Canter Brown Jr. and Larry Eugene Rivers (2004)

Afro-Cuban Religiosity, Revolution, and National Identity, by Christine Ayorinde (2004)

From Garvey to Marley: Rastafari Theology, by Noel Leo Erskine (2005)

Noel Leo Erskine

Foreword by Stephen W. Angell and Anthony B. Pinn, Series Editors

University Press of Florida
Gainesville
Tallahassee
Tampa
Boca Raton
Pensacola
Orlando
Miami
Jacksonville
Ft. Myers

From Garvey to Marley

Rastafari Theology

10 09 08 07 06 05   6 5 4 3 2 1

A record of cataloging-in-publication data is available from the Library
of Congress.
ISBN 0-8130-2807-8

The University Press of Florida is the scholarly publishing agency
for the State University System of Florida, comprising Florida A&M
University, Florida Atlantic University, Florida Gulf Coast University,
Florida International University, Florida State University, University
of Central Florida, University of Florida, University of North Florida,
University of South Florida, and University of West Florida.

University Press of Florida
15 Northwest 15th Street
Gainesville, FL 32611-2079
http://www.upf.com

For Nia, Kimani, and Naomi

Contents

}

Foreword

Numerous scholars have recognized the connections between cultural production and religious expression, and much of the attention to this link has involved an exploration of music and religion. Theologians such as James Cone, Cheryl Kirk Duggan, Jon Michael Spencer, and others have articulated the theological significance and implications of this link. What has been for the most part missing from this conversation, however—especially as scholars of African descent in North America have participated in it—is serious attention to this linkage between music and religiosity within the larger African Diaspora, particularly with regard to a form of musical expression that has had a tremendous impact on North American musical style and sensibilities—reggae. Consequently, we are pleased to offer, as part of our series, this book written by Noel Leo Erskine, one of the premier theologians of liberation within the context of the Caribbean, whose publications include *Decolonizing Theology: A Caribbean Perspective* (1998). In that text and in other projects, Erskine, using a theological framework secured during his studies at Union Theological Seminary, has explored the liberative elements and radical sensibilities of theological discourse within the Jamaican context. In this way, Erskine has broadened the scope of theological discourse related to the struggles of Africa's children. Yet there is more to be said. *From Garvey to Marley: Rastafari Theology* represents the logical extension of his earlier efforts. Recognizing the cultural significance of Rastafari and its musical child, reggae, Erskine reveals the theological sensibilities of struggle and liberation embedded in Rastafari and its contributions to global cultural life. His book enhances the work of liberation theology within the context of the African Diaspora by decentering the Christian church as the context for such discourse. Drawing on key scholarly materials, ethnographic work, and his personal narrative of growing up in Jamaica during the blooming of Rastafari, Erskine exposes readers to the history of Rastafari as a religious movement and to its central ritual and doctrinal components. He insightfully demonstrates the connections and points of disagreement between Rastafari and Christian forms such as the Native Baptists, arguing that Rastafari provides a uniquely creative liberative thrust. We believe readers will appreciate the manner in which Erskine gives needed attention to the successes associated with this religion and also its shortcomings, most notably the questionable positioning of women within the movement. His important study gives much-needed attention to the religious complexity of the African Diaspora that this series seeks to present. We are quite pleased to make it available to a wider audience.

Stephen W. Angell and Anthony B. Pinn
Series Editors

Preface

This book grew out of my earlier work, *Decolonizing Theology*, which places Jamaican ecclesiology in conversation with expressions of religion that are outside the church. I contend in that work that middle-class Jamaica turned its back on religious faiths such as Revivalism and Rastafarianism without any sense of the critical role they played in the formation of popular culture and Jamaican life. While Revivalism continues to survive in the religious context of Jamaica, Rastafarianism has become an international force due largely to the reggae rhythms developed and popularized by the late Bob Marley. In appreciation of his work, the government of Jamaica has bestowed upon Marley the Order of Distinction, which allows us to refer to him as the Honorable Robert Nesta Marley.

The breadth of the appeal of the Rastafarian faith and culture is illustrated with the following anecdote. A couple of years ago, I gave a lecture in the hills of Ferrara, Italy, to about three hundred Italian schoolteachers. When I announced that my lecture would deal with the poet and songwriter from Jamaica, the Honorable Bob Marley, my remarks were greeted with much applause, and I was informed of their familiarity with reggae music. I had similar experiences when I lived in Nigeria in the 1980s and Kenya in the 1990s. Most of the music played for general consumption in these countries was Bob Marley's reggae music. Many persons throughout the world acknowledge that the social criticism of Jamaican society that they find in Marley's songs is applicable to their situation. This has also been my experience while living in the United States. On many college campuses, students and faculty wear the dreadlocks as a symbol of protest and as a way to remember Africa. In the popular culture and on college campuses, people seem hungry to know more and to understand some of the basic themes of the Rasta culture and faith.

Because Rastafari emerges as a religious faith, the church is quite interested in learning more about the religion as well. Jamaica gave to the world in the twentieth century a new religion—Rastafari—that represents a paradigm shift from the perspectives advocated by the Christian religion, with which the Rastas are always in conversation. The Christian approach to the Bible regards the Bible as authoritative for matters of life and faith. The Bible constitutes the central authority of faith for the church.

In the Rasta faith, in contrast, engagement with the Bible occurs outside the church and is not informed by the traditions and teaching offices of the church. Rastas are critical of the church, often noting that the Caribbean church is an extension of the European and North American church and as such is not invested in the alleviation of the grinding poverty of the region. They believe the church represents the bourgeoisie class and that her biblical exegesis represents the theological and exegetical interests of that class. Rastafari connect their struggle for solidarity and dignity in Jamaican society with the struggle of oppressed Israel and claim they are the true Israelites.

To the Rastas, the Bible exists for serving the needs of the community, and Rastafari theology does not begin with a consideration of the historical-critical method but with the circumstances nationally or globally that impinge on the lives of the Rasta community. Their primary concern is the way in which the biblical text affirms Rastas' identity and elucidates issues of dignity in Jamaican society. Because the Bible exists for the community, the Rastas take from it whatever is helpful in their struggle to eke out a meaningful existence in "Babylon," that is, Jamaican society.

Rastafari theology often begins with critical reflection on historical practice in Jamaican society or on the global scene. The Bible is not the definitive source of truth for the Rastas. The authoritative source of truth is "Jah" (God) as Jah reveals Jah's ways in national or world events or in the Bible. Jah's activities are not limited to events of the Bible. Jah is active in national and world events, and these followers often turn to the Bible to find an explanation of what Jah is up to in the world. Because of this, the Rastas are busy interpreting both the sociological and the biblical text. They often begin with the sociological text and then move to the biblical text for elucidation and confirmation of what they presume Jah is doing in the world.

The twin concepts of the divinity of Haile Selassie and the redemption of black people have distinguished Rastafari from other Afro-Caribbean faiths that have sought to promote an awareness of black consciousness in the Caribbean. Further, it must be kept in mind that the discourse concerning the divinity of Haile Selassie and the articulation of biblical warrants to justify these claims are made in the sociopolitical context in which the vast majority of Rastas are at the base of the social and economic ladder. But not only is the Bible being read in a social setting in which inequalities are rife and Rastas are at the base of the society, but it also is being read in a cultural and social setting in which many Jamaicans value those with lighter complexions more highly than their darker neighbor. So, to picture one's God in one's image was a meaningful way of redeeming the image of black people in Jamaica from disrespect and indignity. The blackness of God ensures the dignity and sanctity of black people. This means that blackness is no longer a curse but is taken up into the divinity of God and becomes a point of departure for talk about black humanity. The Rastas claim that they are "sons" of God. Membership in the Rasta community has to do with the unique relationship of the Rasta to Haile Selassie. One does not join the community to become a Rasta. Rather, one has to be born again through a spiritual rebirth, a self-awakening. The believer becomes a son of Jah Rastafari who is God and as such shares in divinity for it is recorded in John 10:34, "I said ye are Gods" and in 1 John 3:2, "Beloved, now are we sons of God, and it doth not yet appear what we shall be: but we know that when he shall appear, we shall be like him; for we shall see him as he is."

The Rastas also use the Bible to justify their use of marijuana, which is popularly known in Jamaica as "ganja." Although ganja has been illegal in Jamaica, the Rastas, with the help of biblical quotations, have designated ganja a "holy herb," and it functions as a religious sacrament for this community. The Rastas cite Genesis 1:12 as their proof text: "And the earth brought forth grass, and herb yielding seed after its kind, and the tree yielding fruit, whose seed was in itself, after its kind: and God saw that it was good." Ganja smoking was one of the ways in which Rastafarians signaled their protest against the unjust ways of the government of Jamaica. Ganja smoking identified them as a "separate people."

There has not been a flurry of books on Rastafari. Several texts treat the group's history and connections with Marcus Garvey in short essays. An example of this approach has been the work done by writers like Rex Nettleford in *Mirror, Mirror: Identity, Race, and Protest in Jamaica* (Kingston: LMH Publishing, 2001), George Eaton Simpson, *Religious Cults of the Caribbean* (San Juan, Puerto Rico: Institute of Caribbean Studies, 1980), Noel Leo Erskine, *Decolonizing Theology* (Trenton, N.J: Africa World Press,

1998), and Barry Chevannes, ed., *Rastafari and Other African-Caribbean Worldviews* (London: Macmillan, 1995). Another important publication is Samuel Murrell, William David Spencer, and Adrian Anthony McFarlane, eds., *Chanting Down Babylon* (Philadelphia: Temple University Press, 1998).

This book is an anthology of essays on Rastafarian faith and practice. Among the more recent texts, this one points in the direction of themes I would like to focus on in a more in-depth and sustained way. In many ways, *From Garvey to Marley: Rastafari Theology* will be a response to *Chanting Down Babylon* as it develops themes that are only hinted at in that text. Robert Hill, the noted Garvey scholar, points out that Rastafari's origins can be traced to the village in Jamaica where I grew up. It was impossible to be reared in this village and not be steeped in Rasta customs and respect for the environment as well as Rasta ideology and theology.

Of particular interest will be "excavating" the faith as this is carried through the medium of music, the trademark of Rasta music popularly known as reggae. The role of music in the development of this religion and in the struggle for identity and dignity will be explored. The basic structure of this work will be historical/cultural and theological. The role of the holy herb (ganja and its significance as sacrament), the meaning of dreadlocks, and the origins of the Ital diet (Rastas were among the earliest vegetarians in Jamaica) will be explored. In the theological realm, particular attention will be given to Christology, ecclesiology, and salvation. I will explore a central question broached by Rastafari: Where does Jamaica stand in relation to Africa?

I would like to thank series editor Anthony Pinn for the many discussions on Rastafari theology. My thanks also go to Dwight Hopkins and John Snarey, who looked at an earlier draft of this manuscript. I am also grateful to Lewin Williams, Donavan Reid, and Velma Grant for much wise counsel as they bring a perspective from within the faith. A special word of thanks to members of the Bobo community, who were most hospitable during my visits, and to my teaching assistants, Douglas Powe, Duane Belgrave, and Eldon Birthright, for the long hours of conversation. Also, to my colleagues at the Candler School of Theology for insightful comments, thank you. For much editorial counseling from Samuel Murrell and Marion Pierre I am truly grateful. This work has been in many respects a community project. Finally, a special word of thanks to Meredith Morris-Babb, my editor at University Press of Florida, for her patience and guidance.

1

} Rastafari Theology

My initial interest in Rastafari theology was sparked during my formative years in Jamaica, West Indies. The village of Trinityville where I grew up—located in the parish of St. Thomas east of the capital city, Kingston—was a stronghold of Rastafari ideology and theology. I recall many a night being lulled to sleep with the drumming and chanting of the Rastafari. It is important to acknowledge childhood in Jamaica during the 1940s and 1950s as being awestruck with the sense of *dread* inspired by the presence of the Rastafari brethren.

Looking back to my childhood, I think that the sense of dread the Rastas inspired must have been similar to the kind of fear inspired by an Old Testament prophet or, for that matter, to the fear inspired by a John the Baptist. I discovered very early that the Rastas were not primarily interested in using dread to frighten members of the community, but rather that the dread I experienced was their way of constituting themselves in the face of colonial domination. Dread Talk became a way of lashing out against the colonial and imperialistic way of life in Jamaica, conditions that the Rastas referred to as "Babylon." Babylon represented the powers that were arrayed against and sought to destroy poor people. Dread Talk became a crucial tool of resistance in fighting the war against Babylon. The dread that was mediated was a way of holding self together in the face of the forces of class and race in the society that were aimed at tearing the self apart.

In "Dread History: Leonard P. Howell and Millenarian Visions in Early Rastafarian Religions in Jamaica," the noted Garvey scholar Robert Hill places the founding of the faith of Rastafari in my childhood village of Trinityville.[1] Howell, the founder of Rastafari, was born in Jamaica, migrated to Harlem, New York, and returned to Jamaica in 1933 after the coronation of Haile Selassie as emperor of Ethiopia. Hill points out that Howell, who was seen on the streets of Harlem with pictures of Haile Selassie, returned to Jamaica, where he proclaimed a message of faith in the divine kingship of Haile Selassie. Howell's central message was that Haile Selassie's ascension to the throne as king of Ethiopia was the fulfillment of biblically and culturally based prophesy from Psalm 68:31: "Princes shall come out of Egypt; Ethiopia shall soon stretch out her hands unto God." Culturally, this text was understood by Rastas as a prophecy by Marcus Garvey that Africa and her traditions would deliver Jamaica and peoples of African descent from oppression mediated by race and class.

On his return to Jamaica in 1933, Howell began preaching in Kingston, but the people in the chief city of Jamaica would not hear his message of the divine kingship of Haile Selassie. It was at this time, because the people in the city were unresponsive to his message, that Howell settled in the village of Trinityville. According to Ennis Edmonds:

> Howell's message, especially in St. Thomas, was revolutionary in its import. To his followers, he advocated hatred and violence against the white ruling class as revenge for their years of oppressing black people. He declared the African race superior to the white race. He admonished his followers to withdraw allegiance from the British Crown, to be loyal only to Haile Selassie, the supreme being and the only true ruler of the African race, and to prepare for repatriation to their African homeland. To buttress his doctrine of repatriation, in December 1933, he sold picture postcards of Emperor Haile Selassie, which were supposed to be passports to Ethiopia. The colonial authorities, recognizing the inflammatory nature and revolutionary potential of Howell's message, arrested and convicted him on a charge of sedition. He was sentenced to a two-year prison term.[2]

On his release from prison, he and some of his followers relocated to the parish of St. Catherine. Here Howell established a commune on property he purchased that was called "Pinnacle," and he continued to preach the divine kingship of Haile Selassie and the need for Afro-Jamaicans to return to Ethiopia.

When I came along as a child in Trinityville in the 1940s, Rastafari was well established with an emerging theology that taught the divinity of Haile Selassie and the deliverance of black people from their harsh life and grinding poverty. This theology that emerged as Dread Talk was literally understood as Dreads talking about God and about life. There was an incipient millennial expectation that the end of oppressive rule was near in Jamaica and the new king would come to Jamaica to deliver Jamaicans by removing them to Ethiopia. Orlando Patterson captures this millennial excitement of Trinityville in his award-winning novel *The Children of Sisyphus*:

> he enquired of the knowledgeable man in front of him, "Brother Solomon, tell me . . . how . . . how long more we goin' 'ave to wait?" He asked the question almost in a whisper, for somehow he felt he should not have asked in the first place. The Great King in the east would send for them and deliver them out of the bondage when he saw fit. . . . Brother Solomon was not severe. He understood his brother man too much for that. "I should say to you, be patient, me Brother, and leave it at that. The delegates we sent to the Holy Emperor to make final arrangements for our return just write us. Their answer show promise. They said they don't speak to the Holy Emperor yet but that arrangement is being made by his holy servants on our behalf. So when we hear from them next time we will hear the good news and know just when we will be leaving this land of Babylon."
>
> "Lawd, Brother Solomon, how me going to pray and pray fo' de day to come."[3]

I recall so very vividly this holy impatience regarding the coming of the awaited Messiah.

Another reason why I am driven to write on the theology of Rastafari is that it is a logical extension of my earlier work, *Decolonizing Theology*. I see *From Garvey to Marley: Rastafari Theology* as a part of my project to decolonize theology. In *Decolonizing Theology*, I looked at attempts by Jamaicans to talk about God from the perspective of suffering and oppression. One of the crucibles from which this theology emerged was the experience of dependency. Growing up in Jamaica, we were taught to look to the metropolis for an answer to our economic and spiritual needs. I recall being a part of a population that grew bananas and sugarcane for export to Great Britain. The fruits we were allowed to eat were those that were not good enough for export. Further, we experienced God as foreigner. This God came to us filtered through other peoples' experiences. We encountered this God in liturgies, hymns, and prayers that came prepackaged from Great Britain and North America. As a consequence, the God we met was an alien. What is interesting as I look back is that during this period of our history from the 1930s on, the pressure for change and for liberation came from religious expressions that were outside the church. In a profound sense, this was true even in the period prior to emancipation.

4 If we look at the contribution of the Native Baptists and of the work of "Daddy" Sharp of Montego Bay in 1831, it becomes clear that the impulse for change came from outside the organized church. In many instances, the church was willing to press for change only because of the pressure of groups—and in this case religious groups—outside the church. Revivalism, Rastafari, and the Native Baptists each constituted a form of resistance that pressed for freedoms. In many instances, the church later followed their lead. So *From Garvey to Marley: Rastafari Theology* is an attempt to follow the lead of *Decolonizing Theology* by confronting the harsh realities of Jamaican life. It takes on the facts that constitute the lives of poor people and that seek to block their efforts and hopes for change. Rastafari theology deals with issues of poverty, illiteracy, and shabby housing that characterize the lot of the vast majority of Jamaicans. Rastafari theology speaks for the vast majority of Jamaicans who are locked into a culture of silence. The Rastas accomplish this through Dread Talk—by speaking out against an oppressive government and targeting the police force and the judiciary, which are often insensitive to the plight of poor Jamaicans and are seen by the Rastas as an extension of Babylon.

Often, like the prophets of the Old Testament, the Rastas dramatize their speech. In a profound sense, we could speak of speech-acts. One of the aims of speech-acts is to bring to the attention of the general public an awareness of the plight of the poor and marginalized in Jamaica. Speech-acts are aimed at making public, exposing the political, economic, and social contradictions taking place in Jamaica. The point of dramatizing their plight is to get poor and marginalized Jamaicans to take responsibility for their liberation. And they do this by modeling for the masses that they do not have to be dependent and wait for handouts from the planter class, but that they can grow what they eat and support themselves through their art and industry. The Rastafarians were among the first vegetarians in Jamaica who insisted on taking responsibility for their health and are admired by other Jamaicans for their creativity and hard work. Rastas insist that they have been hurt by the cycle of dependence and that they cannot wait on other people to liberate them.

They contend that the poor must liberate themselves. They must create their own history. They teach that the poor must guard against false generosity, a generosity that is aimed at keeping things the way they are. Rastas do not trust persons from the oppressor class as they do not believe that the oppressor class genuinely wants to change the system. They believe that people who come from the oppressor class bring their prejudices with them. They refer to these people as being from Babylon—that is, they have a colonial agenda. Rastas teach that to look to the oppressor class is to stay in a state of dependency. The poor must build their own confidence and develop the ability to think and act for themselves. Too often the poor are self-deprecating, dependent, and fatalistic. To break out of this vicious cycle of dependence, Rastas find their own answers to their own questions. Rastas speak their own words; indeed, they fashion their own words as they seize the power to name their world and to change it. This is the key to transformation: the ability to seize the power of definition—to name one's own world and one's own reality.

In *Decolonizing Theology*, I pointed out that middle-class Jamaica turned its back on Rastafari and Revivalism, much as it had turned its back on Marcus Garvey, the prophet of black redemption. However, while Revivalism continues to survive in the religious context of Jamaica, Rastafari has become an international force due largely to the reggae rhythms developed and popularized by Bob Marley.

The focus of this text then is to plumb the depths of Rastafari beliefs. Of particular interest will be excavating the faith as this is represented in the wisdom sayings and rhetorical "reasonings" of Rastas. I will also look at the role of music in the development of Rastafari theology as Rastas articulate the role of religion in the struggle for dignity and identity. The basic structure of this work will be historical, cultural, and theological. The role of the holy herb and its significance as sacrament, the meaning of dreadlocks, and the meaning of Dread Talk will be explored. Particular attention will be given to soteriology, ecclesiology, and Christology. I will investigate whether or not the central question the Rastas pose for us is where we stand in relation to Africa, and I will examine ways in which religion functioned and functions for them as a vehicle for social and economic change.

Roots of Resistance

The Rastas were not the first to make the connection between religion and social and political change in Jamaica. Afro-Jamaicans have always made that connection. This is so because, according to the eminent East African theologian John Mbiti, Africans are never without their religion. They take their religion to the fields. They take it with them to funerals, to the market, and to their festivals, and it shapes their beliefs and rituals.

As Afro-Jamaicans adapted their religion to the Jamaican context, two forms of this religion emerged on Jamaican soil: *obeah* and *Myalism*. In Ashanti, the word for wizard is "obayifo," and in Jamaica this became "obeah." Black Jamaica believed that the person who had the power of obeah had the ability to leave his or her body, to fly at night, and to cause great harm to befall the enemy. One of the main functions of the obeah man or woman was that of making poison with which to kill the enemy. Leonard Barrett explains how obeah flourishes contextually, yet dangerously:

> In Africa, although witchcraft exists and the sorcerer is one of the religious functionaries of the religious system, his work is considered dangerous to society. If he is discovered, he is generally killed or driven out of the community. There are built-in controls by which his polluting influence can be counteracted. In the social and religious system, the evil power of the sorcerer is always in conflict with the powers of the traditional priest. . . . Whenever the society is in equilibrium, that is, when the society is under proper control, there is little need for witchcraft. On the contrary, when the society is in an unstructured state, whenever there is cultural confusion or social disorientation, witchcraft is likely to flourish. This being the case it is easy to see why witchcraft became dominant in the slave societies.[4]

Barrett is helpful in getting us to understand why obeah flourished in slave society. It flourished not only because the society had lost its equilibrium and was in a state of disorientation but because there was a void for a religious practitioner. The traditional African priest had lost his power in this alien society, and as he joined forces with the obeah practitioner they became a formidable force to reckon with in slave society. So powerful was the role of obeah in Jamaican society that there were laws prohibiting Jamaicans to engage in this practice. The obeah man was able to offer Jamaicans protection against the cruelty of the master who had the right to whip, mutilate, or sell any slave at will. There are many stories in Caribbean folklore of house slaves using poison as an effective weapon in the struggle for freedom. The obeah practitioner would give the domestic help particles of a bush that would be hidden under the fingernail, and all the house slave needed to do was dip that finger in the master's drink to poison him.

M. G. Lewis, in his *Journal of a West Indian Proprietor*, in 1816 referred to Christianity as white obeah. What led Lewis to make the connection between Christianity and black obeah was the sense of powerlessness he as a white man experienced in the wake of obeah. Lewis writes of an obeah man called Adam who attempted to poison an attorney and discovered that his plan failed because Bessie, a black woman, betrayed him. Because of this, Adam placed a curse on Bessie, her health declined, and her four children died one after another. Lewis tried Christianity to counteract Adam on two levels. First, he suggested to Bessie "that her pickaninnies were not dead forever, but were only gone up to live with God, who was good, and would take care of them for her; and that if she were good, when she dies, she too would go up to God above the blue, and see all her four pickaninnies again."[5]

According to Lewis, Christianity would work for Bessie if she were good—that is, if she served her master faithfully—and then when she died she would see her children again. In desperation, Lewis pondered Christianizing Adam as a way of diminishing the power of obeah over fellow slaves. Lewis explains that "in short, I know not what I can do with him, except indeed make a Christian of him! This might induce the Negro to believe that he has lost his infernal power by the superior virtue of the holy water, but, perhaps he may refuse to be christened. However, I will at least ask him the question and if he consents, I will send him—and a couple of dollars—to the clergyman—for he shall not have so great a distinction as baptism from massa's own hand—and see what effect 'White obeah' will have in removing the terrors of this professor of the Black."[6] Christianity was no match for obeah, and so Lewis indicates in his journal that he agreed for Bessie to see another obeah man who lived in the mountains to provide the antidote for the spell Adam had placed on Bessie.

Afro-Jamaicans depended on obeah for many reasons. Among these reasons was resistance to white oppression. The obeah man would often kill right and left in an attempt to lash out against the violence inflicted on black people by the oppressor class. But obeah was also a method of keeping the black community in line with the objectives of the obeah practitioner. To be out of step with the program was to run the risk of incurring the wrath of the obeah man. It should also be kept in mind that in a culture in which the enslaved person was defined as property of the master class, for the obeah man to injure, kill, or make ill a fellow enslaved person was to incur the wrath of the master.

Leonard Barrett calls attention to the maroon rebellion of 1760, one of the bloodiest revolts staged by Afro-Jamaicans. Led by Ashanti warrior and obeah man Tacky, the warriors prepared for war by mixing rum with gunpowder and grave dirt. Blood drawn from the arm of each participant was added, and then the mixture was drunk in turn by each warrior. The drinking of this mixture meant that the covenant to fight until death was sealed. After this rebellion, the fear of the obeah man became so pervasive that the Jamaican legislature passed a law against him. The effect of the law was that anyone convicted of practicing obeah faced the possibility of being sentenced to death. This did not solve the master's problems as black people believed "Massa can't kill obeah man."[7]

In West Africa, the worship of the gods was organized in cult groups, often esoteric, which used drums, dancing, dreams, and spirit-seizure as part of organized worship. An aspect of this survived in Jamaica through the ritual referred to as Myal. Perhaps the real difference between obeah and Myal is that whereas the obeah man is usually a private practitioner hired by a client for a specific purpose, the Myal practitioner is a leader of a group devoted to organized religious life. But as was illustrated in the scenario of Tacky calling on the warriors to blend rum, blood, gunpowder, and grave dirt together and then drink to establish a covenant, the lines between obeah and Myal are often blurred.

Winston Lawson reminds us that Myalism embodied African-derived cosmology and is the first documented Jamaican religion cast in the African mold. At the heart of the rituals that highlight Myal is the Myal dance, which was performed in honor of the minor deities or the ancestors who were feared. An important ingredient of this dance was spirit-possession. It was widely believed by participants in Myal that the dance gave them the ability to elude capture when they escaped or made them invincible to bullets.[8]

Citing George Blythe in *Reminiscences of Missionary Life,* Dianne Stewart alludes to many of the ritual practices of Myal and ways in which Europeans could not differentiate between obeah and Myal:

> The superstitions which prevail in Western and Central Africa have been brought to the West Indies and may be comprehended under the two systems of obeahism and myalism; the first of which is entirely mischievous, and the other professes to counteract it. The principal actor(s) in the former are old men, generally Africans. These pretend to have powers over others, even at a distance. . . . One of the plans which the overseers adopted during slavery, for breaking the spell of obeahism . . . was to procure baptism for the Negroes. . . . Latterly, however, baptism or as they call it, christening, has become so common, that it seems to have lost its charm, and the doctor or Myal-man, is resorted to, that he may neutralize the power of the

Obeah-man. Sometimes his remedies are of a very simple character, particularly if his object is to cure some local disease. . . . Sometimes the myalists meet in large companies, generally at night, and dance in rings, till they become excited and frenzied, singing myal songs accusing others of being myal-men, and pretending to discover enchantments which have been made by them. . . . These myal-men also pretend to catch the shadow or spirit of persons who may have lost their lives by lightning or accident. When the spirit is caught, it is put into a small coffin and buried, by which the ghost, as the superstitious of this country would call it, is laid to rest. The myal men are resorted to in great variety of cases, when disease is obstinate, or the nature of it not understood: if a man's wife has forsaken him; if he thinks there is danger of losing the favor of his employers; if he supposes his horse has been bewitched; in all such cases the myal men are consulted.[9]

The rebellions of 1798, the 1830s, 1840s, and 1860s were inspired by the Myalists pressing for social change. It is worth noting that during the 1790s there was a fusing of Myalist beliefs with those of the Native Baptists. The Afro-Christian witness in Jamaica dates from the end of the American Revolution when several hundred loyalists migrated with their slaves to Jamaica. They seized the opportunity to preach their version of Christianity in Jamaica and found ways of merging their understanding of Christianity with Myalism. This was the beginning of the Native Baptist movement in Jamaica. The best-known of the slaves to migrate to Jamaica was George Liele. Liele was born in Virginia around 1751 to a slave couple, Liele and Nancy, and became the property of Henry Sharp of Savannah, Georgia. Liele arrived in Kingston, Jamaica, in 1783 and founded the first Baptist church, which he named the Ethiopian Baptist Church.

Barrett points out that the Native Baptists were the first church to reach out to the enslaved in Jamaica and that one reason for their success among the Africans was the loose structure of the Baptist Church, which enables them to use newly converted lay leaders to supervise the African converts. This flexibility allowed the inclusion of African traditional practices such as drumming, dancing, handclapping—in short, the practices of Myal. Another leader of the Native Baptists was George Lewis, who rejected the white version of Christianity in favor of his own, more African style. "He had been born in Africa and taken to Virginia as a slave. After the American Revolution he was brought to Kingston, where his mistress let him work as a peddler in return for a monthly fee. He mixed peddling with preaching along his route in the parishes of Manchester and St. Elizabeth and spread his doctrine through the southwest part of the island."[10]

Other Africans from the United States in the tradition of George Lewis were George Gibb and Moses Baker. "The organizational basis of both cults was the 'leader system,' an adaptation of the English Wesleyan practice of dividing the church members into classes for teaching. Possibly, the native Baptists picked it up from the few white missionaries who were already at work in Jamaica, but more likely it was part of their American training. In any case the leader system underwent some strange transformations. The class-leaders became something more than just a teacher of the new converts. They were the real spiritual guides, taking a position equivalent to leadership of a myal cult group, and their power over the classes was authoritarian to the point of tyranny."[11]

The class leaders had power to refuse applications for baptism and at times even expelled members. Needless to say, it was not long before the class became the basis for the founding of a new church. It is important to note that from 1783, when George Liele and his fellow African-Americans arrived in Jamaica and started to interpret Christianity from an African perspective, they were unhindered by European theological traditions until about 1814, when the first Baptist missionaries arrived from Great Britain. We must make allowance for the European cultural adjustments in order to get their numbers adequate to deal with the vast number of slaves who were in the island at this time. The important fact to remember is that for twenty-eight years the Native Baptists were unhindered by Europeans as they constructed a theology that would speak to the enslaved situation. Native Baptists adopted a doctrinal position that elevated the spirit and neglected the written word. It is quite understandable that there would be less emphasis on the written word as many of the class leaders were unable to read. "The followers of Baker and Gibb were required to be possessed of 'the spirit' before baptism was administered. This meant that the spirit had to descend on the applicant in a dream, which was then described to the leader. If the dream were satisfactory, the applicant could enter the class. There evolved a regular technique and ceremonial for bringing on spirit-possession, which included a fast according to a set canon followed by a trip into the bush alone at night to wait for the spirit to descend."[12] In a system of slavery that denied them political power, the leaders of the Native Baptists—operating under the aegis of the spirit— were free to make theological connections as they saw fit, carving out their own space in the church. In this church, John the Baptist was seen as the leader since he baptized Christ and accepted Christ into his church, so to speak. It is not surprising that European missionaries later found this theological position shocking and untenable. As the Native Baptists merged African perspectives with Christian beliefs, they formulated a reinterpretation of Christianity that would endure even under the impact of European ideas and beliefs. "By 1830 the doctrine and organization of the Native Baptists had become a thoroughly integrated part of Negro culture—another religion competing with the Christianity of the European missionaries."[13] On the religious state of black people in Jamaica in the 1830s, a missionary organization comments that

> all the Negroes in Jamaica now call themselves "Christians"—generally "Baptists," though their religion differs little from their old African superstitions. The bulk of them are enrolled in Classes under some Black Teacher as ignorant as themselves; and they are connected by the purchase of a ticket with the Baptist congregation in the nearest Town, where they go, and receive the sacrament once a month, or once a Quarter; but they are utterly ignorant of the simplest and plainest of God's commandments. They are too ignorant to understand and profit by the Public Preaching on the Sabbath; and they never see the Missionary at any other time; for they live far away from him and he has thousands attending him whom he does not know. They are perishing in their sins, and stand as much in need of instruction as the Zooloos.[14]

It is quite clear that the arrival of the missionaries did not slow down the Africanization of Christianity along Myal lines. "It was not until 1824, that a potentially strong leader, Thomas Burchell, came to join Baker. Baker urged his followers to accept Burchell's leadership but cultural barriers of communication and a predilection for Africanized, religious celebration, made many of them abandon Baptist orthodoxy for native-led forms of expression."[15] The memory of Africa dominated the consciousness of Afro-Jamaicans, and the class-leader system provided a leadership basis that would press for change in Jamaica. The class-leader system that was an integral part of the Native Baptist system also carried over into both the Baptist Missionary Society and the Wesleyan Methodists.

This undoubtedly was one way in which the missionary church appealed to Afro-Jamaicans. It is reported that by 1830 the Baptist Missionary Society had about 250 class leaders and that by 1832 there were 456 such leaders in the Wesleyan Church. "During slavery, prayer and class meetings under these leaders provided an experience of humanity, dignity, and brotherhood which no other institution could provide. Of more political importance is that this arrangement served as a more-or-less legitimate means of organization and communication in a society that depended for its continued existence on the disunity of Blacks and their absolute subordination to White rule."[16]

The missionary churches that adopted the class-leader system watched their numbers grow as Afro-Jamaicans flocked to those churches. What is interesting is that the masses that attended the missionary church contended they could not understand what the missionary said and would meet after with a class leader who was referred to by Afro-Jamaicans as "Mammy" or "Daddy" to have the missionary's sermon explained. So Afro-Jamaicans would attend the missionary church without any intention of hearing or understanding the sermon. The truth is that this class-leader system became one reason for the failure of the missionary. It must be kept in mind that the missionary did not choose the class leader. He or she was chosen by the people, and it was the task of the missionary to accept the person chosen. Because the class leaders had the people base, they were free to break with the missionary and at times stand over against him. This was what precipitated the rebellion of 1831, which was led by class leader "Daddy" Sharp.

Native Baptists Press for Transformation

It must be kept in mind that the first Christian preaching that most slaves heard in Jamaica was by the original Native Baptists—Liele, Gibb, Baker, George Lewis, and Nicholas Swiegle. Although the Moravian witness on the island dates back to 1754, their influence among the slaves was minimal, partly due to the fact that some Moravian preachers were also slave owners. Perhaps it is part of the pervasiveness of evil that it often contaminates those who come within its purview. Another reason for the minimal impact of the Moravians was that they did not have the class-leader system, which would empower the slaves to provide leadership as Mammies and Daddies. Because the black Baptist Church in Jamaica was started by black leaders and the Baptist Missionary Society came to the island after being invited by the Native Baptists, it is not surprising that two of the pivotal rebellions on the island that prefigure the rise of Rastafari were led by Native Baptists themselves. It is also interesting that because the class-leader system was instituted in the island by the Native Baptists before a single person from the Baptist Missionary Society came to Jamaica, their control of the Native Baptists was minimal. But something of the defiance of the Native Baptists spilled over into a Wesleyan Methodist class leader who enquired of the magistrate if God had made black people apprentices; when answered in the affirmative, he responded that God had done an injustice to black people:

> Mr. Laidlow, one of the special magistrates, informed us that he attended the Bogg Estate on the 4th of August, when James Beard stepped forward and spoke nearly as follows. He enquired "were the Israelites made apprentices when they came out of Egypt?" and being answered in the negative, he asked, "Will you swear upon the Bible that God has made us apprentices?" The magistrate immediately did so, when some of the Negroes said that is not the king's Bible. The magistrate then informed them that the next day he would bring his own Bible and swear upon that which he did; . . . Many of them seemed satisfied and went away. James Beard again asked "has God made us apprentices?" and on being answered in the affirmative he exclaimed, "Then God has done us an injustice!" Afterwards, on their refusal to comply with the law two or three of them were, by the magistrate's orders, laid down and flogged, and James Beard, who thinks himself suffering for righteousness sake, and a few others, were sentenced to hard labour with the penal gang in the workhouse for six months.[17]

The Baptist War

The Baptist War of 1831 led by class leader Sam ("Daddy") Sharp of the Native Baptists signaled the beginning of the end of slavery in Jamaica. The Baptist War as the rebellion of 1831 in and around Montego Bay is said to have brought to a climax the long struggle of Afro-Jamaicans for freedom from imperial rule. The struggle over the years took the form of slaves running away, many—as in the case of the maroons of Jamaica—fleeing to the hills and organizing attacks on the British from time to time. The focus of this war was black people organizing to withdraw their labor, and because of this the brunt of their attack was on institutions of the plantation. A total of about 120 buildings on the estate were torched as black people insisted that because they were human beings who had a right to freedom, they had a right to withdraw their labor and attack the institutions that kept them in slavery. The Baptist War "differed from earlier uprisings, such as that of Tacky's Coromantis . . . from Africa and that of the King of the Ebos with his small band of plantation slaves, in that more than 20,000 African-Jamaicans were involved. The call was to slaves everywhere, not a call to arms but a call to withdraw their labour, and it was issued to people who were determined to win their freedom."[18]

The leader was a deacon of the Baptist Church who had an impressive following among the Native Baptists. Samuel, or "Daddy," Sharp worked as a domestic slave and was impressive as a man of great sincerity, rhetorical powers, and captivating magnetism. A missionary who visited him in prison comments:

> I heard him two or three times deliver a brief extemporaneous address to his fellow prisoners on religious topics . . . and I was amazed at the power and freedom with which he spoke and at the effect which was produced upon his auditory. He appeared to have the feelings and passions of his hearers completely at his command and when I listened to him once, I ceased to be surprised at what Gardner had told me, that when Sharp spoke to him and others on the subject of slavery, he Gardner was wrought up almost to a state of madness.[19]

Edward Hylton, one of Daddy Sharp's followers, tells of being in the hills and receiving a message from Daddy Sharp to attend a meeting at Johnson's house on Retrieve Estate in St. James. The gathering took the form of a prayer meeting. After the meeting, Daddy Sharp, William Johnson—who became one of the leaders of the Baptist War—Hylton, and a few others remained behind. "After a while Sharp spoke to them in a low, soft tone so that his voice would not be heard outside. According to Hylton, he kept them spellbound while he spoke of the evils and injustices of slavery, asserted the right of all human beings to freedom and declared on the authority of the Bible, that the White man had no more right to hold the Blacks in bondage than the Blacks had to enslave the Whites."[20] The meeting went on late into the night as they agreed on a strategy to overturn slavery. They covenanted not to work after the Christmas holidays but to seize their right to freedom in faithfulness to each other. "If backra would pay them, they would work as before. If any attempt was made to force them to work as slaves, they would fight for their freedom. They took the oath and kissed the Bible."[21] It seems as if what Daddy Sharp intended was a nonviolent protest that would be expressed as a labor strike. The plan was that on the day after the Christmas holiday an overseer or a driver would go to the "busha" on each estate and inform him that the slaves would not work until they agreed to pay wages. The bushas were to be kept on the estate until they agreed to pay wages for work.

The leadership of the Native Baptists had organized themselves into a trade union arm of the Native Baptist Church, advocating and negotiating wages for the slaves. Phillip Curtin suggests that what in fact was happening was the Native Baptists skillfully had detached the Baptist missionary organization from white missionaries and were using the Baptist organization as a European trade union leader used the bargaining power of the workers.[22] Later developments attest that this seems to be the case. On December 27 William Knibb, visiting Moses Baker's chapel at Crooked Spring, now Salter's Hill, tried to persuade the slaves that rumors about freedom having been granted were untrue, but his words were received with evident dissatisfaction by many of the slaves present, several of whom left the chapel offended. Others remarked: "The man . . . must be mad to tell them such things."[23] Further, missionary Knibb stated:

> I am pained—pained to the soul, at being told that many of you have agreed not to work any more for your owners, and I fear this is too true. I learned that some wicked person has persuaded you that the King of England has made you free. Hear me! I love your souls and I would not tell you a lie for the whole world; I assure you that it is false, false as hell can make it. I entreat you not to believe it, but go to your work as formerly.
>
> If you have any love for Jesus Christ, to religion, to your ministers, or to those kind friends in England who have helped you to build this chapel, and who are sending a minister for you, do not be led away. God commands you to be obedient.[24]

Fired by the spirit of the Native Baptists, Daddy Sharp responded:

> We have worked enough already, and will work no more; the life we live is too bad, it is the life of a dog, we won't be slaves no more, we won't lift hoe no more, we won't take flogging anymore.[25]

Daddy Sharp and his compatriots Thomas Dove, Linton, Dehaney, and other freedom fighters seized the right to fight for justice and interpreted the message of liberation through the hermeneutic of freedom. They were already able to view themselves from the perspective of freedom. It is reported that when Daddy Sharp was apprehended he said that he "had rather die than be a slave." The price paid by Sharp and his people was very high. "In many instances criminals were condemned during the morning and executed between two and four o'clock. Of 106 slaves tried in St. James 99 were convicted, six executed, one pardoned and two dismissed. Of the

99 convicted, 84 were sentenced to death. In Hanover, 96 of the 138 convicted were sentenced to death; in Westmoreland, 33 of the 64 convicted were sentenced to death. Other punishments in St. James included one sentence of 500 lashes, one of 300 lashes with life imprisonment, one of two hundred lashes with six months' imprisonment, and so the dreadful story of barbarity went. . . . Sam Sharp learned of the executions while in prison. He himself was tried in Montego Bay on 19 April. He was publicly hanged there on 23 May 1832. At no time did his courage, his nobility of spirit shine more brightly than on the day of his execution. . . . He addressed the assembled crowd in a clear, unfaltering voice, admitted that he had broken the laws of the country and declared that he depended for salvation upon the Redeemer who shed his blood for sinners upon Calvary. . . . Sharp declared that the missionaries had nothing whatever to do with the uprising."[26]

In the aftermath of the Baptist War, some six hundred African Jamaicans were killed by British forces. In their defense they killed fourteen whites. But the seeds for the destruction of slavery in Jamaica were sown. On August 1, 1834, Lord Stanley introduced the following act to the British Parliament:

> Be it enacted, that all and every person who on the first day of August, one thousand eight hundred and thirty four, shall be holden in slavery within any such British colony as aforesaid, shall, upon and from any after the said first day of August, one thousand eight hundred and thirty four, become and be to all intents and purposes free, and discharged of and from all manner of slavery, and shall be absolutely and forever manumitted.[27]

Because the British regarded freedom as a dangerous asset, there were conditions instituted for the realization of freedom. One condition was that there should be a period of apprenticeship. Persons six years and older were to register as apprentices and continue to work for their former owners—as field hands for twelve years and domestic help for seven years. Children under six years old and those born after the act's passage were free. Needless to say, African Jamaicans saw this gradual approach to emancipation as a denial of freedom. As it was in the time of Daddy Sharp, so it was in the period of apprenticeship. The system of apprenticeship was resisted. In the first two years, "60,000 apprentices received in aggregate, one quarter of a million lashes, and 50,000 other punishments by the tread-wheel, the chain-gang, and other means of legalized torture." African Jamaicans' refusal to cooperate with an evil system brought apprenticeship to an abrupt end with its abolishment on August 1, 1838. The greatest honor England ever attained was "when she proclaimed the Slave is free, and established in practice what every American recognizes in theory; that all men are created equal—that they are endowed by their creator with certain unalienable rights—that among these are life, liberty, and the pursuit of happiness."[28]

The Road to Morant Bay

After the final emancipation in 1838, two distinct societies emerged in Jamaica: the peasant class and the planter class, or the labor class (ex-slaves) and the ruling class, respectively. For the first time, white Jamaica had the task of managing an economy based on free labor, and so the challenge facing the ruling class—who had heavy investments in sugar and banana plantations—was how to make a success of the new arrangement. "For twenty-seven years after final emancipation, the ruling minority worked at making the 'free system' a success, as *they* understood success. Year by year the failure became more evident. Finally in 1865, there was a new Negro rising at Morant Bay and another bloody repression like that of 1831. In 1866, the Assembly admitted defeat and resigned its powers to the Crown."[29] It had proven too much for European and African Jamaicans who were formed by slavery to adjust to the new environment of freedom. The dilemma was that the new environment posed new issues and new questions that the former environment of slavery could not answer. The critical question facing the African Jamaicans in the new situation was what to do with their newly won freedom. For the ruling class, the dilemma was how to make Jamaica productive and an economic success in the absence of enforced labor. The gist of the problem was that there were two distinct orientations. Black people, as they struggled with their new hermeneutic of freedom, resorted to a worldview and cosmology they knew and understood—religion. The planter class did the same, reverting to what they knew well—economics. It is no secret that slavery in the New World was based on economics. Even in instances where the master class conceded that slavery was morally wrong, they claimed it made economic sense. The dilemma was how to turn free labor into economic success. African Jamaicans did not find profit or monetary rewards an incentive to work. There are several stories of ex-slaves who would work just enough to provide for themselves and their families. In some instances, the planter class increased their wages and were surprised that the African Jamaicans worked less because they only wanted enough. "Sugar production dropped about half between the decade ending in 1833 and the decade of the 1840's. The price of sugar in London was also tending downward, with the result that Jamaica received less money for a smaller crop. The decline in the quantity of coffee exported was even more precipitous, but the problem was not simply one of quantity produced. By the 1850's, the value of the export component of the Jamaican economy was barely one-half that of the thirties, and it never really recovered until well after 1865."[30] The general impression held by both groups was that emancipation had failed because although African Jamaicans were free, both the planter class and the ex-slaves had grown further apart. "They were not only separate in caste and race, but to varying degrees had separate economies, separate religions, and separate cultures."[31]

The transition from a slave economy to a free economy brought attendant problems. One was certainly the need for education, considering that both the ex-slaves and the planter class had the task of fashioning a new society in which the ex-slave was no longer totally dependent on the master class. The planter class was afraid that education would make the peasantry unwilling to work at agriculture. The task of providing an education for the ex-slaves fell to the missionaries, who were helped by the British Parliament through a grant of thirty thousand pounds to the Caribbean British colonies.

There was a great eagerness among the peasantry to learn to read and write as the notion was alive among them that such skills meant acceptance by the ruling class and access to white-collar jobs. Although the success rate was very high among African Jamaicans, the British Parliament reduced the amount for education, and in 1845 funding for education disappeared from the budget of the Jamaican Assembly. Curtin suggests that some of the blame for the disappearance of funds belongs to the dissenting missionaries, who were busy competing among themselves for the loyalty of ex-slaves. In 1864, there were far fewer students enrolled in schools than in 1837.

Another serious problem in this new environment was the lack of health care. It must be remembered that under the former system the planter class provided for the medical and health needs of African Jamaicans. In the 1860s, the number of medical doctors in Jamaica was about one-quarter the number employed at the time of emancipation. In the cholera epidemic of 1850–51, approximately twenty-five to thirty thousand working-class Jamaicans died because of lack of medical care. Many also died from a smallpox epidemic and other tropical diseases. Sanitation problems and the lack of proper attention also exacerbated public health problems in Jamaica.

In spite of the recognition by some planters that their own interest demanded higher public expenditure for health and education, the Assembly refused to spend more, a refusal that was partly a corollary of the decision to spend money on other schemes, such as immigration. But it was also the result of the planters' belief that as illiteracy and disease had been common enough in the great days of the island's past, they were obviously not the cause of decline. Again, there was a tendency, common enough in Great Britain as well, to blame the lower orders for their own misery.[32]

The church was the most appropriate body to bring together ex-slave and ex-master. The established church had the confidence of the planter class, while the missionaries worked very closely with the newly freed African Jamaicans, helping in the areas of education and in the establishment of free villages. Land was not only a socioeconomic necessity for the newly liberated Jamaicans but it had religious significance. The land belonged to the ancestors, and to have land on which to bury the dead was of first importance for Jamaicans. This was one area in which African beliefs and memories lingered in Jamaica. The missionaries did not disappoint with regard to helping the ex-slaves acquire land to raise their families, grow their produce, and bury their dead. Land was an ontological necessity for black Jamaica. In a profound sense, not to have land is not to be. Emancipation meant leaving the cottage provided by the master, the land to rear animals and grow a crop, and, most important, the space to bury the dead. Both Baptist and Methodist missionaries were pro-active in acquiring large tracts of lands that they subdivided into smaller plots and used to create free villages in western parishes. Black Jamaica expressed its gratitude by crowding the churches of the Methodists and the Baptists. The Baptists saw their numbers triple, while the Methodists doubled. These mission churches were convinced that a new day had dawned for them as black Jamaica had renounced drumming, spirit-possession, and dancing as they embraced Christian beliefs.

With this success in membership and the large attendance of black people at worship services, it is understandable that church leaders assumed that black religion had been obliterated. They regarded the influx of black members in their churches as a sign that Christianity had at last won the day, the era of Christian freedom had come, and the long night of black religion and unchristian practices was ended. "The revelries attending births and deaths have given place to the decencies and properties of

Christian life," declared one church leader. "Licentiousness and discord have been displaced by the sanctity of matrimony, and the harmony and comforts of the domestic circle. Revolting and degrading superstition has vanished before the light and influence of truth as 'mists before the rising sun.'"[33]

The missionaries had, however, overlooked the fact that religion was one area in which African beliefs persisted. They had forgotten all too quickly the impact of the Native Baptists, the creative and innovative ways in which they had used the leader system. The African spirit came like a thief in the night and erupted in the mission churches.

> In 1846, the Native Baptist congregations in the sugar parish of Vere were stronger than all the European churches together. Even in Kingston, Native Baptists in 1860 made up half the churchgoing population. . . . To make matters worse, the semi-Christian cults were not the only rivals of the missionaries. At the far end of the religious spectrum, the more African Myal religion revived after the disappearance of the strict control of the slave system, and the practice of obeah increased. Obeah was still essentially private and secret, but Myalism took the form of open outbreaks of local hysteria that were bound to attract attention. One disruption, "the great Myal procession," moved through the northwestern parishes from December 1841 through most of 1842. Another major outbreak came to the southeast in 1846, and there were still other occurrences in the countryside during 1848, 1852, and 1860.[34]

It is safe to say that throughout the island the native form of religion had a firmer grip on African Jamaicans than did European orthodoxy. In a real sense, one could say that Europe and Africa competed for the souls of black people, and that Africa won.

However, the missionaries would not give in without a fight. They felt they had a right to black people's loyalty since they were there during slavery as advocates for freedom. Besides, after emancipation, the missionary churches—especially Baptist and Methodist—were instrumental in establishing free villages for African Jamaicans. The missionaries also heard black Jamaica's expression of preference for preachers of their own hue. Therefore, in 1845, the Baptists founded Calabar College for the training of native ministers. But Calabar did not succeed because the pastors who came through this theological school represented European orthodoxy and were impatient with drumming, concubinage, African Christmas festivals, Sabbath breaking, and African approaches to religion. It should not surprise us then that in 1860 the mission churches launched a united assault against African expressions of religion in Jamaica. In essence, there was a religious revival aimed at converting black people from their heathen ways to Christianity with fasting, dancing, and praying, and the high point came when the Native Baptists set aside the last Sunday of April 1860 for God's arrival in Jamaica. The mission churches were crowded by black people, and for a time it seemed as if the revival was a great success. However, gradually the missionaries began to understand what had happened—the revival had turned African. Insidiously, African religious practices made their way into the revival, and the new convert was usually struck prostrate on the floor; as the revival proceeded, African Jamaicans were given to oral confessions, trances, "prophesying," spirit-seizure, wild dancing, and mysterious sexual doings. The revival became increasingly a rejection of European orthodoxy and an embracing of African beliefs and practices. At the end of the revival, the mission churches were at their lowest ebb.

Another reality we dare not forget is that behind issues of social dislocation and the marginalization of the black population were not only issues of religion but also issues of race. Hiding beneath the issues of economics, health care, education, and justice making, there was always the question of where one stood in relation to Africa. Perhaps one reason for race not being a more explosive issue was that in Jamaica the issue was not only race but racialism. Racialism existed in the sense that there was always a threefold division along racial lines. At the top of the pyramid were white people, followed by colored people, and then, at the bottom of the totem pole, African people. The relationship between coloreds and blacks was always less friendly than that between blacks and whites. One way in which coloreds dealt with white prejudice was to demean their brothers and sisters of the darker hue and deny their own African-ness. The tension between coloreds and blacks was often the most conflict-ridden. One way in which coloreds related to whites was through assimilation and adopting white cultural characteristics. This provided a basis for the hope that since many whites had returned to Europe and many others had succumbed to tropical illnesses, the coloreds were the natural heirs of the political and economic system. Here the seeds were sown for a racial nationalism in Jamaica. The bottom line was that sooner or later Jamaicans would rule the economic and political spheres. Although white people in Jamaica were always in the minority since the majority of the owner class chose to live in Europe, the racial tensions during slavery were never explosive in part because of the systems of control that slavery provided the master class. I suppose one may also argue that the colored class provided a buffer between the whites and the blacks.

Planters had not known much about Negro culture under slavery, and they never came to understand the free working class. In addition, the whites were steadily becoming a smaller minority, not only in relation to the rest of the population but in absolute numbers. The planters who stayed on were more isolated than ever among abandoned plantations and an alien majority. Until the 1860s, the planters' racial fear was only a latent uneasiness, but then, partly through the known discontent of the Negroes and partly through the strange doings of the Revivalists, it grew into something close to a real feeling of terror. White planters began to carry firearms. Whenever the Negroes had a noisy prayer meeting or the Revival drums sounded from a Negro village, the word was passed around that "the blacks are drilling." Such reports were especially common just before the Morant Bay uprising.[35]

The planter class feared what the next move of the black masses might be. There was also an uneasiness concerning the way in which whites regarded the coloreds. Although coloreds were allowed to have political and economic positions, they nonetheless did not overcome the prejudice of whites in social relations. Although there was no evidence of racial hatred of blacks for whites, it is clear that there was little love lost between the races. The bottom line as it was expressed in the Baptist War, for example, was the question of trusting whites to be fair. Black Jamaica felt it could not depend on the planter class or the missionaries to be fair; instead, this trust was placed in the king or queen of England.

The evidence seems to support the claim that the missionaries attached to the Baptist Church such as William Knibb, Burchell, and Phillippo did not practice biological racism. Perhaps one index of their according black people the virtue of being made in the image of God is that in 1845 they established a theological seminary for the training of native ministers and that they were leaders in creating and providing villages for the masses who were socially dislocated after emancipation.

The story of the Methodists was somewhat different. While it is true that they occupied the middle rung between the Baptists and the Anglicans (they were viewed as on the way socially from Baptist to Anglican), it was noted that in the 1940s there was a powerful coming together of blacks and coloreds in the Methodist churches even more so than among the Baptists, who represented more of the lower classes and the masses of blacks. During the slavery period, perhaps because there were a substantial number of coloreds in the Methodist churches, there was the issue of white ministers marrying colored Creoles. But the structure of slavery prevented this issue from exploding or disrupting the internal life of the church. With the end of slavery in 1838, the artificial controls were removed, and the issue came to the fore on two fronts.

A colored politician and publisher named Edward Jordan, along with Thomas Pinnock, a white Methodist minister, spearheaded the movement. It was observed that as early as 1834 there was a measure of discontentment in the Methodist district in Kingston. The problem centered on a number of Methodists wanting to secede from the Methodist Church and call themselves Independent Methodists. One of the colored leaders accused the Methodist Church of racial prejudice, and to compound the problem Thomas Pinnock, chairman of the district, sided with the coloreds.[36] Pinnock also wrote that certain respectable members of color and black parishioners had withdrawn from the Methodist Church in Kingston to form an Independent Wesleyan Methodist Society. Another issue involved two young white missionaries named Walters and Rowden who were romantically involved with women of color. Because of these associations, Walters was placed on probation and Rowden was not given a circuit.

"In several cases of white Methodist missionaries becoming engaged to or actually marrying colored ladies, not once were they successful in acquiring or maintaining full standing as district missionaries. No cases are revealed in the correspondence of any 'respectable' Methodist Missionary marrying outside of their own color."[37] Chairman Pinnock grew increasingly wary of his colleagues in the ministry, whom he charged with racial prejudice. He was replaced as chairman of the district and summoned to answer charges of criticizing his brethren. Rather than attend a meeting, he resigned and formed his own Independent Church with about three hundred members and ten colored leaders.

Although the Methodists started a seminary in 1842, it had only four students in the first three months and was closed within a year. The administration closed the school due to an insubordinate spirit among the students. Robert Stewart indicates that there was no serious commitment by the Methodist Church to train natives for the ministry of the Methodist Church. When Cyrus Francis Perkins, a local preacher, applied to be an assistant missionary, he was encouraged to return to his trade. The problem of racial prejudice was more explicit in the Anglican Church, the church of the planter class. An illustration of the problem centers on Robert Gordon of Jamaica, who applied to the Anglican Church for ordination as a priest in Jamaica. The bishop of Jamaica recommended that he consider attending Codrington College in Barbados for preparation for ministry in West Africa. Gordon migrated to Canada, where he was ordained as the first Jamaican priest of the Anglican Church. However, in 1860 when Gordon returned to Jamaica hoping to be received as a priest in the Anglican Church, he wrote:

> having returned to Jamaica, in the early part of 1860, I threw myself *ad miserecordiam,* on the Christian consideration of the Bishop of Kingston. The recollection of the studied indignities and cruel unkindness which, it seemed, Dr. Courtenay felt an unenviable pleasure to subject me to, because I did not think with him that "Africa was my proper sphere of duty," must ever be bitterly coeval with the existence of my memory. I appealed to him when I was suffering from the want of the necessities of life, and he treated me, not for the first time, as if the God whom we both serve had explicitly told him that He had not created me "after His own image," and that the treatment which he should give to a bad dog would be too good for me. . . . I need not say that I was the first man of my race, in Jamaica, who had ever reached the priesthood. The Bishop's treatment of me has considerably tended, as I can prove, to facilitate the present prostrate condition of the Church.[38]

According to Gordon, the church in Jamaica failed. He had hoped that because the white man in Jamaica had oppressed and degraded the black race they would seize the opportunity to reverse this process through the training of a black ministry since the way to reach black Jamaica was through religion. Gordon argues that the training of a black clergy by the established church would have sent the right message to black Jamaica—namely, that the church was serious about reversing the blight the planter class had inflicted on the people. This effort would certainly help remove the contempt black Jamaica had for white people. But according to Gordon what happened in Jamaica was that the native form of religion flourished because of the dearth of black clergy and the fact that black Jamaica learned that the religion of the official churches was an attempt to keep black people in their place. The Native Baptists saw their churches as spaces of resistance against plantation life.

It should not surprise us then that with the reality of racial turmoil and the sense of black Jamaicans being excluded from institutions on the island in 1865 that a leader from a local Baptist church led another revolution in an attempt to create space for hope to flourish. I noted that there was general unrest in the country prior to 1865. There were issues of health care, labor, land reform, and now racial prejudice. After emancipation, there was a general deterioration in living standards. During slavery, the master had provided the basic amenities for the slave, but now on his or her own, the slave for the first time was required to provide housing, sanitation, and land to cultivate, live on, and bury the dead. A central issue was the enfranchisement of the peasantry and securing of political rights for the masses. A series of issues brought the problems to the fore. On Saturday, October 7, 1865, a court session in Morant Bay was disrupted by protests organized by peasant farmers. The court ordered the leader of the protest, Charles Middleton, arrested, but when the police sought to enforce the order, Paul Bogle, pastor of a Native Baptist church, and others rescued him from the officers. The following Monday, October 9, Lewis Dick, another peasant farmer, was found guilty by the court for trespassing on the Middleton plantation. When fined by the court, he was instructed by Native Baptist Pastor Bogle to appeal the fine because the lands were owned not by Jamaican government but by the British government. As would be expected, the court issued an order for the arrest of Bogle and twenty others for disrupting the will of the court. In an attempt to arrest Bogle, the police proceeded to his house only to discover that Bogle had anticipated their visit and had had the house surrounded with about three hundred members from his church. The members seized the police as Bogle made them swear "to forsake the White and Brown" and cast their lot with them.

The seizing of the police created alarm but the oath created even more, prompting the custos, the chief magistrate of the parish, to call out the volunteers and immediately request reinforcements from the governor in Kingston. The governor communicated the information to the general who readied his troops to sail to Morant Bay by Thursday, 12 October. On that Wednesday, 11 October, a meeting of the vestry was held to enact regular business, but word had already come that troops had been seen coming by land to Morant Bay over the mountains. Alarmed at the turn of events, the rioters struck, killing the custos, Baron Von Ketelholdt; the Rector Rev. Victor Herschell; and other members of the vestry, Charles Price, Capt. Edward Hutchins, Lieutenants Halt and Reid; together with several other members of the volunteer force. Since the court was also in session, several justices were injured along with some police who came to their aid. Meanwhile, Bogle and his followers returned to Stony Gut . . . and in the local chapel . . . he thanked God for the victory that had been given to them by the Divine hand.[39]

Paul Bogle, his wife, and other members of the family were hung. The soldiers launched a full-scale attack against the citizenry, killing many of them. "In retaliation for the 29 white persons killed and 34 others seriously injured, the homes of all would-be protestors were burned and their crops destroyed. The official records state 1,000 homes burned, 354 people executed by court martial, 50 shot without trial, 25 shot by the maroons, ten 'killed otherwise' and 600 flogged."[40] The Bogle rebellion, another religious response to oppression in the parish of St. Thomas, hardly went beyond the Native Baptist church led by Bogle. Bogle used his congregation as a way of launching a full-scale attack against white rule in Jamaica. He and his followers saw themselves as free. They preferred death to the inequities and inequalities that the system of government in Jamaica offered. He targeted local institutions such as the court, the vestry, the police force. They did not die in vain because their blood provided the foundation for a fair and free society and placed Jamaica on the road to a just society.

I would like now to look at the emergence of the Revival Church, which was a logical outgrowth of the Native Baptist Church. I will not dwell further on doctrines or the liturgical structure of the church. It is generally agreed that Revivalism received its name from the Great Revival, which swept Jamaica from 1860 to 1861. Leonard Barrett provides the following important information about Revivalism:

> How can this Great Revival be interpreted? Was it really a revival of Christianity? The answer is no. There was no Christianity to revive among the slaves. What actually happened was a result of the confused state in which the Blacks found themselves after the Emancipation of 1838. Their expectation that Emancipation would result in freedom and self-betterment was disappointed and instead they found themselves disenfranchised, landless, homeless and without the means to support themselves. The missionaries, who played a great role in the liberation movement, had built up their expectations of a better life in a free Jamaica, but this proved to be nothing more than empty talk. The Great Revival is thus better understood as a rejection of Christianity and a revival of the African force-vitale. . . . What really took place was a forcible amalgamation of Christianity with the African ethos.[41]

Among many Jamaicans, Revivalism is associated with Alexander Bedward, the best known and most popular of the Revivalists. Bedward was arrested for teaching that blacks should overthrow white rule in Jamaica. He saw himself in the tradition of Paul Bogle, on one occasion calling on his oppressors to remember the "Morant War." Born in 1859, Bedward models for us some of the traits of the Revivalist spirit. In a visit to Colon, Panama, he received a vision to return to Jamaica and save the souls of his people. The spirit instructed him to fast three times per week, during which time the gift of healing was bestowed on him. With the gift of the Revivalist spirit on him, Bedward began his ministry in 1895 in Kingston, Jamaica. Albert Raboteau captures the essential of Revivalist practices and theology:

> In two of these groups, Revival and Pocomania, services culminate in African-style possession. However, it is the Old Testament prophets, the four evangelists of the New Testament, the apostles and the archangels, and the Holy Ghost who take possession of the members, not the gods of Africa. Revivalists believe that God the Father created the world and dwells in the "highest heaven." He never descends to visit the services or to possess the believers. Jesus, according to the members of Revival, does visit their services and a "love feast" is held in his memory, but he, like the father, does not possess. Deceased members, however, may return to possess their relations among the faithful.[42]

One of the marks of his ministry was the use of the water of the Mona River in Kingston for healing purposes. People came from as far away as Panama and from throughout Jamaica for the water, which is purported to have had medicinal properties. He attracted the most oppressed among the poor, the group at the bottom of the social ladder from which Rastafari would emerge in the 1930s. In a context in which health care was not provided by the government for its citizens and in which thousands among the Jamaican peasants were landless, the Revivalists, through baths and in this case baptisms, provided healing for weary, forlorn, and sick bodies. This was also one way in which the Revivalist churches counteracted the tendency of the mainline churches to focus on healing the souls of the people and to neglect their bodily needs. Indeed, during slavery the master and quite often the missionary taught that while the soul belonged to God, the body belonged to the master. The Revivalists, steeped in African cosmology, made the connection between body and soul, teaching that to heal the body is at the same time to care for the soul, and contending that many illnesses have spiritual causes. The material and the spiritual were connected.

I should like here to draw on my own experience and recollections of Revivalism and the church. The Revivalist spirit had spilled over into the Baptist Church in which I was brought up as a boy in St. Thomas, Jamaica. Although this church was what is referred to by the local people as Regular Baptist in distinction from the Native Baptist, its celebration of the sacraments exemplified the influence of Revivalism. I recall how my baptismal experience at the age of twelve drew upon African cosmology.

It was early Good Friday morning, about 5:00 a.m. All the candidates for baptism met at the church with the "mothers" and the deacons, and being moved by the spirit, we testified and sang. After much praying in the spirit, we all set out with the church mothers and deacons leading—with all of us dressed in white—to the place where our sins would be washed away. It was about three miles that we walked in the early morning, many of us children not quite understanding the ways of the spirit. My father was the minister and being filled with the Revivalist spirit, he asked each of us if we believed in Jesus Christ. Being assured that we did, he then immersed us in the river. Standing close to him with towels in hand to cover us and ready to calm us if we were overpowered by the spirit was the "water mother," who took charge of each of us and safely guided us out of the water.

Alexander Bedward would not have asked those who came to him at the Mona River to receive water for healing and baptism if they believed in Jesus Christ as a prerequisite for salvation or healing. The Revivalists, unlike the Regular Baptists, did not see Jesus as equal with God. Jesus was one of the prophets, like John the Baptist or a biblical figure like Moses. Therefore, it should not surprise us that when the followers of Bedward referred to him as "Shepherd," he changed his title to the "Incarnation of Christ" with the promise that on December 31, 1920, he would ascend to heaven, thereby destroying the rule of white people and establishing the Kingdom of Bedwardism on earth. In the same vein, Bedward could claim that he was Jesus Christ who was crucified. Some Christians may find this sacrilegious because it sounds as if Bedward were equating himself with God. But the Revivalists did not see Jesus as God but rather as a prophet who had the power to heal, prophesy, and change the oppressive order that was killing black people.[43]

Building on Revivalist Christology, Rastafari is able to make a leap of faith and speak of Haile Selassie as the Christ. And for the Rastas to speak of a human being as divine ensures the divinity of his followers. The Rastas represent a move from the Revivalist focus on spirit-possession to actually encountering the Christ-figure. The divinity of the man-God Haile Selassie ensures the divinity of African people. The emphasis here is on the "uplift of the race." To equate himself with the Christ-figure was another way of referring to Psalm 68:31, "Ethiopia shall soon stretch out her hands unto God," a text that Bedward, like Garvey after him, was fond of quoting. But the impetus for this inclusion of divinity within the sphere of humanity originated with the Revivalists.

It is the spirit that is the focus and the locus of divinity. The ideal life is life in the spirit. The goal of the Revivalist is that all who come within the purview of the Revivalists may be possessed with the spirit. A practical consequence of living in the spirit is that one does not sin. The main sin against which the Revivalist counsels is stealing from one's family or one's community; also counseled against are lying, hatred, criticism, thinking evil, deceitfulness, fornication, being unjust, coveting a neighbor's goods, and placing an evil spirit or spell on a member of the community. Other sins include cruelty to human beings, starving oneself when one has money, taking away the freedom of another, and destroying the garden of another person.

The Revivalists are unique not only in their interpretation of life in the spirit but also in their understanding of fornication. One Revivalist leader illustrates the general attitude to fornication: "We know people have to get to know each other before they marry. There is no definite trial period; they carry through marriage when they find money. If a man or woman goes from one to the other, he is a professional fornicator." Another leader said: "I tell young people to take one person and make yourself comfortable. When you find perfection, that is, one who is satisfactory, marry if you can afford it or live holy with that person. Don't take two or more at one time."[44]

A sense of continuity between Rastafari and Revialist ethics can also be seen in the understanding of "living holy." In the Revivalist interpretation of living holy, while polygamy is rejected and monogamy is advocated, these concepts are reinterpreted, with marriage as a legal contract being the exception rather than the rule. Couples were admonished to live holy, but the traditional understanding of fornication was also rejected. Alexander Bedward, much like his successor Marcus Garvey, was the focus of much harassment by the colonial authorities because, like Paul Bogle before him, he spoke out against British colonialism, telling the crowds that "there is a white wall and a black wall, and the white wall has been closing around the black wall; but now the black wall has become bigger than the white wall. Let them remember the Morant War."[45]

Although he spoke in parables, Bedward's reference to the Morant War reminded the colonial authorities of Bogle's defiance of their authority and his appeal to the police officers who were sent to arrest him that they should forsake the white and brown establishment and throw their lot with the blacks. As early as 1891, he was arrested and placed in jail for four months before being taken to court for trial, where he was judged insane. His end as prophet came in 1921, when after an attempted protest march on Kingston, 685 of his followers were arrested and he was placed in a mental institution. That march included casual laborers, cultivators, carpenters, wharf laborers, butlers, and shoemakers. From this social class came, in fact, a number of Bedwardites who were drawn to Garveyism or who retained dual allegiances. One example of the latter tendency was Roman Henry of August Town, who was active in both the Bedwardite and the Garveyite movements at the same time. Garvey himself realized the link between his and Bedward's work when he publicly stated in 1927 that the colonial authorities would have a hard time putting him in an asylum as they had done with "poor Bedward."[46]

Marcus Mosiah Garvey

Marcus Mosiah Garvey, founder of the Back to Africa movement, was the foremost prophet of black liberation in the early twentieth century. He envisioned the return of black Jamaicans to their homeland Africa. Black Jamaicans, like the children of Israel, were captives in the white man's land, and it was God's will that they experience exodus. "As children of captivity we look forward to a new, yet ever old, land of our fathers, the land of God's crowning glory. We shall gather together our children, our treasures and our loved ones, and, as the children of Israel, by the command of God, face the promised land, so in time we shall also stretch forth our hands and bless our country."[47]

Here Garvey gives what was to become the mission statement of his movement. He felt that white and yellow peoples were clear as to the land to which they belonged and that the black people should also be clear that their land was Africa. "Africa for Africans" was the essence of his cry for the self-awareness and liberation of black people. But Garvey was not unaware of the problems associated with repatriation. He counseled that Africans in the Diaspora would have to organize, and that even then freedom would come like a thief in the night. It would, like the wind, come when least expected: "no one knows when the hour of Africa's redemption cometh. It is in the wind. It is coming. One day, like a storm, it will be here.

When that day comes all Africa will stand together. . . . The political re-
adjustment of the world means this—that every race must find a home;
hence Blacks are raising a cry of 'Africa for the Africans,' those at home
and those abroad . . . the only wise thing for us as ambitious Blacks to do,
is to organize the world over and build up for the race a mighty nation of
our own in Africa."[48]

Born in Jamaica on August 17, 1887, he belonged to both the nineteenth
and twentieth centuries. Like many children growing up in Jamaica, he
could not avoid a confrontation with race prejudice. Garvey tells of not
paying attention to questions about race until he was about fourteen years
old. The situation had to do with him becoming a friend of the missionary's daughter, who confided in him on her departure to England that she
was instructed not to communicate with him while away because he was
a "nigger." "Garvey never forgot this incident. He began to observe Jamaican society and was disturbed at the privilege shown to boys of white or
near white parentage. They were given preparation for government posts,
being sent either to the few prestigious schools in Jamaica or England to
study. In contrast, the blacker boys were given menial trades as laborers
on the large plantations, or in a few cases, when they were especially
bright, they became teachers in government and private schools."[49] Garvey
articulated a theological base with which to counter the racial discrimination he experienced in Jamaica as a child and in his travels in the United
States and Europe as an adult. He reminded his audiences that because
human beings were created by God, no one had the right to treat another
human being as a slave or as less than human. "Garvey challenged African Jamaicans and indeed all persons of African descent to set themselves the task of building a racial as well as a national consciousness, to
liberate themselves from colonialism, to build self-esteem and race pride.
These were and remain the imperatives of decolonization."[50]

One of Garvey's important contributions to racial awareness was foster-
ing the acceptance of racial difference. While he affirmed race consciousness and racial harmony, he disapproved and rejected racial segregation.
He felt that an important ingredient in Jamaica's journey to make peace
with blackness or black consciousness was the affirmation of a sense of
self-worth and self-esteem as crucial aspects of a healthy national psyche.
Garvey sums this up succinctly in the constitution of the Universal Negro
Improvement Association (UNIA).

The Universal Negro Improvement Association advocates the uniting of all Negroes into one strong healthy race. It is against miscege-

nation and race suicide. It believes that the Negro race is as good as any other, and therefore should be as proud of itself as others are. It believes in the purity of the Negro race and the purity of the white race. It is against rich Blacks marrying poor whites. It is against rich and poor whites taking advantage of Negro women. . . . It believes in the social and political, physical separation of all peoples to the extent that they promote their own ideals and civilization, with the privilege of trading and doing business with each other. It believes in the promotion of a strong and powerful Negro Nation in Africa. It believes in the rights of all men.[51]

Garvey articulates his vision for African Jamaica and people of African descent everywhere by advocating racial pride, race consciousness, and material and educational attainments. This provided a basis for the motto of the organization Garvey led: "One God! One aim! One destiny!" He had a special mission for the disenfranchised of the race, the needy, and he had a fervent desire to set Africa on a strong footing economically. Perhaps Garvey's central contribution to Jamaica and the rest of the African Diaspora was not only to keep Africa alive in our consciousness but to press us to clarify where we stand in relation to Africa. "Within four or five years the UNIA became both one of the largest Pan-Africanist movements and the largest international movement of Black peoples on the African continent and in the countries of the Diaspora. At its peak it is estimated that there were 1,700 groups in 40 countries with 4 million members. The largest concentration was in Harlem."[52]

Perhaps because African Jamaicans were suffused with religious consciousness, Garvey would couch his teachings on racial uplift in biblical and theological language. It should not be surprising that the Rastafarians—Garvey's logical successors—followed this rhetorical method. Commenting on an understanding of the doctrine of creation, Garvey posits that "when God breathed into the nostrils of man the breath of life, made him a living soul, and bestowed on him the authority of 'Lord of Creation' [God] never intended that an individual should descend to the level of a peon, a serf, or a slave, but that he should be always man in the fullest possession of his senses and with the truest knowledge of himself. But how has man become since creation? We find him today divided into different classes—the helpless imbecile, the dependent slave, the servant and master. These different classes God never created. He created man."[53]

As Garvey used theological language to challenge social inequality in Jamaica, his message of racial pride and self-esteem and his interpretation of everything, including God, through the lens of Africa remained the same. The Rastafarians, Garvey's successors, took his insistence that God gave all people, and by implication especially people of African descent, the capacity and ability to create history a little further than even Garvey was willing to go. While Garvey insisted that African Jamaicans view God through the lens of Ethiopia, he never explicitly stated that God is black. Garvey said it this way:

> If the white man has the idea of a white God, let him worship his God as he desires. If the yellow man's God is of his race let him worship his God as he sees fit. We, as Negroes, have found a new ideal. Whilst our God has no color, yet it is human to see everything through one's own spectacles, and since the white people have seen their God through white spectacles, we have only now started out (late though it be) to see our God through our own spectacles. The God of Isaac and the God of Jacob let Him exist for the race that believes in the God of Isaac and the God of Jacob. We Negroes believe in the God of Ethiopia. . . . We shall worship him through the spectacles of Ethiopia.[54]

Garvey did not attribute color to God, but he insisted that African Jamaicans should see God and view life through the spectacles of Ethiopia.

What does it mean to view God through the spectacles of Ethiopia? For Garvey, this meant coming to grips with your African-ness. It meant racial uplift, racial pride, and recognizing that God who made you "Lord of Creation" imbued you with the capacity and ability to make history and to refuse to be imitators and spectators. In a profound sense, for Garvey this was a statement against the anthropological poverty he encountered among African Jamaicans and people of African descent. Because of this in a country in which many Jamaicans saw self and God in the light of the white ideal, Garvey insisted that they should see God through the spectacles of Ethiopia. But Garvey was not radical enough for the Rastas. Countering anthropological poverty meant an affirmation of one's African-ness, but Garvey was not willing to re-interpret God-talk. This is where the Rastas used Garvey to go beyond Garvey. They understood that there was a theological and spiritual basis for the poor self-esteem and the loss of racial pride that afflicted African Jamaicans. The Rastas understood that for African Jamaicans there was a correlation between construing God as white or colorless and having poor self-esteem. The problem, according to the Rastas, was not that many Jamaicans saw God as colorless, as Garvey implied, but that they saw God as white. The anthropological implications of this view of God were that in a context in which there was a clear religious and theological orientation of the people, they interpreted themselves in the light of this white divine ideal. The Rastas turned this around by seeing God as a black man, Haile Selassie. This reversed the anthropological poverty and gave them permission to re-value themselves and see themselves as made in the divine image.

At the fourth convention of the UNIA in New York City in 1924, the religious question came to the floor. Garvey's theological position was affirmed that God is spirit with the provision that black people should nonetheless visualize God in their image and likeness. "Remarked an old lady from Alabama, 'No white man would die on a cross for me.' A delegate from Mississippi said, 'The man of sorrows ain't nothing else but a colored man,' to which many said, 'Amen, brother.' Rev. J. Barbour of Abyssinia, referred to John caught up in the grand Council of God on the Isle of Patmos, describing Christ as 'a Black man with feet that shone as polished brass, hair of lambs wool, and eyes with flame of fire.'"[55] Although Garvey did not explicitly advocate the worship of a black God, he did not correct others when they did.

The New York Journal reported that at the convention "Marcus Garvey, President-General of the Universal Negro Improvement Association offers one reasonable suggestion. He says, 'God tells us to worship him in our own image. We are Black, and to be in our image God must be Black. He insists, therefore, on a Black God for colored people, with Black saints, and in addition demands the whole of Africa for the colored race.'"[56]

One could argue that Garvey's rhetorical skills were at work, and that by insisting each race view God in its own image he was leaving the door open for God to be or to become black. He contended that God is spirit and therefore transcends race, but at the same time, he asserted that God is race-specific as black people have no choice but to visualize a black God. Garvey sought to institutionalize his views about God and religion by forming his own church. He appointed the Caribbean-born George Alexander McGuire as chaplain-general of the UNIA. McGuire, who hailed from St. Thomas in the Virgin Islands, had roots in the Moravian Church but became affiliated with the Episcopal Church while in New York and Philadelphia. With Garvey's help, McGuire founded the African Orthodox Church (AOC), which became the official church of Garvey's movement. Members of the UNIA were not required to become members of this church, but if a member did not have a church home this was recommended and expected.

The AOC was strongly West Indian. . . . It maintained fraternal relations with the Russian Orthodox Church and when the General Synod of the Independent Episcopal Church met to become the African Orthodox Church, an unsuccessful move was made to omit "African" from its name and substitute "Holy." The AOC admitted persons of all races but according to its Constitution it "particularly sought to reach out and enfold the millions of African descent in both hemispheres." At the . . . Fourth International Convention . . . McGuire advised Negroes to name the day when all members of the race would tear down and burn any pictures of the white Madonna and Child and replace it with a Black Madonna and Child.[57]

One aspect of Garvey's appeal to the masses was certainly the openness the peasant class found in his teaching concerning the nature of God and the nature of black humanity. No one who heard or read Garvey had any doubt that the uplift of the black community in Africa and in the African Diaspora was of primary significance for him. The UNIA motto, "One God, one aim, one destiny," was about empowerment of the black masses. I note the suggestion at the fourth International Convention in New York made by Chaplain General Bishop McGuire to burn white images of the Madonna and Child and by implication to throw out all white images of God. It is clear that the bishop articulated a theology that not only met with Garvey's approval but indeed was Garvey's.

The double emphases of Psalm 68:31, "Ethiopia shall soon stretch out her hands," and of the saying attributed to Garvey by the Rastafarians, "Look to Africa where a Black King shall arise," and Garvey's insistence that each people must interpret God for themselves, provided a rational and reasonable basis for the Rastafarians to look to Ethiopia for the renewing of their hope and for the advent of their salvation. It must be kept in mind that Garvey had a measure of ambivalence toward black religious groups such as the Bedwardites, Revivalists, Pocomania, and Rastafarians. This is rather surprising since groups such as Rastafarians are logical descendants of Garvey and are bearers of his legacy. "Of significance was the censuring of religious cults in Harlem and the West Indies, namely the Father Divine Movement, Holy Rollers, Pocomania, and the Bedwardites. Garvey was also reported to have been critical of the Rastafari movement."[58] Rupert Lewis suggests that there are two reasons at least that may account for Garvey's ambivalence toward other such black religious groups. First was the nervousness among Garveyites that membership in these groups would mean an erosion of the numbers of the UNIA. The members of several of these groups were also members of the UNIA. There was the fear that double loyalty could imperil membership in their organization. The other reality is that the negative attitude toward these groups was voiced at the seventh UNIA convention in 1934. Lewis suggests that the radicalism of the 1920s had given way to a mainstream approach. The point being made is that by the 1930s Garvey had moved away somewhat from the lower classes and had aligned himself with mainstream institutions. This is illustrated in an August 17, 1934, editorial by the *Daily Gleaner* concerning the Rastafarians: "What is to be done to curb an evil that is gathering strength around Kingston, St. Thomas and elsewhere in the island?"[59] Lewis observes that it is ironical that in 1934 Garvey and the *Daily Gleaner* had a similar attitude toward the Rastafarians. There seemed to have been bad blood between the Garveyites and the emerging Rastafarians. "The cult of Ras Tafari in its most fundamental form was not accepted . . . by the majority of Jamaican Garveyites. The better-off Black and the lower-status born elements, the artisans, shopkeepers and clerks who formed the backbone of the UNIA looked to the Emperor with interest and hope, but not worship. It was to the poorest and most exploited, the squatters and laborers of eastern St. Thomas and the inhabitants of West Kingston that Howell and others most appealed."[60]

Another issue that complicated the matter in terms of the relationship between the Garveyites and the Rastafarians was that in 1934 Garvey found himself campaigning for "election to the Legislative Council of Lewis Ashenheim, a Jewish businessman and lawyer."[61] There seems to be a marked difference between Garvey of the 1920s and the 1930s. It is quite likely that the later Garvey had moved to embrace middle-class people and middle-class values as his running for legislative office seems to indicate. I recall, from having lived in eastern St. Thomas from the late 1930s to the 1950s, that at that time the Rastafarians had replaced the Garveyites as the outcasts in Jamaican society. Not only were they at the bottom of the social and economic ladder, but they were regarded as heretics as they not only viewed God through the spectacles of Ethiopia but also identified God with the Emperor Haile Selassie I. While middle-class Jamaicans and certainly many Jamaicans who belonged to the lower stratum of society could relate with pride to a black king in Ethiopia, they regarded it as anathema to regard him as God. It is also clear that Marcus Garvey was not enamored with Haile Selassie. Garvey wanted Selassie to succeed as king of Ethiopia, but he maintained his Christian commitment and regarded Rastafarianism as a cult for misguided people. As Garvey resettled in London in the heat of the Italo-Ethiopian war, he leveled a scathing criticism of Emperor Haile Selassie.

> He kept his country unprepared for modern civilization, whose policy was strictly aggressive. He resorted sentimentally to prayer and feasting and fasting, not consistent with the policy that secures the existence of present day freedom for peoples whilst other nations and rulers are building up armaments of the most destructive kind as the only means of securing peace. . . . And protection. . . . The results show that God had nothing to do with the campaign of Italy in Abyssinia, for on the one side we had the Pope of the Catholic Church blessing the crusade, and on the other the Coptic Church fasting and praying with confidence of victory. . . . It is logical, therefore, that God did not take sides, but left the matter to be settled by the strongest human battalion.[62]

It seems that in the 1930s Garvey's program veered toward the interests of the middle class perhaps because he felt it needed to become mainstreamed as he built the base for a black capitalist enterprise. Is this what the *Black Star Liner* was all about? In the meantime, the colored class in Jamaica looked down on the black underclass of which Rastas were a large part and judged them incapable of success in Jamaican society.

The black underclass was locked out of educational and economic opportunities. Many of the secondary schools were reserved for the children of the colored class. This was also the case with many jobs in the civil service and banking sectors. To make it in the Jamaican society of the 1930s, 1940s, and 1950s, one had to abandon blackness. This means that in many respects Garveyism and Rastafari were on opposite poles of the spectrum. "Garveyism looked to the future and economic progress while Rastas looked to the traditions of an Africanized peasantry. The Rastas never sought to reconcile blackness with modern concepts of economic development, nor did they participate in reformist programs for the humanization of capitalism, such as labor unions and political parties. In the Jamaican labor unrest of 1938, for example, Rastas played no role in the workers' struggles for union representation and governmental regulation of labor abuses. . . . The Rastas also shunned the work ethic and Christian concept of charity, which, along with an acceptance of the inferiority of Blackness, were ideas espoused by the rising White and mulatto middle classes in Jamaica."[63]

Although there were these variants in the ideologies of Rastafari and Garveyism, Rastas were able to separate out what was unhelpful and embrace what was crucial for the practice of their faith. For example, they did not allow Garvey's criticism of their hero and black Messiah Haile Selassie to become a problem for them. They did not seek to second-guess Garvey but inquired as to how they could sign up along with Ethiopian troops to defend the land of their dreams on which they had pinned so much hope. Garvey was merely a prophet of the order of John the Baptist, and for the Rastas this did not exempt him from error. He had fulfilled his mission and ministry. His mission, like that of John the Baptist, was to point to the one who was to come. So it was fine for Garvey and for that matter any other person to criticize Rastafari or Messiah Haile Selassie because his credibility or efficacy did not depend on what anyone said about him. However, to do so one had to be born a Rastafari—meaningful criticism had to come from within Rastafari. The Rastas were not surprised that when Haile Selassie visited Jamaica in 1967 he declared that he was not God or a god, nor was he the black Messiah. The response of the Rastafarians was that this denial was in keeping with the messianic secret. They asked if it were not true that even Jesus the Christ according to biblical reports often denied that he was the Messiah. For the Rastas, criticism does not weaken their resolve to affirm Ethiopia as the Promised Land and to see repatriation as redemption linked to the eschatological hope grounded in Haile Selassie. Criticisms provide occasions for reasoning, that is, discussion among the brethren that serves to deepen the faith. No new ideology or criticism could shake their indomitable faith that Haile Selassie was the Messiah sent by God to liberate black people and get them ready for their journey to the Promised Land of Ethiopia.

Echoing the anthem of Garvey's UNIA, "Ethiopia Thou Land of Our Fathers," the Rastafari assert that Ethiopia is the real Zion referred to in Scriptures. At the same time, they point out that Ethiopia is the only African country never under colonial domination (except for a brief incursion by Italy). This joining of the biblical with the concrete historical extends to their interpretation of the entire New Testament. For the Rastafari, the true children of Israel are the blacks and their descendants in Africa and in exile in the Diaspora. The exodus will be a return to Ethiopia, the Promised Land.[64]

2
The Social Context

The Rastas do not follow their prophet Marcus Garvey uncritically. While Garvey advocated a black capitalism, often reminding his followers of the virtues of wealth and the importance of being competitive and taking advantage of black opportunity, the Rastas—who emerged from the black underclass in Jamaica and who were often frowned on by the colored class and white elite—contend that capitalism and its attendant values of racism and classism are products of Babylon. They regard their current situation of powerlessness and poverty in Jamaica as a consequence of the evils of colonialism and political chicanery, a system they call Babylon. Because they are dealing with the forces of Babylon, they are convinced they cannot make peace with the economic, political, and police powers in Jamaica. Babylon is evil, and the task of the Rasta is not to attempt to transform Babylon but to flee Babylon for Ethiopia. William Lewis, in *Soul Rebels,* succinctly explains that "the Rastas never sought to reconcile Blackness with modern concepts of economic development, nor did they participate in reformist programs for the humanization of capitalism, such as labor unions or political parties. In the Jamaica labor unrest of 1938, for example, the Rastas played no role in the workers' struggle for union representation and governmental regulation of labor abuses. In addition to rejecting reform measures and 'Negro capitalism' the Rastas also shunned the work ethic and Christian concept of charity, which, along with an acceptance of the inferiority of Blackness, were ideas espoused by the rising white and mulatto middle classes in Jamaica."[1]

It is quite clear that the masses of Jamaican people who were sympathetic to the vision of Marcus Garvey were not economically or culturally affected by his vision. In the 1930s, most Jamaicans were landless and unemployed. In 1934, the *Daily Gleaner* reported that "hundreds of thousands of our people are mere squatters on properties off which they may be turned at any time. . . . There is no hope for the prosperity of the peasants until they are settled on lands of their own. . . . There is too much land monopoly in this agricultural society."[2]

The situation had not changed when I came along in Jamaica during the 1940s and the 1950s. There was a sense of economic hopelessness for the masses of Jamaicans who comprised the underclass. It was in this context that Rastafari was born.

> It was the famous Jamaican uprising of 1938, however, which illustrated this process most clearly and became a symbol of the region-wide upheaval. In 1935, unemployment in Jamaica stood at 11%, while another 50% were employed only part of the year. Employers followed a system of "rotational employment" in which they would take on a worker for two weeks and then fire him to make room for another. By 1936, Jamaican workers were organizing under the leadership of Hugh Buchanan, an ex-Garveyite and the first Jamaican Marxist, and G. S. Coombs, a union leader. Throughout the next year, ". . . the whole country rumbled with huge marches and strikes" involving banana workers, sugar workers, ex-servicemen, dockworkers and other groups. By 1938 things had come to a head. Estate after estate went out on strike, protesting not only low wages but also the burden of rents, and thus zeroing in on the key question, control of land.[3]

A number of individuals, among them Leonard Howell, Robert Hinds, Joseph Hibbert, and Archibald Dunkley, drawing on the teachings of Marcus Garvey, turned their attention to what seemed like a strange happening in Ethiopia in November 1930—the coronation of Ras Tafari as emperor of Ethiopia. But, as noted earlier, much of the impetus for this new religion can be found in the Native Baptist churches that flourished during slavery and provided an exodus out of slavery. Leaders such as "Daddy" Sharp, Paul Bogle, and numerous others in the Myal and Revivalist churches are precursors and forerunners of the Rastafari Church. Indeed, what we find emerging in the Native Baptist, Revivalist, and Rastafari churches is what may be appropriately called the church of the disinherited. The economic situation in Jamaica coupled with the cultural dislocation of the majority of Jamaicans forced them to seek a context in which to make sense of God-talk as they sought to carve out social, cultural, and political space for themselves. Faced with social and economic disenfranchisement and terminal poverty, they turned to religion as a form of empowerment and resistance to help them understand local and global events. The person who provided leadership for this resistance to colonial ways of being in Jamaica was Leonard Percival Howell, a Garveyite who migrated to Harlem, New York, and met and worked with Garvey. Howell returned to Jamaica in 1932 and began teaching in Kingston about Ras Tafari, the king of Ethiopia, in January of the following year.

Howell held his first public meetings on the subject of "Ras Tafari, King of Abyssinia" in Kingston in January 1933, but, failing to attract the community of followers he had hoped for, he soon shifted his center of activities from the capital to the countryside, and specifically to that heartland of Afro-Creole countertradition, the parish of St. Thomas in the east, to which he moved in April 1933. It was here—in a human and cultural crucible where the traditions of Afro-Jamaicans meet and merge with those of the descendants of maroons and African and East Indian indentured laborers—where Howell made his earliest converts. And it was here that, after a meeting held in Trinityville on April 18, 1933, he first attracted the attention of the authorities when he urged his audience to sing the national anthem, but before you start, he told them, you must remember that you are not singing it for King George V, but for Ras Tafari, our new king.[4]

Howell and his associate Robert Hinds attracted the attention of the police and were continually in trouble with the authorities for teaching that the people of Jamaica should pay homage to Haile Selassie rather than the king of England. But Howell and his associates went even further than this, contending that Haile Selassie was the Messiah, indeed the black Messiah, and a descendant of King Solomon and the Queen of Sheba who would deliver from oppression all blacks of African descent. Jamaican society never forgave Rastafari for ascribing allegiance to a foreign head of state other than the British royalty. And the second problem, which was related to the former, was Rastafari's looking to Africa for redemption. Marcus Garvey discovered and Rastafari would learn that Jamaica was not at peace with blackness. The central question that Rastafari forced Jamaica to deal with was its relationship to Africa. A third problem, to be considered later, was Rastafari replacing Christian faith with loyalty to Haile Selassie and the acknowledgment of Rastafari that a human being—and in this case an African person—is God. This was dismissed by the church and the majority of Jamaicans as blasphemy.

"The mission also attracted the attention of the police, especially when in 1937 Hinds claimed in public that the new British king, George VI, had not been properly and legitimately crowned and that, accordingly Haile Selassie was the true sovereign of Jamaica, as he was of all Africans at home and abroad."[5] This dismissal of the British Crown was one way in which Rastafari sought to galvanize fellow Jamaicans in an attempt to fight colonialism and the culture of poverty that created disillusionment among the Jamaican masses. Rex Nettleford highlights the critical elements in the social context that provided fertile ground for the flourishing of Rastafari: "the widening gap between rich and poor and the attendant deepening of class differences, the failure of political leaders to find effective answers in the wake of independence, the disinheritance following on increasing foreign ownership of key resources, all served to give the Rastafarian 'rumblings' a rationality and a continued centrality to the quest for identity and for economic security among the Black majority. Inequalities were further underlined in the mal-administration of justice and the indiscretions of the police."[6]

It is significant that one hundred years after slavery had ended, the structure that endured was the one that held sway during slavery. There were a handful of white people at the apex of the society, a fair number of browns in the middle, and the masses of blacks at the bottom of the society. The country was in the grip of a situation characterized by high unemployment, poor housing, and many malnourished children. The black poor benefited the least from any progress the country had experienced.

The people revolted against these atrocities in 1938. The revolt began with the field hands—those who worked on the sugar estates. Very soon they were joined by workers in factories, sanitation workers, and those who worked at the docks. "Inadequate housing, low pay, unexplained wage deductions and unemployment added more fuel to the uprising. Alexander Bustamante and Norman Manley, two rising political stars who were to become major political figures in the ensuing decades, attempted to settle the problems of urban workers and peasant farmers; however, the forces of oppression had been too long in the making to easily placate their protests."[7] The masses of people did everything to disrupt the infrastructure of Jamaica. Eventually the colonial powers, along with the persuasion of Bustamante and Manley, were able to quell the revolt. The prices of bananas and sugarcane increased, making the lot of the peasants in rural parishes a little better. In the ensuing weeks, eight people were killed, thirty-two wounded, and four hundred imprisoned. The government commissioned a study chaired by Lord Moyne of the problems that led up to the uprising.

What is of interest for our study is that the Rastas did not participate in the uprising. They did not join the masses in blocking roads, wielding machetes, and disrupting the infrastructure. They regarded Jamaica as Babylon and did not believe Babylon could be transformed. They focused on talk about repatriation to Ethiopia, where Haile Selassie would provide redemptive space for the healing of black people everywhere. This raises at the onset one of the contradictions of Rastafari—an imbalance between word and activity. While Rastas are known for speech that is often violent and aimed at shocking and pressing one to engage in self-criticism, there is not a commensurate balance with action aimed at changing the situation. The theological and philosophical basis for this position is that Babylon must be destroyed as it is not capable of transformation.

So it is not surprising that toward the end of the 1930s Howell and his group retreated to Sligoville and founded Pinnacle, a commune in the hills in St. Catherine where they briefly received a respite from the harassment of police brutality. Howell called his newfound community the "Ethiopian Salvation Community." "The community which was explicitly compared to a maroon settlement in the *Daily Gleaner* and *Jamaican Times* in 1941 survived several police raids in the early 1940's. In the course of one of them Howell was again arrested, along with sixty seven of his followers, but the community continued to retain a quasi-autonomous existence more on the margins of established society than completely outside it."[8]

Howell's naming the commune at Pinnacle the Ethiopian Salvation Society recalls Garvey's emphasis on Ethiopia. Garvey's UNIA national anthem was titled "The Universal Ethiopian Anthem." And the first Native Baptist preacher in Jamaica, George Liele, named his church the Ethiopian Baptist Church in 1784. There certainly was an Ethiopian tradition in Jamaica, which is surely why Garvey asserted that "we Negroes believe in the God of Ethiopia, the Everlasting God—God the Son, God the Holy Ghost, the one God of all ages. This is The God in whom we believe but we shall worship him through the spectacles of Ethiopia; and as Scripture foretold, Ethiopia shall once more stretch forth its hands to God."[9]

A point worth making here is that for the Native Baptists, Garvey, and now Rastafari, Africa was the organizing principle that gave consistency and coherence to their way of life. It was at Pinnacle that the Rastas developed their community-style approach to life in which they differentiated themselves from Babylon by smoking ganja, the holy herb; wearing dreadlocks; and lashing out against Babylon. It was here at Pinnacle that Rastafari as ideology and theology was born and the "Seven Principles of Rastafari" took root. In his article "The Seven Principles of Rastafari," Ras Ishon Williams, himself a Rasta, gives us some clues of the making of the Rasta community that emerged at Pinnacle. I will look at these seven principles, which provide a frame for talk about salvation in the Rasta community.[10]

Principle 1. The Belief in His Imperial Majesty Haile Selassie I as the One Spoken of in Revelation 5:5

"And one of the elders saith unto me, weep not: behold, the Lion of the tribe of Judah the Root of David, hath prevailed to open the book, and loose the seven seals thereof." A cardinal tenet of Rastafari faith is that King Solomon and the Queen of Sheba are the parents of Menelik I. According to Rasta belief, this places in Ethiopia the Solomonic dynasty, which ended with the disappearance of H.I.M. [His Imperial Majesty] Haile Selassie in 1974. The title he was given when he became emperor was Lion of the Tribe of Judah.

According to Ras Ishon, there is both historical and biblical basis for establishing Haile Selassie as Messiah. He is a descendant of King Solomon and the Queen of Sheba, and he is also the one that Scripture speaks of in Revelation 5:5. Rastas may not be precise in their interpretation of Haile Selassie as Messiah. While some claim he is the Christ returned and others insist he is a new Christ, they are united in the belief that Haile Selassie is God. This is the bedrock of Rastafari faith. But there is openness in the faith as to whether one prefers to relate to Haile Selassie as Messiah or as God. This openness provides an opportunity for reasoning. Reasoning is seen as a forum for the sorting out of Rasta belief and doctrine. "H.I.M. [His Imperial Majesty] is the divine head of the Rasta way of life, and nothing can, or will ever change that. Regardless what the various sects, houses, or branches on the tree of Rasta may say. They must accept the divinity of H.I.M."[11] Howell and his group were the architects of this first principle.

Principle 2. Marcus Mosiah Garvey

Ras Ishon reminds us that one reason for Rastafari's loyalty to the ideology of Marcus Garvey was Garvey's admonition, "Look to Africa where a Black king shall arise." For Rastas, this prophecy provided a horizon beyond Babylon and validated migration as a way of salvation. Coupled with Garvey's admonition to look to Africa was his insistence that God should be worshipped through the spectacles of Ethiopia. Rastafari took this to signify that Garvey prophesied and gave permission for them to worship Haile Selassie as God. It is of interest that Garvey voiced his disapproval of the Rastas' worship of Haile Selassie. Garvey criticized Haile Selassie as unprepared for and of behaving as a coward in his conduct of the Italo-Ethiopian war. But Garvey's critique did not dissuade the Rastas from according reverence and divinity to Haile Selassie. As far as the Rastas are concerned, Garvey was like John the Baptist. His sayings, while prophetic, were not imbued with inevitability or ultimacy.

"The true Rasta knows the reason why Garvey's power will never die. I and I know that our words, actions and deeds represent the living continuation of the prophet that gave us so much. As long as his name is spoken with respect, his works performed in the manner intended, and his lessons taught to the ignorant among us, he will not die, but live on forever as the prophet who point us to the Rastafari."[12] The Rastas claim that prior to Garvey's departure for the United States in 1916, he implored his followers to "Look to Africa for the crowning of a Black king, he shall be the redeemer." All Rastafarians regard Haile Selassie as that king and credit Garvey for this revelation.

Principle 3. Fight against Oppression

Much of the battle that Rastafari wages against oppressive conditions is rhetorical. Words for Rastas have power, and when aimed at oppressors—whom Rastas prefer to term "downpressors," claiming with typical attention to sounds that there is nothing "up" about "oppressor"—these words are judgmental. The words often embody an expression of anger and divine wrath. Ras Ishon reminds us that it was the physical oppression of the Jamaican underclass in the 1930s that created the conditions for the emergence of Rastafari. Perhaps one reason why physical violence is seldom resorted to is that Rastas often refer to the oppression they confront as spiritual warfare. The one exception with which I am familiar is the situation that erupted in Kingston in 1959–60 between Claudius Henry, who referred to himself as Repairer of the Breach, and the police force. Claudius Henry, born about 1900, emerged as one of the powerful Rastafarian presences in Jamaica in the 1950s. Henry had a history of resisting colonialism; in 1929, he was arrested for attacking the Anglican Church in Jamaica as an agent of British colonialism. He was adjudged to be insane.

> In March 1959 Henry distributed large numbers of blue cards to members of the public in Jamaica that purportedly would take Pioneering Israel's scattered Children of African Origin back home to Africa, this year 1959, deadline date Oct. 5th. At least five hundred hopeful "emigrants" turned up at Rosalie Avenue on the appointed day, and in the affray that followed when it became clear that no Africa-bound boat or plane was going to arrive that day or any other, Henry was arrested, fined and bound over to keep the peace for a year. When he failed to do so the police raided his Kingston headquarters on 6 April 1960 and, to their amazement discovered an arms cache consisting of several sticks of dynamite, over five thousand detonators, a shotgun, some twelve-bore cartridges, a revolver, and an array of swords, clubs, batons. . . . Still more astounding, they discovered a letter addressed to Fidel Castro announcing an imminent "Invasion on the Jamaican Government" and promising that "Jamaica and the rest of the British West Indies will be turned over to you and your Government, after this war which we are preparing to start for Africa's freedom is completed."[13]

It was this confrontation with the Jamaican government that caused the government to commission three academics from the University of the West Indies to undertake a study of the movement. This study, which in many respects was sympathetic to Rastafari, sought to help Jamaica rethink policies and perceptions of Rastafari. The issuing of the report two weeks after it was commissioned began the process of middle-class Jamaicans attempting to accommodate Rastafari as a way of life. Coupled with this was also the role that music played in interpreting Rastafari ideology and theology to the populace.

The Claudius Henry affair was one of the few attempts of Rastafari to change Babylon by violent means. Rastas are a peace-loving people and view violence as a means of last resort not aimed at changing society but protecting the individual or community.

Principle 4: Ethiopia the Holy Land

There has been from the arrival of enslaved Africans in Jamaica a tradition of Ethiopianism. This is illustrated by the first African-American preacher, George Liele, arriving in Jamaica and naming his church the Ethiopian Baptist Church. Some time later, Marcus Mosiah Garvey adopted the Ethiopian national anthem as the official anthem of the Universal Negro Improvement Association (UNIA). I also noted earlier that Marcus Mosiah Garvey made Psalm 68:31 ("Ethiopia shall soon stretch out her hands unto God") a seminal text of his movement, and it is one that Rasta-farians imbued with prophetic significance. Garvey's association with this text was one reason the Rastas gave for looking to Ethiopia and finding in Haile Selassie the promised Messiah who would facilitate the emancipa-tion of African peoples. Through Haile Selassie, all of Africa's children would be delivered from bondage of all kinds. Rastas, who are often seen with the Bible in one hand and the newspaper or radio in the other (they are always seeking to discover what the news in the world is reporting), point to Isaiah 43:3: "For I am the Lord thy God, the Holy one of Israel, thy savior: I gave Egypt for thy ransom, Ethiopia and Seba for thee."

Another important text for the Rastas who revere Ethiopia as a holy land is Jeremiah 46:9: "Come up, ye horses: and rage, ye chariots; and let the mighty men come forth; the Ethiopians and the Libyans, that handle the shield; and the Lydians, that handle and bend the bow." Also signifi-cant is 2 Kings 19:9: "And when he heard of Tirhakah king of Ethiopia, behold he is come out to fight against thee." These texts were important indications to the Rastas that Ethiopia was holy and had a special place in the divine plan for the redemption of black people.[14] The sacredness of Ethiopia derives not only from an eschatological hope that their deliver-ance is intimately tied with their return to Ethiopia but from the belief that the biblical Ethiopia is the land of their origins.

An important aspect of the sacredness of this biblical land is that it holds together memory of a sacred past and hope of future deliverance. The messianic hope of deliverance was tied to the land of Ethiopia, from which the Messiah hailed. A robust relationship to the land became the basis for the emergence of black consciousness among Rastafari and for the emergence of a theology of black redemption. William R. Scott cap-tures the power of the tradition of Ethiopianism that swept Rastafari:

> Ethiopianism, as expressed by the Garveyites and other religio-na-tionalists of the day, peaked just before the eruption of the second Italo-Ethiopian war when Haile Selassie I was crowned Ethiopia's

emperor in 1930. The well-publicized and magnificent coronation of the empire's new ruler, who claimed descent from Solomon and Sheba and called himself the Lion of Judah, suggested to a generation . . . much affected by Ethiopian symbology and race oppression that the promised day of universal Black resurgence was imminent. Some cataclysmic event was about to occur, it was felt, that shortly would end the old political order and soon begin a new age when the destiny of the darker races would be perfectly realized.[15]

As has already been made clear, Ethiopia is a holy land and is worthy of pilgrimage.

Principle 5: Repatriation

Jamaicans have always viewed migration as a means of uplift and a form of salvation. The principle of repatriation was directly linked to Marcus Garvey, who insisted, "Africa for Africans at home and abroad." Garvey as leader of the Back to Africa movement insisted that redemption for Africans abroad was tied directly with physical return to Africa. Garvey advocated this at a time when middle-class Jamaicans were ashamed of their African past and associated Africa with the memory of slavery. As did Marcus Garvey, the Rastas received a cold reception from middle-class Jamaica. Because of this, the Rastas modified "repatriation" to mean making a pilgrimage to Africa, not necessarily going to live in Africa. As the Moslems visit Mecca as a place of enlightenment, so people of African descent must visit Africa. Further, after the disappearance of Haile Selassie Rastas came to talk about the Africanization of Jamaica and spoke of Africa being like the kingdom of God existing among us but also found within us: "Rastafari is an African way of life. Our deity is African, our prophet is African, our signs and symbols and philosophy are also African. Therefore, to live according to the principles of Rastafari is to live out the essence of an African way of life. This is the depth to which we are able to take the concept of repatriation."[16]

Principle 6: Ital: The Natural Way

Rastas have been one of the first in the Caribbean to insist on a vegetarian diet. Ital living includes abstinence from meats and salt, but it goes further than this in that it includes a natural approach to life. An anecdote may be helpful here. A couple years ago the Society for the Study of Black Religion had its annual meeting in Kingston, Jamaica. The membership paid a visit to one of the prominent groups of Rastafarians in Jamaica, the Bobo community. The Bobos are constituted as a community with several rituals in place to celebrate community life and the natural approach to living. Most of the members who visited the Bobos and spent the afternoon at their camp were African-Americans. We were eager to understand Rastafari and to identify patterns of living that we felt we had in common with the Rastas. Our first encounter was a shock as we were required to hand over to a member of the Rastafarian community all of our possessions, including passports, wallets or handbags, watches, and shoes. The brethren wanted us to worship and share in reasoning with them, and the first requirement was for us to rid ourselves of material stuff that would distract us from worship. This was a rather transformative experience for many of us; some persons found themselves holding on to their passports, others to their wallets. We were encouraged not to identify self in terms of material possession. We were about to enter into community with members of the Rastafari faith who had turned their backs on material possession. After worship, when we entered into a season of reasoning with the brethren, they explained to us that Ital living had to do with more than being careful about what we ate. "Ital" means natural living in all things. It has to do with a fierce refusal to define self in relation to our passport or our wallets. It includes stripping self of material possessions and discovering that we are organic beings connected with each other and our environment.

The Ital way lends itself to environmental concerns as well. The desire for clean air, water and protection of our trees is of high importance to Rastas as it is to the rest of the world. They need to protect all endangered animals, and more important to protect the Earth. This is the extent to which we desire to develop an Ital way of life.[17]

Principle 7: The Way to Reason

It is fascinating that in the development of Rasta ideology and theology there are several sources at work. I have not looked at Rastas' use of the Bible and other sources of scripture, but beyond a shadow of a doubt the Bible and other sacred sayings are of first importance in the development and articulation of Rastafari faith. One reason they give for the centrality of the Bible in the development of Rasta ideology and theology is that Haile Selassie, like Jesus Christ before him, read the Old Testament. Another source for the development of Rastafari faith is the black experience. That is, they take seriously the Jamaican experience fashioned by slavery and the history of oppression in colonial Jamaica. As mentioned, this experience is viewed through the lenses of Ethiopia. This is brought to the fore in the recognition of a black man as the Christ by black people. Rastas refuse to allow a white Christ or vistas of a white God to devalue or demean the centrality of the black experience. The norm for adjudging these sources is the reality of the black Christ revealed in Haile Selassie I.

I find it intriguing that a central source and way for Rastafari is the Way of Reason. When the Society for the Study of Black Religion met with the Rastas, we shared in worship as we entered the tabernacle and were surrounded with chanting and the language of drums. An important part of the ritual that afternoon was listening to the seven elders expound the faith. Unlike what happens in many Christian churches after the sermon, the Society was invited to the upper room for reasonings. That is, we were encouraged to ask questions about the experience in the tabernacle, to listen to further expositions of the faith, and to propose any questions. According to the Rastas, reasoning is a gift from Jah. There is for the Rastas a thin line between reason and revelation. While there are rules to reasoning, such as study and respecting the views of others, there is a dimension of wisdom present in reasoning that transcends reasoning about Jah or the mysteries of Jah. One reason why Rastas claim that even without formal education they can out-reason academics is that the brethren have wisdom—that is, reason shaped by revelation. Because of this, I noted in the session in the upper room with the Bobo community that the session on reasonings was largely a sharing of revelations that in many cases were esoteric to the group. The Rastas claimed that the give-and-take experienced in reasonings is aimed at keeping the community pure. It was noteworthy that women were excluded from the session on reasonings. When questioned as to why this was so, one of the brethren commented that women were too emotional.

Women in Rastafari

In her informative book *Rastafari Women: Subordination in the Midst of Liberation Theology*, Obiagele Lake wonders out loud how a group such as Rastafari that purports liberation for African peoples could advocate male dominance, hence the subjugation of women. Lake contends that the immediate answer is that the subordination of women in Rastafari parallels that of women in the larger Jamaican and Caribbean context: "Many Rastas believe that a woman can only enter into Rastafari through Rasta men.

Rastafarian women are said to receive guidance from Rasta men and are sometimes dependent on them to gain access to the organization. Rasta men are also considered the spiritual leaders of the movement and the heads of households." The Rastafarian phrase "to grow a dawta," which means to mentally, spiritually, and ideologically initiate women into Rastafari, underscores the childlike status ascribed to women.[18]

Lake points out that although all Rasta women do not live by these principles and guidelines, the majority does. Rastafari is at its very core, Lake contends, a patriarchal movement that looks to the Bible, especially the Old Testament, for its structure and philosophy. The Bible is used in Rastafari to validate the subordination of women, and because this way of life in which the woman accedes to male superiority is also practiced by many Christian churches and has a foothold in Jamaican culture, many people—including Caribbean scholars—are reluctant to criticize.

Another factor that Lake suggests works against women being regarded and treated as equals in Rastafari is that it was founded and organized by men. It parallels the argument given by some Christian churches for the exclusion of women from leadership roles. The argument runs that Jesus, who is the son of God incarnate and the founder of Christianity, exercised his divine prerogative when he chose twelve men to be his disciples. If it were God's will that women should exercise leadership within the church, then Jesus would not have chosen all male disciples. Of course, this argument breaks down in that it is not acknowledged that at his resurrection Jesus sent Mary to tell the disciples that he had risen, thus making her the first apostle. In Christian hierarchy, the apostle has as much power as the disciple.

"The very symbolism of Rastafari is male. The male lion that represents Rastafari is indicative of the androcentric force of the organization. The maleness of the symbol is palpable and suggests dominance and aggressiveness, characteristics that are associated with males. The dreadlocks, even though worn by both women and men, are often worn by men in a style to mimic a lion's mane. The lion is also representative of Haile Selassie who used this symbol to represent the Conquering Lion of Judah."[19]

While Maureen Rowe, herself a Rasta woman, agrees with Obiagele Lake that Rastafari is essentially a patriarchal movement, she is able to nuance her assessment with a historical profile of women's relationship to the movement and their impact on the movement. Because Rastafari emerged from a long line of African religious experiences, Rowe argues that to understand the role and place of women in Rastafari one needs to pay attention to how African patriarchy functions in the Caribbean. Over and against African patriarchy, European patriarchy is based on wealth. In this setting, male authority has a direct connection to wealth. In the European construct of male authority, the male is the chief breadwinner; if the female works, she does so in order to support the male. In instances where the male does not work or makes less than the female, the male is emasculated. Maleness and authority are related to wealth.

Rowe highlights, however, that in African patriarchy maleness is the source of authority. In African patriarchy, authority is intrinsic to maleness and is not dependent on an extrinsic source such as wealth or title. The African male is expected to wield power in the family by virtue of being male. "I have often thought that African women place such a high value on procreation that they allocate a value to the male based on their own valuing of children. The male in this context would have a value assigned to him by the female. The African male, therefore, expects to exercise power and authority in the family by virtue of being male. The male role in relation to the female appears to be one of empowerment. The woman is facilitated by the male, who also supports the family in a manner similar to that of the male in a traditional polygamous household. He will often facilitate her income, generating activities by providing critical support in some areas of domestic life."[20]

To get a meaningful grasp of the role of women in the movement, Rowe suggests the division of Rasta history into three moments: 1930–50, the formative years; 1951–72, the early years; and 1972 to the present. During the formative period, the coronation of Haile Selassie I was celebrated as Jamaica witnessed the crossing of the island by several itinerant preachers extolling the divinity of the emperor. The majority of the membership during this period was drawn from the Jamaican underclass, which shaped the Rastafari belief system. There was an explosion of the membership in the period between 1951 and 1971. During this period, Rastafari became an urban movement and developed a powerful following. In the third period, Rastafari received both national and international recognition through the efforts of musicians who incorporated Rasta beliefs in their music. The most notable among these musicians was the Honorable Robert Nesta Marley. But this was also a time of severe challenges as Rastafari had to deal with the deaths of His Imperial Highness Haile Selassie and Bob Marley, the foremost evangelist of Rastafari.

Maureen Rowe indicates that while it is true that in the chronicling of the movement little mention is given to the role of women, George Simpson, one of the early researchers of the movement, attests to seeing as early as 1948 both women and men who identified themselves as Rastafari dressed in red, gold, and green scarves and caps. "In the now-famous march of 1954 against police brutality and the routing of Pinnacle Hill, females were noted among the marchers, and in the reports of the trial carried by the newspapers of the day, women were very much present in the court. In fact some of them were arrested along with the brethren and incarcerated."[21] Interviews with women who attended meetings and sided with the Rastas against police brutality make it quite clear, according to Rowe, that there was no difference between how women and male adherents of Rasta were treated within the movement between 1950 and 1960. "Jah Bone's describes the involvement of sisters in ritual fasts, where the males were in control of the gathering, which he calls a 'fasting duty.' He speaks of having in attendance, in 1958, five brethren and two sistren. Of the sistren he says, 'Sister Alice and Sister Etta chant up the room, all the classical and new Rasta songs were paraded in the sweetest of voices, rich in their variety of sounds and stylistic rending.' . . . The sisters were good at licking the chalice."[22] But after making allowance for the role of women in the movement during the formative years, sharing and participating in the rituals and even in one case receiving a vision from Jah to go out on the street and testify (which would be quite significant, because in this case women would be the receiver and bearer of revelation), the bottom line is that they belonged to a movement organized and directed by men. Women's participation was limited in the area of doctrine. In this regard, women would not have equal status with men. It is clear that their role was secondary. Perhaps it has something to do with Rastas' view regarding reasoning, which is a role reserved for men. Further, it must be kept in mind that in the formative stages of Rastafari the Old Testament had a key role in the formulation of ritual life and theology. To understand the role of women in Rastafari, especially in the early period when there was not as much openness in Rastafari to Babylonian culture, one has to struggle with the role of women in the Bible. However, I must return to this later.

A breakthrough began for women in the late 1950s with the emergence of "dreadness" as a way of life for Rastafari. Rowe points out that while it is difficult to date the emergence of "dreadlocks" within the movement, it is quite clear that by the early 1950s they were present. Prior to the emergence of dreadlocks within the movement, combed hair and beard identified the male Rastafarian and head-ties and scarves the female Rastafarian. In addition, Rastas were identified by dressing in red, green, and gold. By the 1970s, dreadlocks became a way of identifying Rastas and differentiating between the people of Babylon and the true Rastafarian. It is fair to say that during this period the two defining realities of Rastafari were wearing dreadlocks and smoking herbs. My recollection of the beginning of the movement in Trinityville, Kingston, and Westmoreland, where I served as a pastor in the church founded by George Liele, was that Rastas always felt they had a right to the holy herb ganja. I cannot remember a time in the 1950s or 1960s when Rastas were not associated with the holy herb. On the other hand, my recall of the preponderance of dreadlocks dates to the late 1950s and early 1960s. I do not recall women wearing dreadlocks in the 1950s. I suspect part of the reason why this was not common among women in the 1950s was because dreadlocks and the smoking of marijuana were associated with the criminal element in Jamaica, and during this period there were several confrontations between the police and the Rastafari community. To wear dreadlocks in the 1950s in Jamaica, especially in urban centers, was to pick a fight with the police. The position began to change in the 1960s as I can recall in Westmoreland Rasta families including women and children wearing dreadlocks. Needless to say, the general public saw them as outsiders. No one outside the Rasta faith would consider wearing dreadlocks during this period. To wear the locks was a badge of membership.

> The introduction of dreadlocks into the movement also began the process of clarifying male and female roles. The male, already in the leadership position, took charge of the development process of Rastafari and, in so doing, defined what it meant to be a Rastafari male. The woman's role at this point, was relevant only insofar as certain practices with which members of the movement were familiar were activities in which women played critical roles. In clarifying religious precepts and sharply defining the Rastafari male, the Rasta man, by a process of exclusion, had begun to define the role of the Rasta woman. Locks appear to have been allowed for females; I have observed several elder sisters with locks, which speak to an early dreading.[23]

The charting of the second phase of the movement takes stock of the interplay between popular culture and Rastafari—the phenomenon of the "rude-boy" culture that was quite popular in Kingston during the 1960s. The rude boy—cool, defiant, and macho—was supercritical of the colonial way of life. It was the open criticism of Jamaica as an expression of Babylon that made the connection between rude-boy mentality and Rastafari. Since the rude-boy phenomenon was a youth movement, several scholars wonder whether these young people were children of Rastafari. The rude boys held a low view of women, to whom they spoke in demeaning ways, referring to them as "ting":

> For the rudeboy, women were necessary conveniences. They provided food, sexual favors, shelter, and offspring, but they were never an integral part of the male's lives. The rudies lived on their own or, interestingly, with their mothers. The rudeboy culture became the youth culture of the 1960's with the activities of Walter Rodney and Rastafari, became politicized. The outcome was reformed rudie and the emergence of a youth culture in the society with a strong alliance to Rastafari. That an obvious link existed between rudie and Rastafari is evidenced by the presence of brethren who, when I first began to trod, kept referring to themselves as "cowboys." "Cowboy" was another way of describing the rudie. Eventually, the association must have raised the consciousness of the rudie; for how else could a self-confessed rudeboy/cowboy become a Rastaman?[24]

‍{ 55

Coupled with the strong critique that the rudie leveled against Jamaica as a colonial state—in spite of Jamaica's attaining independence from Great Britain in 1962—was a fierce passion of racial consciousness that was undoubtedly influenced by the civil rights movement in the United States. Another factor that fired the imaginations of the youth in Kingston during the early 1960s was their admiration of Walter Rodney, who lashed out against all forms of oppression. He was certainly one of the heroes of the youth culture.

It was during this period that the term "daughter" emerged as a term of endearment and respect for women in Rastafari: "Around this time, the movement articulated a clear belief system that included a perception of woman as evil and a potential source of weakness in the male. The general use of the term *daughter* became a common feature of the movement. Not only did the male solidify his control, even ownership, of the movement, but the woman's role became cemented in her childbearing functions. Thus, from a position of equality—and certainly one that paralleled women's role in the wider society—in the formative years, the woman had been reduced to helpmate to the male."[25]

There is another factor that I believe influenced the place of women within Rastafari during this period that many scholars do not take into account. It has to do with the place of women within the church. Although Rastas see themselves as standing over against the church, criticizing the church, often accusing the mainline church of being in collusion with the state and focusing too much on life after death rather than life before death, there seems to be always a not-so-audible conversation with the church as they co-opt church language and make splendid use of the church's book, the Bible. But the critical question here is whether or not another factor that influenced Rastafari relegating women to the sphere of the home as they claimed a high place for the family was not the influence of church practice and teaching. Certainly it had to do with their interpretation of the Bible. What is of equal interest here is that religious groups such as Revivalists and Kumina—which, like Rasta, are offshoots of the Native Baptists and shaped by African traditions and culture—give a more prominent role to women because they, unlike Rasta, depend more on the moving of the spirit. Because Rasta faith is steeped in doctrinal statements and is often the outcome of reasoning, primarily among males, it does not have the openness to the surprise of the *new* that we find in Revivalist groups led by women. This, I wager, is one area in which Rasta ideology more closely approximates the European pole than the African. There is much more of a dependence on the spirit in African-derived religions.

There was a radical infusion of women in the movement during the 1970s. Many entered as part of couples, and others joined as part of the youth movement. Many scholars indicate that this was a time for organizational clarity and also for doctrinal purity. One of the factors that facilitated this development was the creation of camps that were centers of learning and reasoning for Rastas. It was in this context that Rasta theology was hammered out and explicated. The woman who had become a convert to Rastafari was not a part of these camp experiences and therefore would have to depend on the male to interpret her role in Rastafari. The man reaffirmed his position as head of the household and representative of His Imperial Highness Haile Selassie I. The woman's role approximates that of the empress in relation to Emperor Haile Selassie.

However, another reality that decisively shaped the emerging image of the Rastafari women was their reading and interpretation of the role of the woman in the Bible. They did not regard it as coincidental that Eve, the first woman the Bible mentions, was portrayed as weak and an instrument of evil. She was a temptress who led Adam astray; hence, men in Rastafari must be careful not to allow women to lead them astray.

> The first female character is Eve. She it was who, tempted by the devil, in turn became Adam's temptress. Next is Sarai, who when asked by her husband to pose as his sister in order to safeguard his life, did so unquestioningly. Following Sarai is Rebekai who schemes

against her husband to ensure that her favorite son would receive his blind father's blessing. Rachael and Leah, both sisters, vied with each other for their husband's affection, each relying on her fertility to win favor in his eyes. Potiphar's wife attempts to seduce Joseph then, thwarted in her attempts to do so, reported that he had attempted to rape her.[26]

It is clear that Rastas use Scripture to suit their own ends. Here, no mention is made of Queen Esther, after whom a book in the Bible is named, or even of the important role of Miriam in safeguarding Moses. Again it must be observed that the selective use of Scripture to serve their own ends and to keep women in their place in Rastafari is not unique to them. I do not even believe we can say with a clear conscience that Rastas took this proof-texting of Scripture to a new level. The Christian church in Jamaica during this period also used Scripture as a weapon against the oppressed. Unlike the Rastas, who turned to the Old Testament, the mainline churches would turn to the letters of Paul and from them construe through their interpretation that women are ordered by Paul to be quiet in the church and to take a secondary role to men in the home, society, and church.

Rastas also used issues of "purity" to subordinate women to men. Basing their arguments on the Levitical code, Rastas contended that during the menstrual cycle women were impure and should not participate in worship and their roles in the home should be limited. In 1996, when I visited the Bobo community outside Kingston with scholars from the Society for the Study of Black Religion, women were not allowed to enter the tabernacle for a worship experience unless they first had a conversation with one of the empresses of the faith to determine if they were clean. The women later explained that this depended on the time passed since their last menstrual cycle. Several women were not allowed to enter the tabernacle but had to catch the preaching and music through the window. Also, after worship the Rastas invited only the men among us to enter the upper room for reasonings. It cannot be emphasized how much conviction and courage it took for a Jamaican woman to become a member of the Rastafarian faith, especially during the early evolution of this faith.

We must remember that Rastas were treated as outcasts by the middle class as they reinforced values that colonial Jamaica despised. They wanted to remember Africa, and their language heaped judgment on Jamaica for affirming Eurocentric values and seeking to obliterate the memory of Africa. Jamaica, as it was shaped by colonial values, saw whiteness or things European as symbols of freedom and saw blackness or things African as symbols of slavery, bondage, and backwardness. The following system of classification documented by Edward Brathwaite aptly illustrates how middle-class Jamaica valued whiteness and brings into sharp relief the values Rasta stood against:

Sambo: child of mulatto and Negro

Mulatto: child of white man and negress

Quadroon: child of mulatto woman and white man

Mustee: child of quadroon by white man

Mustiphini: child of mustee and white man

Quintroon: child of mustiphini and white man

Octoroon: child of quintroon and white man.[27]

What was at stake was the obliteration of the black stain; hence, the octoroon was legally free in Jamaica during the colonial period. The Rastas took on the valuing of whiteness and the devaluing of blackness and things African. This had a direct bearing on women who would convert to Rastafari as this would run counter to the way upward mobility in Jamaican society worked in relation to women. For many women, the way out of poverty and invisibility was to marry up, and this meant marrying brown or white. To marry someone with a darker pigmentation was to marry down or to put the brakes on upward mobility. Therefore, to become a couple with a Rasta was to turn one's back on the way Jamaican society defined progress. This means there were not a great many women rushing to become Rastafari. It is estimated that in a population of about 2.5 million Jamaicans, about fourteen thousand are Rastafari with approximately 2,600 women. Of course, in addition to the social ostracism that women experienced from the general population, there were the strictures within the movement itself that kept women marginalized. And yet women continued to become a part of the movement both through conviction and involvement with male Rastas. Many Rasta women observed that because the Rasta man had to fight against the colonial powers and often endure police brutality, women's role was to be supportive and to quietly engender change from within. When we come to look at the role of music, we will see the contributions women made to the movement.

3
{ The Origins of Rastafari

Rastafari have progressed from being a group on the outskirts of society to becoming a religious faith that is no longer ignored in Jamaica and is known in many parts of the world. It is clear that Rastafari was a response to poverty, unemployment, economic deprivation, cultural alienation, and the colonial way of life in Jamaica. The colonial lifestyle expressed itself in Jamaica in a system in which a handful of white people at the apex of Jamaican society gave the orders and ran the country's affairs with their power enforced by the police. This was one reason why when Leonard Howell, the first preacher of Rastafari, called on Jamaicans to give allegiance to Haile Selassie, he was arrested and thrown in jail for two years. The Rastas continue to fight this kind of oppression. For example, since national independence in 1962, Jamaica has had a Jamaican governor-general of its own choosing who is nonetheless viewed as the representative of the queen of England. So Rastas have always seen their primary role as that of building a racial as well as a national consciousness to liberate themselves and Jamaicans from colonialism as they seek to build self-esteem and bring about racial uplift.

The catalyst that provided a theological and ideological base for Rastas' protest and an attempt to construct a new social reality in Jamaica occurred in November 1930, when the prince regent Ras Tafari was crowned emperor of Ethiopia. The economic and political situation in Jamaica and the coronation of Haile Selassie were the triggers that led the Rastas to search their Bible for the meaning of these events. Commenting on the socioeconomic situation in Jamaica, the Jamaican scholar Leonard Barrett states that

60 }

> the decade beginning in 1930 may well be called "the decade of despair" for the average Jamaican. The political situation was stagnant. The country was still in the hands of men who had little or no feeling for the hungry masses. The average wage for a full day of unskilled labor was twenty-five cents for men and fourteen cents for women. ... These were the years of the great depression, which saw lines of hungry people. .... Most scholars agree that the movement originated soon after the coronation of Haile Selassie in Ethiopia. The coronation of this African king caused some Jamaicans of African descent both on the Island and in New York to study their Bibles more closely. They remembered a pronouncement by Marcus Garvey: Look to Africa where a Black King shall arise—this will be the day of your deliverance.[1]

It is not surprising that Barrett makes the connection between Garvey's prophecy and Rastas looking to Ethiopia for signs of deliverance from oppressive Jamaica, or Babylon. The Rastas made a connection between Garvey's prophecy that a black king would emerge in Ethiopia and the need for deliverance and liberation in Jamaica. The Rastas felt that what was being signified in the coronation of this African emperor in Ethiopia was nothing less than the death pangs of colonial rule in Jamaica and the signal for black peoples to repatriate to Africa.

Here I would like to call attention to Leonard Howell, Joseph Nathaniel Hibbert, Henry Archibald Dunkley, and Robert Hinds, the early leaders in the movement who define the central teachings of Rastafari.

Leonard Howell

I noted earlier that Leonard Howell first introduced the idea of Haile Selassie as the messianic hope of black people in Jamaica. In the parish of St. Thomas from 1933 to 1940, Howell preached a version of Garveyism. Howell suggested that black people were superior to whites. Because of the injustices perpetrated on blacks by the colonial class, they should withdraw their allegiance to British authorities and pay homage to Haile Selassie, emperor of Ethiopia, the divine who is the only worthy ruler of the black people. Also, black people should get ready for their return to Africa. As early as December 1933 Howell was seen selling pictures of Haile Selassie that were supposed to serve as passports to Ethiopia. Barry Chevannes sums up the main teachings of Howell:

> From the earliest years Howell's main drive was toward the establishment of a *community* of believers. According to informants this was why he moved to St. Thomas in 1933, a parish with a proud history of anti-colonial resistance. This was also his reason for later buying and settling on Pinnacle estate in St. Catherine in 1940. Between living in these parishes, he lived with a small community in Kingston, which earned its living by running a bakery. . . . His very approach to organization was a criticism of colonialism. . . . the bakery was run in such a way that "when a poor man go there and buy a piece of bread you get a little sugar free and a little cornmeal."[2]

} 61

Howell formed the Ethiopian Salvation Society and founded a Rastafarian commune at Pinnacle in St. Catherine. In this commune with more than five hundred members, Howell established a farm community that supplied a local prison in Kingston and at the same time kept a great deal of the food in storage. "Gungo peas, cow peas, sweet potato, yam, coco. You have some store houses . . . full at all times with these things. Livestock included fowls, cows, goats, and beasts of burden. Pigs, ducks, and pigeons were taboo. Howell utilized the free labor of the community to stockpile food. . . . The food stored away also provided entertainment for the visiting Rastafari who came to Pinnacle for celebrations or for visits. . . . Some of these functions were feasts to celebrate the Passover and the anniversary of the emperor's coronation, before which there would always be fasting."[3] Although Howell formed this commune in the seclusion of the hills to escape the gaze of the police authorities, there soon would be frictions between the Rastas and the farmers in the Pinnacle community.

Some reports claim that the early Rastas informed the farmers that taxes should not be paid to the Jamaican government but instead to them as representatives of Haile Selassie. As early as 1941 there was confrontation with the police authorities, who charged several of the members of the commune with perpetrating violence against the farmers and for selling marijuana (ganja). "The Pinnacle community gave to the Rastafari movement its close association in the mind of the public with ganja. 'Anywhere through the island a man want ganja to buy is right there him come. . . . He carry the best herbs.' Howell, it would appear, was the first ganja *farmer*, as opposed to small cultivator. He produced this substance on a sufficiently large scale to meet its growing demand in Kingston. Ganja was Howell's main cash crop."[4]

Two principles from this experiment at Pinnacle have survived and continue to influence Rastafari. These are the reality of the commune and the importance of ganja for ritual purposes.

The Pinnacle commune is an important phase of the early develop- ment of the Rastafarians because it established several facets of the movement. It began a communal pattern of living which has contin- ued among a large segment of the Rasta community. (Today, an ex- ample of the Pinnacle experience is being carried out in the group headed by Prince Edward in St. Thomas.) The use of ganja may have been adopted as a ritual practice in the hills where it was easily grown in abundance and the freedom to indulge was unimpeded. Pinnacle, then, was the wilderness experience which became the "bridge-burn- ing act," solidifying the movement around certain rites and practices with which they are now identified.[5]

The commune was a residential community with each family provid- ing for its own needs. In addition, there was the practice of communal labor for the good of the community and for the sharing of their life to- gether. Each family was responsible for its own upkeep and expected to contribute to the common good. Howell, who lived apart from the com- mune on the top of a hill, functioned as an African chief. "Social organiza- tion at Pinnacle was based on Howell's charismatic leadership. At the head was the 'Gong,' beneath him several deacons, and below them the rest of the people. The Gong lived apart, on the hill that overlooked the estate. He alone ruled the community, and alone gave the punishments, which could be harsh."[6] It seems as if the disquiet between the commune and its neigh- bors and the continual dis-ease between the colonial powers and the com- mune caused Pinnacle to be raided again in 1954. During this raid, the buildings were demolished and the members scattered. "Early in 1954, the police again raided the cultists and 163 members were arrested. Howell and his lieutenants were also apprehended and tried, but by this time the government had become tired of sending them to prison. The judge ac- quitted them as nuisances—but the Pinnacle experience did not end here. The commune was destroyed by the police who then turned the members and their leaders loose in the slums of Kingston."[7]

This scattering of the membership at Pinnacle and the destruction of its buildings by the police marked the decline of the leadership and influ- ence of Howell. In 1960, he was committed to a mental hospital (as had been Alexander Bedward, the charismatic anticolonial leader before

Howell). After his release, Howell lived quietly, refusing to give interviews or to meet with the public; he died in 1981.

Joseph N. Hibbert

Another Rastafari pioneer was Joseph Nathaniel Hibbert, who was born in Jamaica in 1894 and died in 1985. At the age of seventeen, Hibbert migrated to Costa Rica, where he lived for twenty years. There he became a member of the Ancient Order of Ethiopia, a Masonic Lodge. George Eaton Simpson, who met with and interviewed Hibbert, claims, "I have been told that he was regarded as a 'scientist,' that is, as one of the early leaders who was thought to have formidable powers of an occult nature that enabled him to withstand the forces of the colonial period."[8] Barry Chevannes supports Simpson's claim that Hibbert was a "scientist" as "occultism" was the very cornerstone of his Ethiopian Coptic League. Hibbert claimed that there were hidden secrets in the book of Maccabees and in the publications of DeLaurence. These claims represented an ethos that was quite common among Rastas in Trinityville during the 1950s. I remember very clearly members of the Rastafari faith suggesting that the riddles of the universe were hidden in books of the Bible that ministers would not share with their members. Some even suggested that books such as Maccabees and Tobit were hidden in secret places in the Baptist church in Trinityville. Hibbert was able to tap into that mysterious culture and dread that was embodied in Rastafari presence and faith.

> Hibbert gathered around him many such men, awed by his reputed powers and desirous themselves of learning the art of magic. According to an informant, an Englishman wanting to get a true picture of what was going on back home in his domestic life visited Hibbert. Hibbert sent for his former common-law wife, and, using her as a medium, told the man the whole story. The Englishman was so impressed that in addition to paying Hibbert a fee, he gave the medium a one-pound note. Up to his death in 1985, Hibbert continued to be known for his occult powers.[9]

Chevannes gives two reasons for the decline of the organization within Rastafari that Hibbert represented. First, he was unwilling to impart his secrets to new initiates. Several members of the organization claim that Hibbert would allow one to go so far in the organization and no further.

Like many teachers, he would not allow his students to learn his special secrets.

Second, Hibbert could not accept challenge to his leadership, which occurred with the establishment of the first chapter of the Ethiopian World Federation (EWF). According to Brother Duggie, the EWF came to Jamaica through the initiative of Brother Paul Earlington, who saw an EWF advertisement in a copy of the *Ethiopian News* sold on the streets by a man named "Polly." This was late in the 1930s, following the fascist invasion of Ethiopia, a period during which Rastafari and the Garveyites showed intense interest in Ethiopian affairs. The advertisement made it clear that a minimum of twenty-five dues-paying members in good standing were necessary to establish a charter. Earlington appealed to Hinds first, then to Dunkley—both of whom turned down his request for sponsorship—then finally to Hibbert, whose place on the executive committee was as far down as third vice president. Because he could not be president, he ordered all his members out of the local branch.[10]

It seems on the surface that Hibbert functioned as an African chief. Parallels today are found in the black church in the United States or in several Afro-Caribbean communities. Revivalist communities differ, however, in their dependence on the spirit and in their belief that one cannot prejudge how the spirit will lead. Hibbert, on the other hand, saw himself as an ambassador of the Christ figure Haile Selassie. The ambassador could both act and speak on behalf of the Messiah.

Archibald Dunkley

The unwillingness to accept spirit-possession within the movement and the sense that Rastafari was driven by a strong sense of the divinity of Haile Selassie came to full flowering in the life and ministry of Archibald Dunkley. It is reported that he used a sword at meetings and was against any manifestation of spirit-possession by any of his members. A report from a meeting called by Dunkley states:

> We went to Highholborn Street and the meeting was so powerful that I find myself couldn't stand up. All I try to keep down myself I was just wheeling and spinning. And I hear him say him don't want that in here, and continue talking. I feel that I want to stop to steady myself, but I couldn't control, and him say that him don't want that there. I din't say anything, but I never go back. Because if you living

clean, the Spirit of Almighty God lives in you and if him find a clean body him will move in you.[11]

It is instructive that Dunkley was clear that Rastafari was to be differentiated from the practices of the Revivalists. Spirit-possession was a central element in Revivalist teaching and practice but not in Rastafari. While it is clear that Rastafari borrowed Revivalist practices such as chanting, drumming, and dancing, it is also clear that Rastafari did not deem dancing in the spirit to be acceptable. Rastafari, like Revivalists, believed in the Bible. For the Rastafari, the category of blackness—both in relation to their Messiah and in relation to themselves—functions as the hermeneutical key; for the Revivalists, the key was the power and presence of the spirit.

Robert Hinds

Robert Hinds is the fourth founding member of Rastafari. As a Garveyite and follower of Alexander Bedward, Hinds was the most successful of the early Rastas. At one time, his King of King's Mission numbered over eight hundred persons. Unlike Dunkley, Robert Hinds's organization was similar to that of the Revivalist Church. In Hinds's King of King's Mission, the connection with Garveyism, Alexander Bedward, and Rastafari is apparent. It seems clear that a part of the mystique surrounding Hinds was that when Bedward was arrested and taken to be tried at Half-Way-Tree, Hinds was a part of that group. He was admonished by the court and told to return to Linstead, from which he hailed.

Hinds also had a close association with Leonard Howell when Howell got into trouble with the police for exhorting Jamaicans to give loyalty to Haile Selassie, emperor of Ethiopia, rather than to the king of England. After experiencing a Revivalist vision similar to the one Marcus Garvey had concerning the naming of the UNIA, "Hinds launched out on his own instead of returning to St. Thomas with Howell, and set up his headquarters first at 82 North Street then at 6 Law Street, where he remained up to the early forties. His headquarters were known as the 'King of Kings Mission.'"[12]

The King of King's Mission was organized along the lines of a Revival group. "Leader," or "Shepherd," was Hinds himself, whom the members regarded as a prophet. Beneath him were the secretaries, two chaplains, an armor bearer, twelve male officers, and twelve water-mothers. The secretaries were recording officers; literate, they read lessons at meetings and were responsible for correspondence, such as asking for permission from the police to hold a march. The chaplains, water-mothers, and officers were indispensable at baptism rituals, which took place twice a year to mark the reception of candidates into full membership. The process be-

gan when a person accepted the doctrine and at the end of the street meeting gave his or her name to be entered on the register. The candidate then attended the regular weekly meetings, learned more about the religion, and received the instructions of Mr. Hinds. "You only sit and then Mr. Hinds tell you how you must walk and how you mustn't walk in the street with a wantonness, and all like that."[13]

It is quite clear that in the King of King's Mission as established and led by Hinds the Revivalist spirit broke out. Although Hinds purported to be Rastafari, it is clear that one reason for his success was his merging of Rastafari and Revivalism. At this mission there were fasts, feasts, and baptisms—all carryovers from Revivalism. Another feature of Revivalism was a preponderance of women, and, in fact, women did outnumber men at Hinds's mission. It seems as if in the early years of Rastafari, when the influence of Revivalism was still strong, the place of women was not an issue. In both Howell's and Hinds's communities, women were key players. One area in which Hinds's mission differed from the Revivalist community was that he established a court for hearing grievances internal to the mission. Related to the court were seven security guards who were charged with the safety of meetings and also served as members of the court. We should not forget that Leonard Howell had guards at Pinnacle.

It seems to me that Hinds's version of Rastafari is of first importance and thrived because it provided continuity with the Revivalist past on the one hand and a forging with the new practices and beliefs on the other. For example, while Hinds would not allow members to smoke ganja in public or at the mission, there was no problem with them smoking ganja in the privacy of their homes. Hinds was not against the smoking of the herb. As he brought in the new, there was also the millenarian hope that Haile Selassie would answer the question concerning the oppression of black people in Jamaica. While his former shepherd, Alexander Bedward, saw himself as the Christ, Hinds saw Haile Selassie as the messianic figure who would deliver black Jamaica from the shackles of poverty and colonial harassment. Being a Garveyite, he could talk about the Messiah through the lens of Ethiopia and affirm himself as ambassador of Haile Selassie. But this new religion was rooted in the African past through the incorporation of the practices of Revivalism. For Hinds as for his former shepherd,

Alexander Bedward, baptism was a pivotal ritual of the new faith, but he also celebrated the Passover to remind the membership that they were exiles in Babylon who sought to return to Ethiopia. I believe this blending of the old and the new is what gave the King of King's Mission its popularity among the people in Kingston in the early years. Also, it must be kept in mind that the incorporation of the practices from the Revivalist community was at the same time tapping into practices that were current in many mainline churches. Incorporating these practices gave legitimacy to Hinds's mission, and it raises the issue as to whether the future of Rastafari is not an incorporation of practices that emerge from King of King's Mission.

Rastafari Beliefs

Rastafari base a great deal of their teaching about the Messiah and themselves on the Bible. They believe that the Bible was written by black people about black people, which accounts for the preeminent place the Bible has in Rasta theology. At the outset it is worth mentioning that Rastas' approach to the Bible differs markedly from that of the Christian church, with which they are always in conversation. The Christian church regards the Bible as authoritative for matters of life and faith. The Bible constitutes the central authority of faith for the church. With the Rasta faith, there is a shift in perspective and outlook. First, their engagement with the Bible occurs outside the context of the Christian church. The Rastas are critical of this church, often pointing out that the Caribbean church is an extension of the European and North American church and as such is not invested in the alleviation of the grinding poverty in the region. Rastas regard the church as representing the bourgeois class, and the church's biblical exegesis as representing the theological and exegetical interests of that class. Alliance with the state is one of the weightiest charges that the Rastafari levy against the Christian establishment. "Government" and "Jesus" are two closely associated words in Western society, and both bespeak oppression in the Rastas' view: the "tribulation and tormentation that we pass through is not from our own doings, but from them that claims themselves over us, which is the heads of governments and Je-sus. I say Je-sus because the state cannot run without the church. They are all one thing."[14] The Rastas connect their struggle in Jamaican society for solidarity and dignity with the struggle of oppressed Israel and claim that they are the true Israelites. As far as the Rastas are concerned, the Bible exists to serve the needs of the community, and hermeneutics does not begin with a consideration of the historical-critical method but with circumstances nationally or globally that impinge on the lives of the Rasta community. Their primary concern has to do with the ways in which the biblical text affirms Rastas' identity and elucidates issues of dignity in Jamaican community. To Rastas, the biblical personalities, writers, and common people were all black, and the books were all written to teach black people of all ages the proper way to live and worship Jah (God). But "the Europeans, after enslaving the Black man, took his scriptures and attempted to translate them, even though they hardly understood the language in which they were written."[15] Because the Bible exists for the community, the Rastas take from it whatever is helpful for their struggle to eke out a meaningful existence in Babylon, or Jamaican society. Rastas' approach to the Bible often begins with critical reflection on historical practice in Jamaican society or on the global scene. The Bible is not the authoritative source of truth for Rastas. The authoritative source of truth is "Jah" as "Jah" reveals Jah's ways in national or world events or in the Bible. Jah's activities are not limited to the Bible. Jah is active in national and world events, and Rastas often turn to the Bible to find an explanation of what Jah is up to in the world. Because of this, the Rastas are busy with exegesis of both the sociological and the biblical text. They often begin with the sociological text and then move to the biblical text for elucidation and confirmation of what they presume Jah is doing in the world.

Thus the Rastas sit and read with the newspaper in one hand and the Bible in the other. They search out the manifold correlations between contemporary events and the sacred recorded history. Where correlations are found, they are used to help interpret the precise meaning of the present reality and to divine the course of future events. The biblical prophecy that the Rastafarians see being fulfilled in current events has a compelling strength: it must be accomplished.[16]

This seems to be what happened in the 1930s during the founding of the Rastafari movement in Jamaica. According to Leonard Barrett, who worked closely with the Rastas, the economic and political situation in Jamaica during the 1930s and the coronation of Ras Tafari were the triggers that led the Rastas to search the Bible for the meaning of these events:

> When Marcus Garvey left Jamaica for the United States in 1916, his followers in Jamaica fell into disarray. Although the movement continued to exist with local leadership, no one could fill his void. . . . This situation existed until 1930 when Ras Tafari, great grandson of

King Sheka Selassie of Shoa, was crowned Negus of Ethiopia. He took the name Haile Selassie (Might of the trinity), to which was added "King of Kings" and "Lion of the Tribe of Judah," placing himself in the legendary line of King Solomon. His coronation in St. Georges Cathedral, Addis Ababa, in November of that year brought representatives of all the great powers as well as journalists and correspondents from every part of the world. The crowning of a young Ethiopian king, with this Biblical title, together with the pomp and grandeur of the fabled empire, was more than a secular occasion. For the people of Marcus Garvey's leaning, this came as a revelation from God. In Jamaica an almost forgotten statement of Garvey—who, on the eve of his departure to the United States was supposed to have said, "Look to Africa for the crowning of a Black King; he shall be the redeemer"—came echoing back like the voice of God. Possessed by the spirit of this new development, many Jamaicans now saw the coronation as fulfillment of Biblical prophecy and Haile Selassie as the messiah of African redemption.[17]

As events unfolded in Ethiopia and Rastas felt trapped in Babylon, they remembered Garvey's pronouncement, "Look to Africa where a Black King shall arise—this will be the day of your deliverance," and turned to the Bible for answers. The Rastas feel that there is a sense of inevitability to prophecy. The fact that Garvey—for the Rastas, a modern-day John the Baptist—forecast in his pronouncement the coming of a deliverer who would be crowned king of Ethiopia and would in time deliver people of African descent was enough for the Rastas to claim prophetic certainty in this regard. The Jamaican scholar Barry Chevannes supports these claims:

> The year, 1930; the month, November. In the remote kingdom of Ethiopia, then also known as Abyssinia, kings, princes and heads of state from all over the Western world assembled to witness the elevation of Prince Tafari Makonnen as the new Emperor of Ethiopia, Haile Selassie I. "Haile Selassie" means "power of the trinity." . . . Not only is Ethiopia one of the earliest countries to have adopted Christianity, but a part of the Ethiopian nobility, including the Makonnens, had at least since the middle ages claimed descent from King Solomon of Judah and the Queen of Sheba. Self-consciously, therefore, the new Emperor in appropriating as his title "King of Kings," "Lord of Lords," "Conquering Lion of the Tribe of Judah," was reaffirming the ancient roots of Ethiopian civilization and its independent place in the Judaeo-Christian traditions.[18]

The Origins of Rastafari

The Rastas' search for God is grounded in the Scriptures. A biblical text that became crucial for Rastafari as they seek to make theological sense of the events that were unfolding in Ethiopia is Revelation 5:2–5: "And I saw a strong angel proclaiming with a loud voice, 'who is worthy to open the book and loose the seals thereof?' And no one in heaven or on earth or under the earth was found worthy to open the scroll or to look into it. Then one of the elders said to me, 'Weep not: lo, the Lion of the tribe of Judah, the Root of David, has conquered, so that he can open the scroll and its seven seals.'"

As far as the Rastas are concerned, the correlation between the claims made by the new emperor of Ethiopia and the biblical injunctions is ample proof that the new king is divine. Another text the Rastas found helpful in interpreting the titles chosen by Haile Selassie is Revelation 19:16: "On his robe and on his thigh he has a name inscribed, King of Kings and Lord of Lords." The Rastas looked to Africa and to the Bible and became convinced that Ras Tafari was none other than Jesus Christ returned to redeem Africa and people of African descent. A young Rasta man gives us the sense of the process in which knowledge of God emerges in the community: "I started really thinking unto myself, who was really god or who in this time as a man upon earth present himself as god unto man? I began to hear of this man who was Emperor of Ethiopia. And I started checking back and relating stories about him with stories in the Bible. Well more or less these stories start bringing a certain amount of life within me."[19]

In the interplay between the biblical story and the contemporary narrative, the Rasta found an infusion of new life. Robert Hill points out that another event that helped convince the Rastas that Ras Tafari is Jesus returned was the homage paid to him by Western heads of state. According to Hill, one of the dignitaries to visit the new emperor and pay obeisance was the Duke of Gloucester, son of His Majesty King George V. The duke presented the emperor the gift of "a scepter of solid gold twenty-seven inches long which had inscribed on one side 'Ethiopia shall make her hands reach unto God' and on the other side 'King of Kings of Ethiopia.'" The gift and the obeisance of the royal envoy convinced the Rastafarians that prophecy was being fulfilled as Howell, one of the early leaders, read Psalm 72:9–11 for validation: "They that dwell in the wilderness shall bow before him, and his enemies lick the dust! The kings of Tarshish and of the isles shall bring presents: the kings of Sheba and Seba shall offer gifts. Yea, all kings shall fall down before him." The reading of Genesis 49:10 was another confirmation by the Rastafarian community that Haile Selassie was of divine origin: "The scepter shall not depart from Judah, nor a law giver from between his feet, until Shiloh come; and unto him shall be the gathering of the people be."[20] How did the Rastafarians know these things and how could they be sure that the Scriptures referred to Haile Selassie? The answer is found in Jah's revelation to the righteous, which was made plain both in world events taking place in Ethiopia and in their interpretation of the Bible.

The Rastas are convinced that the day is fast approaching when all nations must acknowledge the kingship of Haile Selassie and affirm his universal reign. Ultimately all nations will come to see and all tongues will confess his supremacy. Joseph Owens captures the logic that drives Rastafari:

> When Selassie was crowned in 1930, some seventy-five nations felt obligated to send representatives to pay their respects at the throne of the new Emperor, but such homage was only a foreshadowing of the universal recognition that will inevitably take place, as the following verse declares:
>
> KING NEGUS IS AN ETHIOPIAN BLACKMAN
>
> Born and grow up in Judea
>
> Religion tells us that he comes from heaven;
>
> But the heaven is King David's Royal Throne
>
> HE IS THE FATHER OF ALL NATION
>
> UNTO WHOM THE WORLD MUST NOW OBEY.[21]

The Rastas also find conclusive evidence in the Bible's Song of Solomon (1:5–6) that their Messiah is black: "I am Black, and comely, O ye daughters of Jerusalem, as the tents of Kedar, as the curtains of Solomon. Look not upon me because I am Black, because the sun hath looked upon me."

According to the Rastas, the color of God is also made clear in Jeremiah 8:21: "For the hurt of the daughter of my people am I hurt; I am Black; astonishment hath taken hold of me." Not only were Solomon and Christ black, but there are biblical warrants for claiming that the chosen people of God are black. Some of the main texts cited are Lamentations 4:8, 5:10; Joel 2:8; Habakkuk 2:10; Job 30:30; Psalm 119:83; Jeremiah 14:2; and Revelation 1:14. While Rastas engage in proof-texting to make the point that their God and the chosen people are black, they also point out that the Bible is not the only source for this unique knowledge. A more important source is the inner knowledge that comes from their likeness to that of the Israelites of biblical history: "The Rastafarians constantly point to the glorious age of the Black Race in Africa before the coming of the European. Habitually they refer to the historical figures of Egypt, Ethiopia, and Greece as Blacks of the past who once occupied intellectual and political positions far superior to any achievements of the Caucasian race."[22] The Rastas, like the early Native Baptist George Liele, are constantly relating their story of oppression to that of those people they refer to as their first ancestors, the children of Israel. They see a common history between the children of Israel and Rastafari. They mark off similar events such as slavery, exile, and the scattering in the Diaspora: "Our foreparents was first enslaved by the Assyrians, who worked them, showed them no mercy. We were brought into the West as slaves as early as 1518. The present-day black Israelites are, in fact, viewed as suffering for the very same sins for which those ancients were scattered. 'Jah' say: 'I shall scatter my people among the wicked, for in the times when the people should have known the fullness of Jah, they have turned their backs against I.' That is why the Black inhabitants of the earth have been scattered throughout the whole creation."[23]

One of the important marks of Rastafari is fidelity to the faith, and this is reflected in faithfulness in relationships both to Jah and to the Rastafari community, especially to the family. I recall that during a visit to the Bobo community on the outskirts of Kingston, as we sat down for a conversation of reasoning, I respectfully asked what the brethren thought about Bob Marley, the father of reggae and the one who was in a profound sense an evangelist for Rastafari. Through reggae, Marley proclaimed many of the tenets of Rastafari throughout the world. The response of the brethren was a very sophisticated give-and-take of stating and then examining the problem. They acknowledged that the Honorable Robert Marley did a great deal for Rastafari through his visibility around the world and the fact that his appearance and his message were symbols of Rastafari. But no sooner had they acknowledged Marley's contributions with seeming gratitude than one of the brethren asked, "But is that what make a Rasta a Rasta?" And the hidden presupposition of this question pointed in the direction of election. Another would suggest that what qualified Marley to be a Rasta was not his visibility or notoriety "because Rasta don't call attention to himself, Rasta call attention to Jah."

To suggest that Marley's popularity and visibility may have been enough to make him Rasta said that I did not understand that Rastas are born, not made; Rastas are begotten. As the reasoning session went on, another offered an assessment: "Rasta don't have no heap a children outside." While they would not directly disavow Marley's identity as Rasta, they raised questions concerning what makes a Rasta a Rasta; in an indirect way, they characterized the traits of Marley that seemed intended to make me both affirm and disaffirm Marley. My sense was that this process of give-and-take, of thesis and antithesis, was aimed at forcing me to name the truth myself without their revealing to me their own position. In the end, I was clear that the whole issue of Rasta identity was simple and complex at the same time. It was clear that Rastafari was not a faith or a church that one joined. The Bobo community, which seemed to have much in common with the early Rastafari communities such as Pinnacle or the King of King's Mission, seemed to function as a church in the sense that they had worship, liturgies, and rituals that informed the worship experience. But I came away from there being clear that Rastafari was not a community or church that Marley or anyone could join. One becomes Rastafari by being born into the community as one discerns that one's identity is inseparable from that of Jah's. What I found interesting in the reasoning session on the question of Rasta identity is that although it was made clear that Rasta is of Jah (God), and therefore one is born Rasta or elected by Jah to be Rasta, there was implied discomfort with the fact that Marley had many children outside of marriage.

The implication was clear that although a Rasta is born of Jah and elected by Jah, faithfulness to Jah is expressed in fidelity to the Rastafari community and to the Rasta family. The brethren at the Bobo reasoning session did not explicitly disqualify Marley as a Rasta. The reasoning session offered up the possibility that if one is born of God and elected to be Rasta, then one could not be disqualified. On the other hand, if one is born of God and elected by God, then one will do the works of God. One will be faithful to Jah and to the family.

As clearly as the Scriptures reveal to the Rasta brethren their special position in the plan of God, these indications are only scant evidence compared to that provided by the sheer devotion of Rastafari to their God. Love of God is the foremost proof of one's being called to share intimately in the life of God, and the Rastas can see no other people more devoted to God than they are themselves: "We are the loves of the Most High, because it is only us who love him. It is seen and known in the whole earth that it is only I-n-I who love Rastafari. . . . I testify on I own behalf and the father who sent I also testify on I own behalf. You know neither I, or I father, if you knew I you would know the father also."[24]

Divinity of Haile Selassie and Black Redemption

The twin concepts of the divinity of Haile Selassie and the redemption of black people have distinguished Rastafari from other Afro-Caribbean movements that have sought to promote an awareness of black consciousness in the Caribbean. It must be kept in mind that the discourse concerning the divinity of Haile Selassie and the claims concerning biblical warrants that justify this claim are being made in the sociopolitical context in which the vast majority of Rastafari are at the base of the social and economic ladder. The bottom line is that the Rastas have to contend with life in Babylon on a daily basis.

For the Rastas, Babylon is the ultimate evil; much more than an emotive symbol, it is an everyday reality, something tangible, the effects of which could be experienced through day-to-day pressure. A Rasta man exclaimed that "each and every day pressure bears down on the black man: racism, unemployment and I would say injustice in the courts. . . ." The police more than any other group personified the Rastafarian conception of evil; they were the living proof that Babylon was alive, active and waiting for any opportunity to suppress them.[25]

It is rather clear that the discourse concerning Rasta identity as this relates to Haile Selassie occurs in the social setting in which inequalities are rife for the Rastas at the base of the society but that talk about self and Jah occurs in a cultural and social setting in which many Jamaicans value those with lighter complexions more highly than their darker fellows. It should not be surprising then that the most important belief of Rastafari is that the late emperor of Ethiopia, Haile Selassie, is God. This has been the consistent belief throughout the years and has endured in each period. We noted earlier that Robert Hinds named his congregation the King of King's Mission. Although Hinds raises for us the question of Rastafari ecclesiology, it is clear that even for Hinds the cardinal belief was that Haile Selassie offered the possibility of redemption through repatriation to the land ruled and governed by a black king in Ethiopia. The good news as it related to the black king and Rastafari was that through this king the promise of black people's return to the land of their destiny, Ethiopia, was at long last ready to be fulfilled. Rastas explain:

We know before that when a king should be crowned in the land of David's throne, that individual would be Shiloh, the anointed one, the Messiah, the Christ returned in the personification of Rastafari. (On his vesture and on his thigh is a name written, "King of Kings and Lord of Lords.") He (Ras Tafari) is the "Ancient of days" (the bearded God). The scripture declares that "the hair of whose head was like wool (matted hair), whose feet were like unto burning brass (i.e., black skin)." The scripture declares that God hangs in motionless space surrounded with thick darkness (hence a black man).[26]

The Rastas would chant:

Babylon is a wicked one
Babylon is a wicked one
Babylon is a wicked one
O, Jah Rastafari O, Selah.

Our forefathers were taken away
Our forefathers were taken away
Our forefathers were taken away
O, Jah Rastafari O, Selah.

Open up the gate mek I repatriate
Open up the gate mek I repatriate
Open up the gate mek I repatriate
O, Jah Rastafari O, Selah.

There is confidence among the Rastas that they are the true Israelites and that as God emancipated the children of Israel, so in similar fashion God will deliver them from colonialism and neocolonialism, especially as expressed in Jamaica. The Rastas would also chant this song:

There is a land, far, far away,
Where there's no night, there's only day.
Look into the book of life and you will see
That there's a land, far, far away.

The King of Kings and the Lord of lords
Sits upon his throne and he rules us all.
Look into the Book of life and you will see
That there's a land, far, far away.[27]

Beyond a shadow of a doubt that land was Ethiopia. It was clear that Ethiopia provided the liberative lens through which Rastas viewed self and

God. There was a great deal of emphasis on escape to Ethiopia because Babylon (Jamaica) was hell. As Caribbean cultural critic Rex Nettleford points out, there is a sense in which many upwardly mobile Jamaicans who see their fortunes in the United Kingdom and the United States are not very different from the Rastas who see emancipation and deliverance from poverty and social injustice through repatriation to Ethiopia. Middle-class Jamaicans see deliverance from the vicious circles of poverty and crime not in Ethiopia but in the United Kingdom and the United States. Nettleford wonders whether this desire to relocate in the United States and the United Kingdom does not in fact make these Jamaicans "white Rastas."

The wider society was particularly critical of this Rastatenet (repatriation to Ethiopia) since it represented a threat to the fundamental idea of "a nation of Jamaicans for Jamaica." Yet when one takes into account Jamaicans' heavy migration to the United Kingdom, where many Jamaicans were seeking their fortune, as well as the fact that privileged Jamaicans— or white Jamaicans, as journalist Frank Hill once called the upper classes—habitually looked to England for example and inspiration, the Rastas' other-directedness seems typical of conventional Jamaicans. What the Rastas did was to substitute Ethiopia for the United Kingdom, the United States, and all those other places to which Jamaicans have migrated since the late nineteenth century.[28]

It is precisely at this point that the University Report had a significant impact on the Rasta movement and on the wider society in which they lived. After the Rev. Claudius Henry was charged with an attempt to take over Jamaica in 1959—when a couple of soldiers were killed and several members of Rev. Henry's group were tried and sentenced to death—a number of leading Rastas, disturbed by the events and by a large slice of the public associating the Rastas with the events, asked the University of the West Indies to investigate their doctrines, complaints, and way of life and tender a report to the Jamaican government on their behalf. The three university professors who undertook this assignment were Rex Nettleford, M. G. Smith, and Roy Augier. "The study not only revealed the socio-economic conditions of the movement to the general public, but also, for the first time, articulated the history and doctrine of the movement. The report found that the vast majority of Rastafari brethren are peaceful citizens who do not believe in violence. Rastafarian doctrine is radical in the broad sense that it is against the oppression of the Black race, much of which derives from the existing economic structure."[29]

Rex Nettleford pointed out that there were vast cleavages in Jamaican society, many of which were caused by the colonial education system. The system trained the middle class, who had matriculated through the secondary school system, to view Jamaica through European eyes. This placed the middle class on a collision course with Rastafari, who viewed life through Afrocentric lenses. The University Report helped middle-class Jamaica see that the Rastas were not as unpatriotic as they had originally thought. Their desire to repatriate to Ethiopia was presented as not un-Jamaican but rather was likened to the migration of middle-class Jamaicans in search of their destinies. The report helped the wider society understand that the desire to physically move to Ethiopia was fueled in part by the lack of an infrastructure in Rasta communities. Rastas resided in some of the worst slums in the urban centers, and the report recommended "the building of low-rent houses in greater numbers and the introduction of self-help co-operative building, the extension into slum areas occupied by squatters of such facilities as light, water, sewage disposal and garbage collection, the establishment of civic centers in Kingston with facilities for technical classes, youth clubs, child clinics, an invitation to establish a branch of the Ethiopian Orthodox Church in Western Kingston."[30]

Professor Nettleford informs us that the focus of the recommendation was the rehabilitation of the Rastas into the wider society. This aspect of the report was well received by the majority of the brethren except for some who were more militant, belonging to the "Church Triumphant." Members of this group declared that they were interested only in going back home to Ethiopia.

The second recommendation by the university professors was that the Jamaican government should send a delegation including Rastafarians to visit African countries on an exploratory visit. According to Nettleford, the wider society was livid as these two recommendations "turned on those very tenets of the Rastafarian doctrine which posed fundamental threats to Jamaicanism. First there is the implied allegiance to a foreign head of State. Second, the emphasis on Africa brought uneasiness to a country which had never regarded itself as Black. Third, the adoption of the Rastafarian faith was to the orthodox Jamaican Christians blasphemous and anti-Christian."[31]

While colonial Jamaica could not deal with blackness and did everything to escape African-ness, the University Report accomplished two things. It signaled a rapprochement between Rastas and the wider society, with the university serving as broker between them in that the report that portrayed Rasta in a favorable light. The report then gave Rastas a new

confidence to articulate their views even in the context of further persecu-
tion (since the oppression of the Rasta by the state did not disappear overnight). Perhaps the primary consequence of the report was that it gave
Rastas a stake in Jamaica as the report called on the government to provide
employment, housing, and other necessities to rehabilitate Rastas into Jamaican society. I contend that Rastas were never a passive community
sitting on the margins of Jamaican society waiting for change. They would
threaten the colonial system—Babylon—and critique the educational and
church establishments that they considered oppressive. However, it was
not until after the University Report that they began to consider the
Africanization of Jamaica. Although Ethiopia was their spiritual home,
they lived in Jamaica and now had a vested interest in their homeland.
They began in practice to parallel the approach of some Christian
churches that regard heaven as their home but must come to grips with
the reality that they live on earth. While they had not given up on Ethiopia,
in the meantime they worked to change Babylon. So Rastafari began to
move from being only a millenarian community to one that would work
for social change as well.

The government of Jamaica took the University Report seriously in
spite of the ridicule that much of Jamaican society accorded it. The government sponsored two missions to Africa, in 1960 and 1962. The delegation
was comprised of civic leaders and members of the Rasta faith. The mission was aimed at finding which African states would provide space for
Jamaicans to repatriate. The delegation visited Nigeria, Ghana, Liberia,
and Sierra Leone and met with governmental and religious leaders. "On
returning to Jamaica, the Rastas on these missions maintained that the
African governments were committed to the repatriation of Jamaicans
whose forebears were displaced by the Middle Passage. However, the majority report of the first mission . . . concluded that, while there was an
outpouring of good will from the African states visited, they were only
interested in receiving professionals and other skilled persons who could
contribute to the building of their post-colonial states."[32] Since the majority of Rastas were unskilled, this criterion virtually excluded them. "In
1964–1965, a delegation of Rastas made another mission to Africa in the
hope of pushing their repatriation agenda. Though the Rastafarian delegations were well received in the countries they visited, their mission failed
to lead to an official policy of repatriation by either the African governments or the Jamaican government."[33]

The high point following the University Report came in a state visit by
His Imperial Highness Haile Selassie to Jamaica in 1966. It was a pro-

found gesture of accommodation to Rastafari beliefs for the Jamaican government to invite to Jamaica a black man regarded as divine by Rastafari. To say that thousands flocked the airport would be an understatement. It took a great deal of persuasion by one of the leading Rasta elders, Mortimo Planno, to get Rastas to make room for their Messiah to deplane. "Many had broken through the police line and were surrounding the plane. Repeated attempts by government officials failed to bring them under control, and the emperor could not deplane. . . . Rastafarian representatives were invited to participate in state ceremonies and found themselves socializing and dining with the upper and middle classes at King's House (the residence of the governor general). In addition, the Rastas sought and received a private meeting with Selassie."[34]

The visit of Haile Selassie and the exposure of the public to Rastas, coupled with the remarkable way in which they conducted themselves, opened a new chapter of Jamaica's making peace with blackness and with Africa. There began in the wider culture an embrace of Rasta theology and ideology. Many young people began to wear their hair in similar fashion to the Rastas as well and became more open to conversation with Rastas, who were always willing to impart their teachings to whomever would listen.

In addition, many Jamaicans would now wear African attire, especially the bright colors that were popularly associated with Africa. They began to experiment with ganja, the holy and sacred herb regarded by Rastafari as a weed of wisdom. Rastas began to adjust to Jamaican society and to change their posture from one of resistance to one of accommodation. In a sense, there was accommodation on both sides. The wider society began to see Rastas as hardworking and to value their art and industry. If indeed, as seems likely, the invitation by the Jamaican government to Emperor Selassie was intended to quell the Rastas' desire for repatriation, it seems to have succeeded in large measure. It is reported that during the emperor's visit the phrase "liberation before repatriation," attributed to Selassie, emerged as a directive for the Rastas to work for the freeing of the Jamaican people prior to their return to Ethiopia. "The credibility of this directive seems to be buttressed by the fact that after the visit there was a noticeable cooling of the repatriation fervor that had been evident in the movement for over a decade."[35]

Another move by the government that was aimed at tempering the quest for repatriation was the invitation extended by the government to the Ethiopian Orthodox Church to establish churches in Jamaica. This church would provide a Christian compromise that would offer the Rastas a

Christian frame of reference, yet at the same time the government of Jamaica decided in 1969 to meet the needs of the Rastas for grounding in
Ethiopia. In 1970, the first Ethiopian Orthodox Church was established
in Jamaica, and by the mid-eighties there were several such churches
throughout the island. I have attended the Ethiopian Orthodox Church in
Kingston and observed many Rasta members. However, it is widely reported that there is often doctrinal disagreement as Rastas continue to
hold on to their convictions. But these gestures of accommodation on the
part of the Rastas were not signals that the wider society was about to
become Rastafari. In fact, the Jamaican government–owned radio station
decided to cancel two weekly broadcast programs sponsored by two Rasta
groups known as "Disciples of the Great King and the Sons of Negus
Churchical Hosts due to the 'un-Jamaican' nature of their content. The
broadcasts ('Speak Love' and 'The Lion of Judah Time') proclaimed Rastafari (Haile Selassie I) to be God, the Returned Messiah, asserted that Jesus
was not white, swore allegiance to the Emperor of Ethiopia and threatened
destruction if there is no Repatriation, with prophetic biblical support
from Isaiah 48:20."[36]

It became clear that although Rastas had become more socially acceptable and sought through the news media to share their views with Jamaica, they had not abandoned their central beliefs in the divinity of Emperor Selassie and the importance of Ethiopia as homeland. The reasons
given for the discontinuance of the broadcast were that "the Jamaica
Broadcast Corporation is not prepared to accept for release to the wider
society views which claim His Majesty Haile Selassie is God, such views
could threaten the racial harmony of Jamaica, . . . adversely affect the practice of law and order in the land and run counter to Jamaica's national
motto: 'out of many one people.'"[37]

It has remained clear that doors of acceptance were being opened to
Rastas by the government, which was willing to sponsor delegations to
Africa; invite His Imperial Majesty Haile Selassie for a state visit to Jamaica; and make it possible for the Ethiopian Orthodox Church to establish churches in Jamaica. Coupled with this were private employers who
were willing to provide jobs for Rastas. In spite of these accommodations,
the Rastas would not give up the basic doctrines that served as foundation
stones for their faith. First, they would not budge on the belief that Haile
Selassie, emperor of Ethiopia, is God. Coupled with this belief is the principle of the blackness of God. These claims were non-negotiable. To assert
the blackness of God in colonial Jamaica—which was never at peace with
blackness—was a revolutionary strategy. To portray God as black in an

environment in which white is right and where people of darker hue are victimized is to begin to force the society to take a second look at their system of values. To picture one's God in one's image was a meaningful way of redeeming the image of black people from disrespect and indignity. Jamaica's history is replete with oppressed people prior to the Rastas who used the strategy of fashioning their own religion as a means of survival and liberation in a hostile environment. The Rastas borrow from Native Baptists, Myalists, and Revivalists—especially Alexander Bedward—who used religion as a means of not only dreaming a new world but as a source of invective against the forces of oppression.

> The Rastas have turned to a major strategy of de-marginalization: religion. Having one's own God in one's image was a grand flowering in Rastafari of what earlier began in Myal and developed in Zion Myalism and Pocomania with the hijacking of the oppressor's God in a move that sought to discommode the oppressor. . . . Wresting *the Christian message from the messenger* as a strategy of de-marginalization helped bring slaves and free peasants nearer a perceived mainstream as "children of God." . . . The divinity of all black people —in fact, of all human beings—here, becomes the basis of equality, liberty, dignity and mutual respect, and equity in terms of access to economic resources, and all the values claimed by civil or democratic society but yet to be achieved in what, to exiles from Africa, is Babylon.[38]

Black people are able to enter into solidarity with Jah because Jah is black, and the humanity of all black people is included in the divinity of Jah. The blackness of God ensures the sanctity and divinity of black people; therefore, that blackness is no longer a curse that has to be avoided. It is now taken up into the divinity of God and becomes a point of departure for talk about the divinity of black humanity.

It is appropriate to query the ultimate view Rastas have of white people. Do Rastas believe, as the leader of the black Muslims stated, that white people are devils and incapable of being reformed? Rastas believe that it is possible for all people to see the light. Therefore salvation is not outside the purview of whites, provided they are willing to reject their evil ways and manifest the ways of Jah. I believe for Rastas this is more of a philosophical opening than a practical hope.

The Ethiopian Zion Coptic Church, which claimed to be Rastafari, has come to international attention for its passionate defense of the right to smoke and use ganja, claiming that it was a "holy sacrament," and this has endeared many young Rastas to the ideas that the Coptics promote. The Coptics, linking themselves with local blacks, introduced the concept that "white Americans" could be Rastas, calling into question one of the fundamental tenets of Rastafari that "the Rasta is one who never forgets he is an

African."[39]

> Race consciousness is what Rastafarians are constantly seeking to promote among Jamaican people. One of the brethren found such consciousness to be more developed among black people of the United States than was the case in Jamaica. . . . Rastas do not believe in full-scale integration of the races; they feel rather that each race has an identity that should be preserved, though this need not prevent them from living together in unity. "All man will live in oneness, as the Bible says: each man under his *own* vine and fig tree. Each nation represents itself, but while doing so, would live together and help each other. What a world this would be."[40]

Here we have a poignant illustration of Rasta dialectics: "Rasta is one who never forgets he is an African." Yet one does not have to become Rasta to find salvation. What is of primary importance is to find your own vine and fig tree—that is, to find your own identity and live out of that identity. This is especially so as it pertains to the races. One can hear Marcus Garvey in the background of Rasta philosophy, "Africa is for the Africans." Haile Selassie is about the liberation of black people because Selassie can be separated neither from his blackness nor from his social location in Ethiopia. It is only required for black people—Africans and people of African descent—to come through the gate of blackness. As mentioned earlier, this is in stark contrast to Elijah Muhammed's version of black nationalism that sees white people as devils and therefore hopelessly lost. Muhammed viewed Christianity as the white man's religion.[41]

However, the Rastas are unable to adopt this position because they "hijack" elements of the Christian religion in the articulation of their faith. For example, they use the Christian Bible as the primary source for the explication of their faith. Further, Rastas are willing to associate with all peoples and races provided they are willing to view them as equals and accord them their God-given liberty. The focus here for Rastas is self-affirmation that highlights dignity and naturalness, which in no way necessitates the vilification of other people. The truth is that Rastas are at peace with being black. They live in harmony with that reality. There is no pressure or desire for other people to come to know the Rastas' God or to become like Rastas. Again, the hand of Marcus Garvey is at work as Garvey instructed that every people should see God through their own lens. Like Bishop Henry McNeal Turner before him,[42] Garvey taught that white people should not be faulted for presenting their God because it is natural and healthy for any people to see God in their own image. On theological and philosophical grounds, it would be impossible for a white person to become a Rasta. Even if they could adopt certain rituals, beliefs, and practices of Rastafari, they are unable to participate in the mystical knowledge of "I and I." Paget Henry captures this difference:

> The directness and originality of this mystical knowledge is captured in the I-language of the Rastafarians. Among Jamaicans, Rastafarians are unique in their use of the pronoun "I." It is substituted for "me" and "my" which represents the old self before awakening to the divinity of Haile Selassie. "I" represents the new identity that emerges from participation in the divinity of Haile Selassie. Thus, all things and persons that have acquired this new identity through mystical participation, have "I" attached to them in some form. Thus Selassie himself becomes Haile Selassie I. The Rastafarian individual becomes an "I." He becomes "I-man" or she becomes "I-woman." A plurality of Rastafarians produces not a "we" or a "you and I," but "I and I." "My children" becomes "I children." One often hears sentences like: Haile Selassie—I I rated (created) this universe, and his truths I-dure (endure) forever. Or, I and I have been made strong by the almighty GOD—JAH-I. These unusual uses of "I" all signify a participation in the divinity of Haile Selassie.[43]

The awakening that takes place facilitates participation not so much in the community as in Jah. In a profound sense, this leads to becoming a son or a daughter of Jah. This is how one becomes a Rasta. The Rastas claim this divine kinship and membership in the Rasta community has to do with the unique relationship of the Rasta to Haile Selassie. One does not join the community to become a Rasta but is born again through spiritual rebirth, self-awakening, and knowledge of Selassie I. This experience awakens one to the reality that he or she is divine. The believer becomes a son or daughter of "Jah Rastafari who is God" and as such shares in divinity as it is stated in John 10:34, "I said ye are Gods" and in 1 John 3:2, "Beloved, now are we sons of God, and it doth not yet appear what we shall be: but we know that when he shall appear, we shall be like him; for we shall see him as he is." This undoubtedly is an important part of the Rastafarian project of salvation in black. The challenge is how to constitute the self, how to maintain the "I" in its relation to "I" granted all the forces that are seeking to tear the self apart. There are the forces of unemployment, security forces of Babylon arrayed against the Rasta, and the inadequacies in the society that give the Rasta little hope—the widening gap between rich and poor, the sense of disinheritance engendered by Jamaica's key resources being owned by foreigners.

Coupled with these problems is the reality of color. The vast number of black people is at the bottom, while a handful of browns and whites thrives at the apex of the society. The Rastas find hope in Jah as they are existentially related to Jah through son-ship and daughter-ship, through "I-and-I" relationship. Rastas believe they are gods, that is, that the divine resides within them. The mystical relationship between Rasta and Jah is so consuming and embracing that Rastas take on the form of Jah. If one should ask the Rasta what form Jah takes in the world, the answer would be unequivocal. Those who see the son or daughter have also seen the father.

> Fully aware of their humble position within society, the Rastas understand it paradoxically as a sign of their prophethood; they castigate those who refuse to sit in the dust with them to share some reasoning: "They won't come near to even say: 'let us reason a while.' You know what cause that? No one will humble himself to come down and hear what the base things of this world have to say." The Rastafarians appear to be of no account, but since only they have been courageous enough to call themselves by the very name of their God, they alone will be found to have known him truly: "We are of the base things of the earth, that Christ speak of in the Bible. We shall confound the wise and prudent and shall set up a new world through the power of His majesty. For no one did know him but those who were called by his dreadful and terrible name, Rastafari."[44]

4
Organization and Ethos

How Rastas constitute themselves as a people and as a religion is thought to be something of a mystery. A cursory look at Rasta meetings and conversation would give the impression that they are disorganized as there is no central organization holding them together or accountable. Neither is there an overarching framework in terms of doctrine or management style that prescribes the worldviews, cosmologies, and lifestyles of the Rastas. That said, it will become clear nonetheless that there are commitments and principles of discernment that shape the Rastas' approach to God, humanity, and the world. This is one reason that Rastas resist the notion that their relationship to God and each other should be spoken of in terms of church. They resist the association with the church as they know it because of its penchant for hierarchy and because of the close relationship in Jamaica between church and state. Rastas often complain that one steps out of the church into the state and out of the state into the church without knowing the difference.

Although Rastas borrow the church's book, the Bible, and interpret from their own frame of reference, they nonetheless observe that the church's appropriation of the Bible is Eurocentric and therefore antithetical to the dismantling of Babylon. It strikes me that the Rastas are correct in their assessment of the mainline churches in Jamaica, whose practices would not suit the purposes of Rastafari. It seems to me that there would be some value in Rastas taking a second look at the Native Baptists and even the Revivalists to see if their models of church are closer to what Rastafari is about.

Characteristics of the Rastafari have a remarkable similarity to Revivalists, whose origin is traced to the incorporation by Myal of Christianity. The first Baptist to convert slaves, George Liele, was himself a black slave who was brought to Jamaica by his Loyalist master fleeing the American Revolution. But the more slaves Liele converted, the less control he had, as converts went on to preach their own understanding of Christianity, which in effect was Myal. Thomas Gibb, George Lewis and Moses Baker were three such preachers. They had no central organization, no mutual cooperation. Their movement reproduced itself in a cellular way.[1]

Barry Chevannes is onto something here in terms of the freedom that characterized the ethos of the Native Baptists and later manifested itself in "Daddy" Sharp standing over against the established Baptist Church and seizing freedom. But what Chevannes alludes to in terms of the freedom of the Native Baptists could be attributed to the polity of the Baptist Church itself, which is based on the autonomy of the local church and is a characteristic of most Baptist churches. However, Chevannes instinctively placed his finger on something that was going on in the Native Baptist churches that seems to be a carryover in Revivalism and Rastafarianism. What occurred was the class leaders taking charge of the ticket and class system, an important principle in Native Baptist churches. This principle originated with the Wesleyan Methodists but was introduced to the Baptists by George Liele. The way it worked was that a local congregation was divided into classes, with each class having a leader who had power to call the class together. This class leader in the Native Baptist tradition became a "Mammy" or a "Daddy."

I have discussed "Daddy" Sharp and "Mammy" Wellington, who had power to forgive sins. It was this principle that gave power to class leader Paul Bogle. The truth was that they turned their classes into churches. As I will note shortly, this principle was carried over into Rastafari in terms of the concept of "yards" and "houses." But I suspect one reason among others for the unsuitability of the Revivalist model for Rastafari is not only the Revivalist nonengagement with Africa in terms of repatriation but also their strong reliance on and fascination with the work and function of the spirit. Revivalism teaches about a pantheon of spirits, with different spirits serving different needs. In a discussion of the organization and ethos of Rastafari, it is important to note that although Rastafari stakes its theological reason for being in relation to Africa/Ethiopia, it is not a religion that takes the spirit seriously.

The elevation of Man to the status of shared identity with God is at the same time an elevation over the world of the Spirits. Rastafari do not recognize the existence of, let alone communicate with, those beings which are so central to Revival. They have no need of them. If there are no spirits but only God and Man, and if Man is also part God, then God himself no longer is the distant "Big Maasa," without a real role in the affairs of Man, but a loving Father. When Rastafari speak of "the father," they do so with great reverence and with an awareness of His central place in their lives. To some extent the identity with the father gives coherence to the strong patriarchal orientation for which the movement is noted. This alteration in how the spirit world is conceived marks a radical departure from the African tradition.[2]

It is quite clear that the Rastas' focus on Haile Selassie as Christ-returned has not left any room for engagement of the spirit. This focus rather than engagement with African cosmology—which would of necessity force them to deal with the spirit world—allows Rastas to keep intact their patriarchal worldview. One of the lessons learned from Revivalism in Jamaica is that its dependence on the spirit world lends it structure and openness that makes room for women in leadership positions. A religion open to the movement of the spirit—whether it is an African spirit or Christian spirit—means that the structure could not be closed because it is difficult to tell ahead of time which way the spirit will move.[3] It is somewhat surprising that Rastas—who carved out their religious faith in Jamaica and in conversation with Africa, which to the average Jamaican is peopled with "duppies" and varied spirits—would insulate themselves and their theology from any expression of faith that takes the spirit seriously. This raises a central question: To what extent may we regard Rastafari as an African-derived religion?

It is interesting to note that although Rastafari does not rely on any understanding or dependence of the spirit, be it African, Jamaican, or Christian, the end result of its open-ended structure is rather similar to that of the Revivalist or Native Baptist movement. What happens in these cases is that there is no central organization holding the different houses or groups together. They relate together through a network and belief in certain basic doctrines and rituals. At the foundational level, there are many Rastas who do not belong to any specific group or house or mission but who share the fundamental belief in the divinity of Haile Selassie, in the need for repatriation, and that Jah will engender this repatriation in Jah's own time. The bottom line has to do with a relationship between the

Rasta and Jah, a relationship I referred to as "I and I." The movement here is from the Rasta as subject to Jah as subject. It is this "intersubjectivity," this new consciousness of the self in relationship with Jah, "I-and-I consciousness," that defines the parameters of the new style of life that we call Rastafari. In a profound sense, we could say that theology for Rastafari is subjectivity. This, however, is not uniquely Rasta because there are antecedents in the popular culture. From my childhood, I recall hearing that Haile Selassie was none other than Jah. I remember being taught in my father's church that Baptists neither believe in any defining creeds nor subscribe to any liturgy or prescribed order of worship. What was defining for us was a personal relationship between the believer and Christ. This was the defining experience in the life of the believer. And this was not peculiar just to this church but was true of many Methodist, Moravian, and Pentecostal churches.

The difference between these groups and Rastafari is that Rastafari meant this literally. The key for these foundational Rastas was that there was no hierarchy that one could presuppose or a community called church to which one was answerable. There was a degree of freedom to go and come as one pleased, to belong to a group or not to belong to a group, or to belong to several communities and still maintain intact the sense that one was a Rasta. For members of my father's church in Trinityville, to be a person or a Christian meant to be in community. We could say "the church is therefore I am." What makes a Rasta a Rasta is communion with Jah. That is why "I-and-I consciousness" is the key to Rasta identity and ethos. Everything else finds its meaning in relationship to this primal event. Because of this central commitment to "I and I," it not unusual to meet Rastas who belong to more than one Rasta house, yard, or organization. Ennis Edmonds puts the issue succinctly:

"Houses" and "yards" describe another level of Rastafarian social organization. Houses and yards are small, informal groups of Rastas whose members sustain an ongoing relationship. The term *houses* expresses the idea that each gathering of Rasta (usually males) attach themselves to a "leading brethren" and frequently gather at his house or in his yard to partake of the sacramental herb (marijuana) and to engage in the dialectical discourse called "reasoning." The discourse is usually about their faith and current or historical events impinging on their understanding of their place in the world. Within the house leading brethren are often regarded as elders. However, eldership is

88

not a formal position, attained through election, but rather an "inspirational position" that is informally conferred on those who meet at least two criteria. Elders must have a record of uncompromising commitment to and defense of the principles of Rastafari—a commitment that often leads to confronting the establishment and even suffering imprisonment as a result. Elders must also have the ability to "speechify," that is, to expound the philosophy of Rastafari, to interpret historical and contemporary events through the Rastafarian prism, and thus to inspire the brethren to greater understanding and fortitude.[4]

The position of elder is not one conferred by community; rather, it is recognized through the exercise of the power of persuasion through facility with words. This fascination and facility with words is one of the most striking and memorable characteristics of Rastas I have encountered. It is clear that there is a sense in which Rastas, like the Old Testament prophet, engage in word-act—that is, the word is enacted and is indistinguishable from deed.

"More formal groups of Rastas are organized around particular leaders or groups of elders. These are either communes led by charismatic or voluntary organizations (sometimes legally registered) dedicated to the accomplishment of particular goals. Some Rastas refer to these as 'mansions,' because compared to the houses which comprise maybe ten to fifteen Rastas, these groups often have hundreds of members. These more formal groups fall into two categories: 'churchical' and 'statical.'"[5] The churchical group focuses on the development of Rastafarian religious culture and bringing to the fore African consciousness and lifestyle. The statical group is primarily interested in political and social goals. The important thing to remember here is that Rastas do not feel that membership in one group excludes membership in another: "A member of the Rastafarian Theocratic Government may also belong to the Rastafarian Movement Association and vice versa. In the case of Rastafarian communes, various patterns of participation have emerged. Some make their domicile in the commune on a permanent basis. Others alternate between the commune and some other place of residence. Still others belong to a certain commune for a short period, then move to another or abandon communal life."[6]

In a profound sense, a rugged individualism runs through Rasta life and ethos. Rastas are ultimately free of organizational strictures. It is cru-

cial that the organization exists for Rasta and not Rasta for the organization. This freedom allows Rastas to belong to the Ethiopian Orthodox
Church even though it is not a Rasta organization. Rastas are free in relation to any organization that remembers Africa. On a visit to Jamaica in

2001, I visited the Ethiopian Orthodox Church in Kingston and noted that
a large percentage of those in attendance were Rastas. Many Rastas who
were not in attendance entered the sanctuary in time to receive the blessing. The tendency to belong to multiple groups is not unique to the Rastas
in Jamaica. When I served as pastor of a Baptist church in the parish of
Westmoreland, there were several loyal members who after Sunday morning worship would go to the Revivalist service Sunday night and dance to
the music of the drums all night long. There was no sense of conflict. It
was clear that although for social purposes these persons would identify
themselves as Baptists, they were also Revivalists.

Certainly it would be much easier for a Rasta to negotiate his or her
relationships within the different organizations in Rastafari. The bottom
line is that the Rasta is free in relation to all groups and organizations
because the truth comes from within. Because Rastas are sons and daughters of Jah in terms of the "I-and-I" relationship, the truth is that the divine
inheres in each Rasta. Rastas are accustomed to claim "we are Gods," and
they say this on the basis of the divine inhering within each Rasta. Rastas
do not have to go outside in search of truth or God because God dwells
within. The authority to act and to be comes from within. It is clear that
what unites all Rastas irrespective of the groups or yards or houses to
which they belong is the claim that Haile Selassie is God and that Rastas
are sons and daughters of God.

This provides the basis for "I-and-I consciousness." The "I-and-I consciousness," which is the result of a new awakening of the self, results in a
high anthropology that contradicts the "anthropological poverty" that was
the lot of Rastas before this new consciousness. The mark of anthropological poverty in Babylon is the need to look to authorities outside of self, the
tendency to deprecate self and to marginalize self as was typical in colonial
and neocolonial Jamaica. The mark of anthropological poverty is to associate blackness and African-ness with bondage, psychological dependency,
and the spirit of victimization. "I-and-I consciousness," which is anchored
in Haile Selassie, breaks this cycle of poverty as through the process of
"intersubjectivity" a new collective self emerges—a new self in terms of
collaboration and cooperation. This is the basis for a unifying matrix for
Rasta ideology, theology, and organization. A Rasta never loses his or her
African-ness, and this is what makes it possible to negotiate life in Baby-

lon. It is this African-ness that provides the interpretive and unifying key in which doctrine, lifestyle, and organizational ethos are mediated.

Although there was no ritual accompanying the break with the old order as represented by other blacks, comparable to, for example, the Mau Mau initiation rites and oaths which involved extreme violations of Kikuyu taboos there was the suggestion of a total rejection of their past: "I now look to myself as a proper person; I wasn't myself before; I and I didn't know ourselves . . . now we are making positive steps to find our true selves." This break with the old "brainwashed" order and the entry into the new meant that black youths realized not only fresh ways of looking at the world but also a new way of understanding themselves: "It's for I and I to revive the true self." This realization of the true self was conditional on the break with the old order and everything representative of it.[7]

The bottom line is the transformation of the individual as the Rasta renounces the ways of Babylon and takes on the new lifestyle of being a child of the King of Kings, Haile Selassie. The new initiate discovers the inseparable link between freedom and responsibility. "I-and-I consciousness" means a new self-awareness and taking responsibility for one's actions. In a profound sense, the highest court of appeal to which one may turn for clarity concerning doctrine or ethos is self. One is free in relation to self as the self takes responsibility for its utterances and action. There is no individual, no super Rasta man who is able to impose his will on organizations and groups. Rastas affirm the divinity of Haile Selassie and the sacredness of the African homeland and then take it from there.

It goes without saying that Rastas seek in their living to preserve a rhythm between themselves and nature. Nature is closely related to the power of Jah and as such demands respect from everyone. Rastas proceed at a very local level to advocate that streams are not polluted and that pesticides and chemical waste are not buried in Mother Earth: "Nature is not essentially a force external to man; it works within his innermost being. If man allows the natural powers to be corrupted, then he himself will be corrupted as well. Already Western man has begun what appears to be a systematic destruction of natural forces—through the reckless pollution of the atmosphere and waterways of the earth. Selassie's kingdom by contrast is one that builds upon nature, not against it, and it has no room for those who would seek to vitiate it."[8] But there is also a sense in which nature expresses the will of Jah. Nature is not merely neutral; it is the vehicle of Jah's judgment. There are times when, as the Rastas use judgment, they call on nature to embody the word. As often as judgment is pronounced on Babylon or the agents of Babylon they will call on nature to assist: "May lightning and thunder strike the downpressors."

One of the realities that Rastafarians have reminded Jamaicans of is to cultivate a healthy respect for the land, for Mother Earth. Respecting and honoring the land is not only Rastafarian but Jamaican as well. For Rastas, the key to understanding self in relation to Mother Nature is to get to know Mother Earth: "They try to stay close to the earth, they are not afraid of dirt and grime; they call others 'to sit in the dust with them.' They long to cultivate a piece of land; and they laugh at those who try to escape into space. Because of their fidelity to earth, secrets are revealed to them, from that revelation they are inspired to bid others simply to 'behold the earth.'[9] This recognition of the importance of being close to the earth and reaping results from being organically related to Mother Earth is not merely a Rasta phenomenon. Jamaicans have always felt it important to marvel at the wonders of Mother Nature. A hurricane or earthquake may be interpreted as God's punishment for not living in harmony with God's will; if one's property is spared when a hurricane or earthquake strikes the island, it is often viewed as a sign of divine favor. The Rastas have picked up on this tradition and will speak of a hurricane or earthquake as God's judgment on Babylon. But the positive inference is also true as it is widely viewed that a relationship to Mother Nature through playing in the Caribbean Sea or planting a garden will be rewarded with good health or peace of mind. Some years ago I asked Rev. Maxwell of a Congregational church in Kingston the secret of his good health and long life. At the time he was in his nineties. Without any hesitation he said it was his relationship to the land as he planted and cared for a garden. He proceeded to instruct me that in the Gospel resurrection narratives, it was not coincidental that Jesus was mistaken for a gardener. What then differentiates the Rastas' attitude toward nature? Rastafari view the earth as a loving mother and even as God.

"The earth is mother. Hurt not the earth, for Jah is the earth." . . . Earth and nature are seen as a unity, and both are identified with the Lord: "That is how I would say God again: God is nature." Not only is Jah said to rule over the earth, but he is at times identified physically with the earth. The Rastas hear the Psalm which proclaims: "The earth is the Lord's and the fullness thereof," and they drop the 's from Lord's and state simply: "The earth is the Lord and the fullness thereof." The same scriptural text, along with others, is used by the brethren to assert the rights of squatters against removal from the little piece of earth that they claim. Since the earth is the Lord and belongs above all to those who love Jah, what right has any government to displace people and leave them landless? The Rastas maintain firmly that land should never be sold, since no individual can claim ownership rights.[10]

The Rastas raise a profound question for theology and ethics: What ought to be our attitude to the land if the land belongs to Jah? For the Rastas, there is a giftlike character to the land, and they believe the real owners of the land are not the ancestors, as in African religion, but Jah. The relationship between Jah and the land means that because God is the landowner, the neighbor has a right to the land. The Rastas who are steeped in Old Testament thought would agree with the mandates of Deuteronomy 19:14, "In the inheritance which you will hold in the land that the Lord your God gives you to possess, you shall not remove the neighbor's landmark." Each citizen is entitled to a bit of land. In the context of Deuteronomy, landlessness severs the binding relationship between the people of the covenant and Yahweh. The land is sacred because it ultimately belongs to God.

In Jamaica, the land is of first importance to the people as the homestead often provides space to plant a garden in which food is provided for the home, as well as space for games and meeting for family and friends. In Jamaica it is not unusual to meet and socialize in the yard, to sit with Rastas under a tree for a game of dominoes, or to stay outdoors all day for a game of cricket. In many cases, the house plot is also used as family cemetery, especially in rural areas. Because identity issues in Jamaica cannot be properly discussed without reference to land, Jamaicans are grateful to the Rastas for raising this central issue of access to the land.

"Ital Livity"

Closely related with Rastas' organic view of human beings' relationship with Mother Earth is their understanding of natural living. Natural living does not mean to live naturally but to live in an awareness of the organic relationship between human beings and Mother Earth. The way of wholeness is to live in harmony with the principles of creation. Everything is given in Mother Earth for sustenance, healing, and wholesome living. "The brethren proclaim themselves to be a natural people in virtue of their conception of God. They announce that God is not in another world, but is here on earth and in man. Their God is a God of nature and 'naturality,' not one of superstition and imagining: 'God is in man, and God is man, because things are natural. We are a people that deal with naturality.'"[11]

Emerging from this notion that the earth is sacred and that it provides everything for human beings' wholeness and healing is the notion of "Ital living." "Ital" means springing from the earth—earthy, natural, or organic. "Livity" is to live according to the strict principles of Rastafari. "'Ital living' is therefore a commitment to use things in their natural or organic states."[12] This is one way in which Rastas distance and differentiate their lives from those lived in Babylon.

One can easily identify the ways of Babylon that are expressed in artificiality. For example, the people who embrace the Babylonian way of life use tobacco, alcohol, synthetic materials, and chemically treated foods. Rastas warn against the use of manufactured foods, especially canned foods, as they contend that these foods are intended by the Babylonian authorities to destroy the minds of black people. Most Rastas try to adhere to a vegetarian lifestyle—rarely eating meat, and prohibiting the consumption of pork, shellfish, and scaleless fish.

> One of the prime staples of the Rastas is fish, but only of the small variety, not more than twelve inches long. They are fond of small herring known as "sprat" and all fish with scales that meet this strict size rule. All larger fish are predators and represent the establishment—Babylon—where men eat men. But the food of the greatest worth to the cultists is vegetables of almost every kind. Like ganja, the earth brings forth all good things. Food is cooked with no salt, no processed shortening. . . . The word "I-tal" is another Rastafarian word that is fast becoming part of Jamaican speech. It means the essence of things, things that are in their natural states.[13]

Rastafari also has a "fresh food" tradition that bans the use of salt. Rastas observe that Mother Nature, who knows what is best, has already placed in the food what is needed, and therefore extra salt is superfluous. Rastas also acknowledge times when cooking fresh foods, fruits, nuts, and vegetables is unnecessary. "Our chief delicacies use to be fruits, and peppers, and coconut . . . we have a stage where we never really cook . . . but we roast— like a roast breadfruit and we eat jackfruit and roast the seed which become a 'bean' fo' we. Dat is a complete food in itself, ya know. And yuh know is what we eat out of? De coconut dat cut in two. Dat is our cup. And every one of our pot is made out of clay. We were so I-tal we daon use spoon or even bowl . . . maybe we just eat off a leaf."[14]

The turn to Ital living focused on the purity of foods and took seriously questions concerning the preparation of food. This complicated the Rastas' relationship with women as they contend that when women are menstruating they should not be allowed to prepare food. This argument is used to reinforce the patriarchal privilege that is already a part of the Rastas' way of life, providing a basis for male domination. This, in essence, caused a redefining of gender roles in the family.

In the traditional Jamaican family, it is understood that the woman is supposed to perform domestic chores. Rastas, however, redefine this. For them it is not unusual for a man to be in charge of cooking and instructing the family in Ital living. In addition, it must be kept in mind that Ital food is mostly raw. I noted earlier the fastidious concern Rastafari have about the consumption and preparation of food. But I must observe here that some of their reservations concerning food that they do not themselves prepare may be a carryover from the wider society. For example, when I was growing up in St. Thomas in the 1940s and 1950s, it was standard practice in my home not to eat food given to the family. Although it was not unusual for members of my father's church to give us puddings, cakes, and sometimes cooked food, most often it was thrown away even though we needed it. My father's rationale was that we lived in a village and parish in which obeah was rife, and he would not put it beyond people to use food as a weapon. It was the belief in my village that one of the main ways in which obeah was effective was through ingested food. So it may be that some of the Rastas' concern about the preparation of food arises from a similar response to conditions in the wider society, which illustrates in a real sense the way in which Ital living is a critique of the ways of Babylon at a number of levels.

This attention to the preparation of food forces the society to stop and think about the role of food, which traditionally has functioned as symbol of fellowship and invitation to fellowship. Food has always had a central place in our culture, but the Rastas have reminded and informed us concerning rules governing nutrition. In the wider society, the woman cares for the house and children and prepares the food. As Rastas struggle with Levitical codes, they contend that women should be banned from food preparation when they are menstruating. While not all Rastas impose this prohibition, I believe the majority of Rastas hold fast to it. Ital living serves the function of making the community more conscious of food preparation. In a culture in which people have used food as a weapon, the Rastas' injunction about who prepares the food is heeded seriously.

Another important effect of Ital living is the reverence for the environment and the looking to the earth to provide for the needs of the family. This had important implications for one's relationship to money in a context in which one did not have to buy everything. Again there are precedents in the wider culture, especially in the rural settings, where people depended on the family garden to provide for their daily needs. It raises important questions concerning one's relationship to economics. Although economic hardships caused some Rastas who were ravished by poverty to eat what they could get, by and large Ital living was a standard to which Rastas aspired.

> Central to the ideal of ital living is the belief in herbal healing. Rastas believe that the entire universe is organically related and that the key to health, both physical and social, is to live in accordance with organic principles, as opposed to the artificiality that characterizes modern technological society. In addition to the Rastafarian commitment to a virtual vegetarian diet, there is a commitment to the use of various herbs which they believe promote human well being. Foremost among the herbs, that Rastas treasure is ganja, which they often refer to as the "holy herb" or "wisdom weed."[15]

Rastas have been closely associated with the use of marijuana, or ganja. They feel that Jah chooses to reveal God-self to human beings through herbs. Herbs, they contend, are intended for the healing of the nations, and if a people would seek to understand Jah it will be through the use of herbs. And chief among these is ganja. Rastas who are versed in the Bible cite Genesis 1:29 to provide biblical warrants for their use of the "holy herb": "And God said, Behold, I have given you every herb bearing seed, which is upon the face of the earth, and every tree, in which is the fruit of a tree yielding seed; to you it shall be for meat." Another text that underscores their use of ganja is Revelation 22:2: "the leaves of the tree were for the healing of the nation." Using Scripture for their own ends, Rastas suggest that even God enjoys smoking by citing Psalm 18:18: "There went up a smoke out of his nostrils, and fire out of his mouth devoured: coals were kindled by it." Because Rastas live in a fractious society that is divided by inequalities of class, economics, and privilege, they contend that in this society the smoking of ganja is for the healing of the nations.

> The very act of smoking ganja is considered a form of religious worship among the Rastas. Almost always, when lighting the chalice, whether alone or in a group, Rastafarians will stop talking, doff their caps, and pray for a blessing upon themselves and in praise of Jah

Rastafari. Frequently the prayer consists of various verses taken from Psalms 19 and 121. . . . Smoking the herb is freely compared to both the sharing of the communion cup and the burning of incense as these are practiced in the various churches. One Rasta, as he puffed deeply on his pipe told me: "This is the cup Je-sus said we should take from: He who sippeth of this cup, sippeth of me."

In the brethren's view, smoking the holy herb is the purest and most natural form of attaining communion with God. Further, while alleging a certain similarity between their own smoking of herbs and the Catholics' burning of incense, the Rastas emphasize a fundamental difference that relates to their whole critique of traditional Christianity: the true church is not a building but rather is the person of a believer—and only when the incense is burned in the true church is it really sacred. "We smoke our herbs as a incense unto our God. The Roman Catholics burn fi dem kind of things in their building what them *call* church. We burn our herbs in our temple, in our *structure*, for our structure is our church."[16]

For Rastas, smoking ganja is the medium of contemplation, inspiration, and insight. Through this sacrament they are able to plumb the depths of wisdom and discover the revelation of God that is given to reason. Smoking the herb intensifies the reasoning process and opens up new worlds of illumination, visions, and enlightenment. "Ganja smoking is also a means of creating and celebrating community. In this respect, the Rastafarian perspective on Ganja smoking is opposite to the generally held view (in Jamaican society) that ganja smoking predisposes the smoker to violence."[17]

I recall several clashes in the 1950s and 1960s between Rastafari brethren and the police, and in each instance the public claimed that the confrontation was caused by Rastas smoking ganja. This perception changed in the 1970s and 1980s as the public came to better understand Rastas. It was discovered that Rastas were peace-loving people and that much of the conflict with the police was caused by others in the society posing as Rastas. The difference in perception came as many Rastas began to make it into middle-class Jamaica and as ganja use in Jamaica began to be demystified.

The smoking of the herb is a deeply religious ritual. Rastas concoct a pipe specifically for the smoking of ganja that is called the chalice.

The smoking paraphernalia reserved by Rastafarians for communal rituals is particularly interesting. A type of water-pipe is often employed, constructed from a variety of containers (including gourds, cow or goat horns, sections of bamboo, or tin cans), to which is attached a clay or wooden bowl in which the cannabis is placed. Not only are these pipes of a design similar to those described in oral traditions as having been used by the post-Emancipation Central African immigrants, but they resemble several sorts of water-pipes made from gourds or animal horns—documented among a number of Central African peoples. Rastas refer to this kind of water pipe (and sometimes specifically to the bowl on top) as a chalice or *kochi* (the latter term, usually spelled "cutchie" or "kouchie," is of uncertain origin). At the bottom of the *kochi* bowl is placed a small object, called *gritty* stone—a small piece of nutmeg, stone, or clay—upon which the cannabis rests and through which the smoke is drawn. Also commonly used is the *chillum* (from Hindi, chilam), a conical or cylindrical pipe, the mouth-end of which is sometimes covered with a piece of cloth known as the *sapi*.[18]

Before the smoking begins, the pipe is blessed as a prayer is offered to Jah: "When the pipe is ready it is invariably blessed. Whatever the level of activity there is a temporary respite as attention turns to the brother giving the blessing. It is generally he who has prepared the herbs, although younger brethren often give it to their elders to light as a gesture of respect. . . . According to the Rastas the secret of herb-smoking is to bless the pipe and give Jah praises. . . . A communion bond develops among those sharing the pipe, and it would be a transgression to leave the circle until the last draw is taken."[19] Smoking frees the mind from the trickery of colonialism and provides through the reasoning process the means of transcending the limits imposed on the brethren by the system of Babylon. Through the smoking of ganja the Rasta attains the "I-and-I consciousness," which is the breakthrough of the intersubjective experience of the individual and Jah.

The Rastas insist that ganja enhances their understanding and assists them in praying, contemplation, reasoning, and exposing the trickery of Babylon. There is clear potential for collision between the Rastas and the government that has made the smoking of this herb illegal. Rastas attest to the sacramental value of this herb and to its potential for awakening of mind and spirit; the government prosecutes for possession of it. Confrontations are unavoidable. A young Rasta dramatizes the problem:

Before I start to smoke herb, the world was just good and pleasant to me. Me never have to work, and my people always give me money.

Them try to push me into society. They try to make me white. But from I start to herb now, I start to read between the lines. Is like wool was removed from before my eyes. That is when my rebirth start, my reincarnation, when I start to smoke herb. The government knows from a man start smoke herb he be aware of some things. That is when he start come off the brainwash, when he start to smoke the herb. That's why them is against the herb so much.[20]

The young Rasta man is expressing deep feelings regarding how Rastas view the relationship of their use of the herb and the government's injunctions against their use of it. According to the Rasta, the use of the herb facilitates the reasoning process and inspires them to ask awkward questions of the society—questions concerning the disparity between rich and poor and the violence of the state against the poor. "The Rastafarians will admit, then, that there is a sense in which the herb is a 'dangerous drug,' and that society has good reason, therefore, to fear it. The herb endangers the corrupt society which condemns it. Herb is against society. It is harmful in that it makes poor people think about the system and want to change it."[21] In Rasta discourse, the herb facilitates an awakening, a bringing to consciousness of the "downpressive" conditions that confront Rastas, who for too long have been "the least of these" in Jamaican society.

In the wider society there has also been a mystical belief in the power of the herb both among the poor and the middle-class community. When I was a pastor in the Baptist Church in Jamaica during the 1960s, many of my parishioners would use the herb for making tea for their children from infancy on and would attest to its medicinal value: "My child has never had to go to the doctor because from he was three months old I give him the tea." Others attest to making a bath in which they would soak, causing malaria or related illnesses to leave. This is widespread throughout Jamaica. Most Jamaicans would at some time have used ganja as tea or as a form of medicine so there is much more tolerance and understanding in the wider society of Rastafari and their confidence in the salvific use of this holy herb.

Barry Chevannes suggests that there is a real possibility that the Rastas may have taken the practice of smoking from the East Indian community in Jamaica. There was a tradition among the Indians to meet in a "camp" for the smoking of ganja. A camp was any yard where ganja was retailed and smoked. "A very old informant remembered taking part in the ganja-smoking contests in the yard of an East Indian who used to peddle it, around the time of the First World War. The East Indians, he said, would take offence if the 'Creoles' (his word) smoked more than they, and once he himself barely managed to escape without injury. From this it may be inferred that as many as eighty years ago ganja smoking, still very much an East Indian activity, used to take place in yards."[22] It seems as if ganja smoking among the East Indians was recreational, like gambling, alcohol drinking, and playing Indian music. "These practices were in striking contrast to those of the African-Jamaican Rastas, among whom the smoking of ganja became an act of serious import. Thus, while the idea of the herbs camp may have had antecedents in the East Indian herbs yard, new elements seemed to have been introduced by the African population, of which the idea of the *camp* was one. . . . Traditionally, ganja smoking was done by male East Indians, using a chillum pipe with a dampened rag, called a *saapi*, wrapped around the mouth. Females smoked only tobacco, but they used the huka, or water pipe. In the camps, however, the huka became the preferred vessel and passed from left to right in the circle of partakers."[23] A profound difference between the Rastas' and East Indians' practice of smoking the herb is that for the Indians it was primarily a recreational activity, an attempt to socialize and to relax. The Rastas imbued this activity with divine significance as it was transformed to a sacrament and an occasion for reasoning. Through my visit to the Rasta community I can attest to the seriousness of the reasoning sessions. Rastas who seemed inspired by the holy herb refuse to be satisfied with surface answers but probe beneath the surface for a richer and fuller encounter with truth. For Rastas, smoking the holy herb does not incite one to do evil or mischief unless of course one is evil and mischievous. They believe the herb allows one to express one's essential nature.

"The Rastas maintain that, unlike alcohol and other 'non-natural' drugs, ganja does not incite violence and disruption, but assists a man to inner peace and concentration. The herb can have no bad effect upon a man unless the man has evil in his heart already. The brethren cannot be bewildered at society's reluctance to control the use of alcohol, despite the manifest harm caused by it, but they are doubly confounded that such severe restrictions are placed upon ganja, which they know to be far less dangerous than liquor."[24] They fear that a double standard is at work in Jamaican society as the large distillers who produce rum serve as a lobby for preventing the legalization of ganja, which they fear would cut into their profits.

Never, the brethren argue, has a man been declared dead as a result of taking ganja, although many have clearly died from rum. Although ganja has the reputation of breeding violence, there is real evidence only for rum doing so. . . . Definitive proof of the peace-engendering qualities of the herb was given in the behavior of the Rastafarians at the Palisadoes Airport the day that Selassie came to visit. The brethren delight in telling how everyone smoked ganja that day, right under the eyes of the police. . . . "And Rasta prove fruitful during that whole day! Palisadoes was without no disturbance, without no war, without no struggles."[25]

The Rastas contend that in the wider society there is the common perception that ganja smoking is the cause of frictions and disturbances between them and the police. But, the Rastas argue, the more careful observer will note that ganja is merely the smokescreen that veils the deeper problems of poverty, inequality, and police brutality.

I suspect the Rastas are correct that a person's essential nature comes to the fore in the smoking of the herb. This does not and should not imply that I approve of ganja smoking as I do believe that all forms of smoking are injurious to one's health. But for the Jamaican society to blame many of its ills on Rastas because they smoke ganja is to miss the mark and hide behind a smokescreen of its own choosing. Horace Campbell points to the connection that Jamaican society often makes between Rasta, ganja, and violence.

The links between Rasta, ganja and violence were once again fervently discussed in the Jamaican press after the Coral Gardens rebellion in 1963. Easter weekend 1963 witnessed an important intervention by the Rastas because they asserted their right to walk across the Rose Hall land to their small lot of ground provisions. Rose Hall at that time was being developed as a tourist attraction, and the whole area was being built up by real estate developers to be renamed Coral Gardens. Young Rastas such as Felix Waldron—a promising mathematician—had turned their backs on the miseducation of Cornwall College and had spent their time out in the hills behind Rose Hall in the gullies preaching about Lumumba, the Congo, Nasser and Haile Selassie. They had defended their right to walk across the area (regardless of whether their presence horrified tourists) and in the altercation that followed one incident on Holy Thursday, a petrol station was burnt and the policeman who had come to prosecute the Rastas was attacked with a spear. The State called out the army, and after the deaths of eight persons, the military and the police carried out mass arrests of Rastafarian women, men and children. Not since the Sam Sharp revolt, in the same region, had there been such a mass arrest of black people. The prisons were full, and when the heat of the sun caused uncomfortable conditions in the detention centers where the Rastas were held, the police turned water hoses on those arrested.[26]

The local newspaper the *Daily Gleaner* carried stories claiming that the disturbance and mass revolt by the Rastas was caused by their being under the influence of ganja. There was no discussion in the press or the pulpit concerning the rights of Rastas as citizens of an independent Jamaica. The perception of Rastas reflected in the national newspaper was that they were lazy, did not want to work, and were always smoking ganja. As I look back on those fateful weeks of uprising and police brutality, I must confess that there was in 1963 such a disconnect between middle-class Jamaica and Rastafari that it is not surprising Rastas were dismissed by middle-class Jamaica as lazy criminals and seen by the society-at-large as receiving what was their due by being arrested en masse and thrown in jail. I recall feeling, as a young minister in the Jamaican church, that Rastas were heretics for preaching that Haile Selassie was God and for underscoring that view by publicly smoking ganja. The truth is there was much antipathy between Rastas and the church since Rastas regarded the church as the servant of the state. They regarded the religion of Jesus as preached and practiced by the church as one of the main roadblocks to social and economic liberation in Jamaica. In the Rastas' view, the churches openly sought the favor of the government and refused to criticize the government in its neglect of those who were socially marginalized.

Rastas were known to prophesy destruction of both government and church. The church, aspiring to become a middle-class institution, saw Rastas as irredeemable and undesirable for church membership—as outside the pale of salvation. The public shared this perception of Rastas, whom they saw as nobodies. So it would not be surprising that police would get popular support for arresting and killing Rastas with the charge that they were unproductive and spent their time smoking ganja. The wider society refused to raise questions concerning Rastas' rights as citizens, and the church did not view them as children of God.

Horace Campbell helps us understand a profound sense in which working-class Jamaicans entered on a collision course with the government. The church took sides with the Jamaican government as it took a popular custom—ganja use—and made it illegal, with penalties for violating the law that included imprisonment. To outlaw the use of ganja was to set a trap for the imprisonment of a large percentage of the population, with Rastas—who were most unlikely to hide their use of this herb—being the chief among them. "Arrests for unlawful possession went up 300%, and it was not until the Rastas helped to defeat the Jamaica Labor Party regime (the one they termed Pharaoh) that the People's National Party amended the provisions for mandatory imprisonment, so that now there was a fine for those arrested for possession for the first time. This amendment had come partly because many of the children of the petty bourgeoisie and political careerists were now being attracted to the power of Rasta, including the spiritual use of ganja. Michael Manley's administration understood that they could not deal so repressively with a popular custom."[27]

Theological Identity and Dreadlocks

The sociologist Barry Chevannes suggests that the early Rastafari were concerned with the problems of their identity and the identity of God. This was true of Howell, Hibbert, Hinds, and Dunkley. The point of departure for talk about their identity and the redemption of African people and people of African descent was the identity of God. Chevannes explains:

> The early preachers of the new religion concentrated on the question of the identity of God. All informants confirm that this was so. This thrust accomplished at least one objective: it undermined the racial values of the colonial status quo, which to a significant extent had gripped the poor peasant into compliance. Regardless of the nuisance Bedward was thought to be to the status quo, he never challenged the identity of the colonial Christian God. The Rastafari did. God was none other than the little black man ruling over Ethiopia. What was more, God has always been black. He was King and all true believers were to serve him.[28]

The blackness of God was the unifying theme that held all Rastas together in the early years, and it is still the central belief to which all Rastas subscribe. Smoking ganja is desirable but not required. There are also different stages of Ital living.

While some Rastas eat meat and others do not, they are united in the decision not to eat pork and shellfish. Wearing dreadlocks was also not required in the early years as Hinds himself and certainly the primary founder Leonard Howell did not wear dreadlocks. I can recall Rastafari brethren in the late 1940s and 1950s who did not wear dreadlocks. The

Rasta who made the most significant impression on me was a man in my village called Eddie. Eddie was a barber prior to becoming a Rasta, and he maintained his skill as a barber. I remember he had a rather large afro and facial hair that were neatly combed. But I recall that what set Rastas aside those days was neither dreadlocks, nor Ital living, nor for that matter ganja smoking (as there were many people in the village who were not Rastas who smoked ganja). What set them apart and identified them as Rastas was their talk about this black man in Ethiopia who was considered by them to be God. Most people in my village did not take Rastas seriously on two fronts. Rastas were viewed as supplanting the Christian God, the God embraced by the majority of people whether they belonged to a Kumina, Revivalist, or mainline church. The Christian God was approved by the colonial class, and no supreme being who threatened allegiance to this God could stand. And allegiance to Emperor Haile Selassie, a black man as God and king, meant disavowing one's loyalty to the king of England. Further, Rasta preachers, especially Howell, taught that taxes should not be paid to England or any foreign head of state as Haile Selassie, the emperor of Ethiopia, was the head and deliverer of all black people. It should not surprise us then that Howell and Hinds were imprisoned and charged with sedition and blasphemy. The Rastas' attempt to focus God-talk in relation to a black man from Africa ostensibly decolonized the Christian God and provided another frame of reference from which black people could identify themselves. Haile Selassie was not just another head of state who would send papers saying black people are free as the king of England did in 1834. This king would deliver his people not only because he was divine but because he was black. The identity nexus for black people hinged on the reality that they could not separate divinity and blackness. He was divine because he was black and black because he was divine. The unity of blackness and divinity merged exquisitely in him.

There are two realities that are important to note here concerning Rastas' openness and relationship to their king and God. His divinity and his blackness were equally important to them. The importance of the divinity had to do with the reality that Rastas felt trapped in Babylon, which represented principalities, powers, and wickedness in high places. Rastas were clear that the Babylon that confronted Jamaica was the legacy of slavery expressed in a confrontation with racism, cultural resistance to things African, and the widening gap between rich and poor. God-talk became a form of resistance as hope for deliverance in Babylon was linked to the man-God Haile Selassie. God-talk was for liberation from the trickery and violence of Babylon.

The thrust of the Rastafarian messianic ideology puts it in tension with the present "Babylon" order, which is undesirable and unacceptable since it represents and subsists on the denial of human rights and freedom of Africans. . . . Babylon constitutes oppression and exploitation of the black race in general and is therefore an evil system. Rastas have a very strong expectation of a new order of existence in a radically new setting. In this new environment, current wrongs and wickedness perpetrated against Rastafarians will be corrected. Freedom, righteousness, justice, peace and love will prevail. . . . Rasta orthodoxy has declared Selassie to be the returned Messiah, "the King of all African kings and a descendant of David. . . ." Every Rastafarian recognizes HIM. . . . Haile Selassie of Ethiopia to be the returned messiah; the only mediator between God and man representing Christ. We base these beliefs on the interpretation of the Scriptures and can quote many passages in the Bible which endorse these beliefs and the concept of the divinity of HIM. He is the 225th rebirth of Solomon. . . . He is the black Christ of this era.[29]

Rastas place their hope in God for deliverance from exile in Babylon. Hope for Rastas is not in patterning the church and declaring that Christ is dead but rather in embodying the good news that the black Christ lives and is active in their affairs. Although they are willing to participate in the creation of a just society based on biblical and fair principles that would benefit the poor and marginalized, they are clear that they will not participate in perpetuation of Babylonian principles. The truth is that Jah's judgment will fall on Babylon as Babylon is destined for destruction.

I now move to the question of the significance of the dreadlocks as an index of identity. The Rastas are clear that a part of the meaning of wearing dreadlocks is that it differentiates Rastas from those who are committed to the Babylonian way of life. The people who wear the dreadlocks are those who have the "I-and-I consciousness" and experience a rebirth due to their relationality, are open to the new future made possible by the man-God Haile Selassie, and are no longer held in cultural captivity to the ways of Babylon. "I-and-I consciousness" allows Rastas to share in the son-ship of their God, the black man from Ethiopia. Sharing in son-ship means that Rastas are divine because they are sons of the man-God, but they are also black. The modern sign and signal of blackness, which is at the same time a signifier of son-ship, is the wearing of the dreadlocks.

It is difficult in this age, when it has become fashionable for many professors and students on campuses to wear the dreadlocks, to remember that Rastas were persecuted, prosecuted, and often imprisoned because the dreadlocks were a sign of anti-Jamaican-ness and a refusal to accept what they saw as Babylonian captivity. The appearance of the Rastas with their locks threw greater fear into the hearts of the ruling class, for the popular version of beauty at that time suggested that the black who wore his or her hair long and in its natural form was ugly and offensive. Parents would sometimes curse their children as "nattie-head pickney." Some black people, both men and women, went to great lengths to process and straighten their hair so that it would look European. Because of the opposition of the wider society to the appearance of these bearded black men who called their beard "precepts," there was a sense of solidarity among the Rastas, while the state, in its effort to humiliate the brethren, attempted to shave their locks. The more the police tried to humiliate the Rastas, the more they were determined to keep their appearance, which was called "dread." It was in this period that the concept of "Natty Dread" became part of the vocabulary of resistance.[30]

The appearance and acceptance of dreadlocks as a statement of resistance and dignity flip-flopped the divine blackness equation in Rastas' understanding of the man-God Haile Selassie and their relationship to him. It seems to me that in the early years of the movement, the emphasis was on the divine rescuing Rastas and the black oppressed from Babylon. As Rastas began to adopt an accommodating attitude to Babylon, the emphasis changed from divine rescue and a resettlement in Ethiopia to the affirmation of blackness as a means for social change in Babylon and as a badge of dignity. The dreadlocks became a symbol of the new dignity associated with blackness. The wearing of the dreadlocks became an outward sign of "I-and-I consciousness," an outward sign of an inner transformation. The wearing of the dreadlocks was a merging of inner and outer. It was a sign that a rebirth had taken place, and it meant that the wearer had a commitment to redefine self in relation to Africa, to say yes to Africa and no to Europe. This was problematic for colonial Jamaica, which was accustomed to seeing itself through the lens of Europe. Dreadlocks signified the struggle against neocolonialism and all forms of oppression in Jamaica.

Recently I visited the Marley Museum in Jamaica. After the tour, I conversed with a Rasta man who introduced himself as Ras Tafioritta. We had a lively conversation about Bob Marley, and then I inquired into his "overstanding" [understanding] of the dreadlocks and the beard. "Why do you wear the dreadlocks," I asked? He replied, "You know brethren, my overstanding is that the locks and the beard is about the lion look. His majesty Haile Selassie is the lion of the tribe of Judah; therefore, we represent the lion look. You, my brethren represent the lamb look, but Rasta man the lion look."

The dreadlocks were intended to evoke the confidence and strength of the lion. According to Brother Tafioritta, the lion look helped him shake off the legacy of slavery and colonialism that told black people they were un-important, inconsequential, and that their bodies belonged to the master. Brother Tafioritta emphasized that the lion look emphasized that black people were no longer buying the false gospel that kinky hair equals bad hair. The lion look was an affirmation of the natural, allowing the hair to grow as Jah intended. As brother Tafioritta said, "After all is Jah hair, mek Jah hair grow."

> To begin to repair this psychological damage the Rastas declared their identification with the *lion*—in its roar, its hair, its body strength, intelligence and total movements. The mane of the lion's hair was compared favorably with the locks of the brethren, while ordinary Jamaicans were reading about Tarzan and Phantom pacifying lions and Africans, the Rastas emerged in Jamaican society as *lions*. . . . The African lion symbolizes some of the same black ideals and hope that Brer Anancy symbolized in our "ancient" conscious-ness, but the lion is more of a fitting ideal for a people bent on a militant march forward towards their own maximum and ultimate self-realization and self-discovery. The African lion expresses more of the natural and ideal spirit and ideal strivings of the enslaved Afri-cans. The lion image offers a more universal and wholesome defini-tion of how man ought to organize himself outwardly and how he should feel inwardly. It represents the Brethrens' supreme symbolic yearning for wholesomeness and power to compensate for their powerlessness and their alienated existence. As such they have gone well forward of the mass of working class people in becoming con-scious of the need to develop an independent philosophy of life, in ways more appropriate to and reflective of our experiences, needs and vibrations as Africans. Rastas express a vision of life radiating from the ancient memories of our deepest longings.[31]

The lion is the cardinal symbol of Rastas that gave rise to the expres-sion, "Rasta man a lion": "For the dreadlocks were supposed to be a 'sym-bolic reincarnation or imitation of the lion in man form, both in face and body, as well as in the spirit and structure.' The picture of the lion began to appear on Rasta dwellings, on their meeting halls, on their push carts. . . . painted in the colors of Marcus Garvey—red, black and green."[32] And the

Rastas would sing, "The lion of Judah shall break every chain and make us free again and again."

Father Joseph Owens, in his much-cited work *Dread: The Rastafarians of Jamaica,* reminds us that the wearing of the dreadlocks was another expression of Rastas' commitment to the natural way of life. Rastas seek to offer ritual expressions of their religion in the growing of the dreadlocks, the smoking of the holy herbs, and through Ital living. The natural environment of Rastas' way of life is expressed in and through their commitment to the natural environment. "Beards and locks are cultivated by the Rastafarians because they are seen to be the fullest expression of nature. Not those who grow their hair long but those who trim it off are required to explain their actions. 'They that don't like the hair, it's because they are afraid of nature themselves. Hair play a very important part upon man. Everyone that have the color brown would know that hair is nature. Anyone who fight against the hair fight against self. . . . We the African should let our hair grow as much as we desire, so as to fit nature, which is the force that we the African should let control our system.'"[33]

A number of sources seem to be credited for the practice of wearing dreadlocks. Barry Chevannes suggests that one of the first groups to wear the dreadlocks was a group of young militants known as the Youth Black Faith: "Sometime in the 1950's a change took place in the physical appearance of the 'beard.' . . . This was largely the work of a group of young militants grouped together in the Youth Black Faith, a name which captured their youthfulness, Black Nationalism and idealism. A quasi-group, they undertook to enforce a fresh image of Rastafari as a force opposed to the entire Jamaican society. . . . they symbolized in their adoption of the illicit ganja as a sacred herb, their illegal marches, and, to be sure the dreadlocks."[34] Chevannes chronicles the history of dreadlocks:

> At the time of the founding of the Youth Black Faith, locks were not in vogue. This is not to say that there were not Rastafari who did not trim. It had not taken long after the movement was founded, in fact, for some to wear beards in the manner of Selassie (and of course Jesus). It was believed that only those who wore beards would be repatriated on August 1, 1934 [the date suggested by Howell for the return of Rastas to Ethiopia]. From the 1930's, therefore, beards became a practice, and a biblical reference was found to justify it, namely, the Nazarite vow of Samson. What the Youth Black Faith debated now, however, was whether to comb. The issue was largely a social one at first because society did not accept unkempt hair. Not to

comb one's hair was to declare oneself not merely antisocial but extrasocial, like mad derelicts and outcasts such as Bag-a wire. It was precisely this concern that was the issue. The side that won was the side of the Dreadful, the warriors, the Bonogees. "It appears to I many a times that things that the man comb would go out and do, the man with the locks wouldn't think of doing. The appearance to the people when you step out of the form is outcast. When you are Dreadlocks you come like a outcast." Locks had a shock value but they were also a way of witnessing to faith with the same kind of fanaticism for which the prophets and saints of old were famous, men gone mad with religion.[35]

I am grateful to Chevannes for this chronology of Rastafari. His pointing to these Rastas who wore beards and their hair uncut calibrates with my experience and memory of Rastas. What is helpful is Chevannes indicating that the only people who wore matted hair in Jamaican culture were homeless persons and those edged out of the society because they were insane. The Youth Black Faith, according to Chevannes, took on the matted hair of the despised and rejected in the society, and for many years the society chose not to differentiate between the Rastas and the derelicts. Like the outcasts, they were regarded as dirty and were often placed in asylums for the mentally ill. Rastas entered into solidarity with the outcasts and by association they became outcasts. It is incredible that in the latter part of the twentieth century the dreadlocks that were the sign and signal of the rejects have been transformed to become an emblem of dignity. It seems that the Rastas entered so deeply into this ethos of the outcasts that they transformed it into a sign of hope and dignity.

Horace Campbell traces the roots of Rastas wearing the dreadlocks differently. He relates it to the Rasta settlement that Leonard Howell established in Pinnacle community of St. Catherine: "The colonial state showed such unrelenting opposition to the settlement that with hindsight it is now possible to assert that they wanted to kill the seed of cooperation and open love for Africa before it blossomed in the society. . . . Extra powers had been given to the police under the Defense Regulations and more than 173 armed policemen, under the direction of the Commissioner of Police, were deployed to break up Pinnacle."[36] A part of the problem was that the police charged that the Rastas at Pinnacle taught as part of their doctrine that Jamaicans should not pay taxes to the colonial state. In addition, Howell and twenty-eight of his followers were placed in jail and charged with growing ganja. Because of the constant raids by the police, Howell instituted guards at the gate of the commune who were called *Ethiopian Warriors*. "When the struggle of the land and Freedom Army (called Mau Mau) in Kenya exploded, and Rastas saw pictures of the freedom fighters with their natural hair, long and matted, the Rasta positively identified with these fighters and began to wear their hair in 'locks.'"[37] The dreadlocks hairstyle made the guardsmen fearsome and frightening.

Ennis Edmonds supports Campbell's claims that the dreadlocks hairstyle originated in the 1940s as Rastas observed that African Freedom Fighters wore the matted locks: "It was apparently inspired by the appearance in the Jamaican Press of Africans wearing a similar hairstyle. Those whose pictures have been variously identified as Gallas, Somalis, Masais, or Jomo Kenyatta's Freedom Fighters. Along with the implicit justification of the dreadlocks hairstyle that comes from its alleged African origin, Rastas also invoke the biblical teaching concerning the Nazarites, whom the Levitical laws forbade to trim their hair or shave (Num. 6:5), as a means of validating their hairstyle."[38] Father Owens also seems to support Horace Campbell as he recollects: "In a Rastafarian publication, *Our Own* (No. 2), a picture of a Mau Mau leader showed him with a magnificent set of long Rasta-styled locks. The brethren also cite *National Geographic* (December 1970) because it pictured some Ethiopian monks with locks, and they bring forward the example of the Ethiopian soldiers during the Abyssinian war, who were known to have their hair quite long. The official symbol of Ethiopia, a standing lion, provides further justification for the locks, since they are often compared to a lion's mane."[39]

Regardless of how this significant tradition began, it is perhaps the primary mode of identifying Rastas, and even within Rastafari it used to be a significant symbol of commitment to the movement. This has changed as the dominant culture—what the Rastas would call Babylonian culture—has co-opted this practice, and it is now common to see fashionable persons wearing the locks who have no commitment to the movement.

However, Rastas claim that additional reasons for their wearing locks are because Christ and the prophets of Israel were all locks men: "The locks and beard are a sign of the anciency of the ways of the Rastafarians. The ancient times saw people much closer to nature than today. The locks and beard is the fullness of the precepts. We are an ancient people. We are a nature people. Now I could not create a strand of hair; therefore it would be wrong to destroy it."[40] Rastas take great pride in citing the story of Samson and Delilah as an indication of the importance of not putting a razor to one's hair. But the most important scriptural citation is Numbers 6:5, where Jah instructs Moses to inform the children of Israel of the

Nazarite vows: "All the days of his vow of separation there shall no razor come upon his head: until the days be fulfilled, in which he separateth himself unto the Lord, he shall be holy, he shall let the locks of his head grow long." Other important texts include Leviticus 19:27: "Ye shall not round the corners of your heads, neither shall thou mar the corners of thy beard," and Leviticus 21:5: "They shall not make baldness upon their head, neither shall they shave off the corner of their beard, nor make any cuttings in the flesh." Rastas refuse to cover their locks, while they insist on women wearing a covering such as a head scarf or a turban. They find scriptural warrants for these claims in 1 Corinthians 11:4–6: "Every man praying or prophesying having his head covered dishonoreth his head. But every woman praying or prophesying with her head unveiled dishonoreth her head: for it is one and the same thing as if she were shaven. For if a woman is not veiled, let her also be shorn: but if it is a shame to a woman to be shorn or shaven, let her be veiled."

Obiagele Lake, a Rasta woman, points out that all Rasta women and men wear locks but that only the women wear covering. The woman must wear a covering as her hair is at once her beauty and her shame.[41] She points out that the primary Scripture cited to keep women in compliance is Ephesians 5:22–24: "Wives, submit yourselves to your husbands, as unto the Lord. For the husband is the head of the wife, even as Christ is the head of the church: and he is the savior of the body. Therefore as the church is subject unto Christ, so let wives be to their own husbands in everything."

Lake adds that the vast majority of Rasta women take these scriptural texts with the utmost seriousness and are seen covering their heads in public. Lake observes, however, that the truth is that the hair is not a symbol of shame but of woman as an ontological reality. Barry Chevannes agrees with Lake and purports that among Rastas all women regardless of age are below men in status. The male is the "King-man" or the "God-man" and as such is naturally superior to women, even though women are often referred to as "empresses." "The subordination of women to men is characteristic of Dreadlocks in general, only the Bobo carry it to a greater length. In the commune all females must cover their legs and arms. Women are confined to looking after children and performing other household chores such as cleaning and washing. . . . Women give deference to men."[42] The bottom line, says Lake, is that both in Jamaican society and in Rastafari community women are subordinate. But the problem becomes more complicated in Rasta ideology and Christian theology, which provides the overarching rubric for Jamaican society. The problem is that in both Christian theology and Rasta ideology woman is polluted. "Pollution is used in this context of sex and gender and refers to the capacity that women have to endanger men through their bodily substances and through their overall femaleness."[43] Citing biblical warrants, Lake explains that "a woman who becomes pregnant and gives birth to a son will be ceremonially unclean for seven days, just as she is unclean during her monthly period. On the eighth day the boy is to be circumcised. Then the woman must wait thirty-three days to be purified from her bleeding. . . . If she gives birth to a daughter, for two weeks the woman will be unclean, as during her period. Then she must wait *sixty-six* days to be purified from her bleeding" (Leviticus 4:12).[44]

Although according to Leviticus 4:15, a male's discharge is also considered unclean, the days of atonement are considerably fewer than those of a woman. The fact that when a woman has a female child her period before being received back into the community is much longer than that of the male child indicates the female's inferior status. While Jamaican society as a whole accepts the notion of women's inferiority based on Christian dogma, this is enhanced in Rasta culture and practice. For example, in the Bobo community women may serve guests but may never serve Bobo males. In Jamaican society, the woman usually cooks and serves, but in the Bobo community the men cook and serve. If the women so choose, they may cook for themselves but never for the males.

Velma Grant, a member of the Bobo community, supports the claims of inequality between men and women made by Lake and Chevannes. She points out that in the Bobo community, male and female housing is located on separate sides. The menstrual status of the female is made evident by a flag displayed at the entrance of the female's quarters. A white flag indicates that the female is "free" and is not on her menstrual cycle. During that period, she is allowed to have female or male visitors. A red flag means she is not "free" and is menstruating. During this time, she is confined to her residence and off limits to visitors. According to Grant, this focus on the menstrual cycle enforces a separation that carries over into the temple:

> The separation continues even in the Bobo Shanty house of worship, which the female may only enter while she is "free." The men are seated on one side and the women if "free" are seated on the opposite side. There is no interaction between the two genders during the worship services. The only exception to this rule is evident at the culmination of a fasting period where a male priest will administer a

ceremonial piece of bread and a cup of water to a female to "break" the fast. The ceremony that is part of the worship service is reminiscent of the communion meal that is a unifying factor between the various Christian traditions. Along with the priest that administers the fasting elements there are usually six other priests on the altar and four guards stationed at the doors, one in each direction and they are all males. Within the Rastafarian faith and particularly this group, there is no place for women in any of these roles or functions. It is strictly a male dominated culture that relegates the function of women to that of mother and wife and only at particular times of the month.[45]

The recounting of life as a Rasta woman by Velma Grant seems to lend support to the subtitle of Obiagele Lake's book *Rastafari Women: Subordination in the Midst of Liberation Theology.*

Rasta Theology as Liberation Theology?

In her book, Lake concedes that a liberation motif informs the Rastafari way of life and so concludes that what we have in Rastafari doctrines is a liberation theology:

> Since the inception of Rastafarianism in the 1930's, Rastas have protested against European colonial control over African descended people in Jamaica. Freedom from colonial, capitalistic hegemony and self-determination for African Diaspora people has constituted the cornerstones of their philosophy. As adamant as many Rastas are in these beliefs, they have not seen liberation as a right of women. To say that Rastafarian women are subordinated to Rasta men is not tantamount to claiming that women are pawns, that they have no agency or influence, or that they have no personal power. Neither does the claim of women's subordination mean that they do not respect themselves or are not respected in certain ways by males in the organization. Women are respected if they respect the rules that suppress them. Having said this, it is important to point out on a case by case basis, there are Rastafarian women who are confident, active and self assertive. But, these women, who would probably not be servile to anyone, are in the minority. . . . Based on women's presumed inferiority, many believe that they must be brought into the organization by a man. Women's status is further denigrated by

dress codes which conceal their bodies and symbolically shroud them in a veneer of feminine protection. Language which refers to women as "daughters" also diminishes women in relationship to men. In addition, reggae music, which has become a vehicle for the spread of Rastafari to almost all continents, acts as a fifth column in its derogation of women as sex objects and as dependents of men.[46]

Obiagele Lake contends that Rastafari is a liberation theology. I will first examine this claim. It seems that if we are to define liberation theology as the attempt of oppressed people to relate the freeing power of the black Christ to the situation of oppression in such a way that the chains of oppression are broken and the people begin to "emancipate themselves from mental slavery," then Rastafari is on the right path. Liberation theologian James Cone, who espouses a black Christ as the basis for black liberation theology, writes:

> On the American scene today, as yesterday, one problem stands out: the enslavement of black Americans. But as we examine what contemporary theologians are saying, we find that they are silent about the enslaved condition of black people. Evidently they see no relationship between black slavery and the Christian gospel. Consequently there has been no sharp confrontation of the gospel with white racism. There is, then, a desperate need for a *black theology*, a theology whose sole purpose is to apply the freeing power of the gospel to black people under white oppression. In more sophisticated terms this may be called a theology of revolution. Lately there has been much talk about revolutionary theology, stemming primarily from non-Western religious thinkers whose identification lies with the indigenous oppressed people of the land. These new theologians of the "Third World" argue that Christians should not shun violence but should initiate it, if violence is the only means of achieving the much needed rapid radical changes in life under dehumanizing systems. . . . Unless theology can become "ghetto theology," a theology which speaks to black people, the gospel message has no promise for life for the black people.[47]

There are clear congruencies between the theology of James Cone and that of Rastafari. Both speak of the liberative task in terms of liberation for Africans at home and abroad. Both are persuaded that the key to liberation is the black Messiah. For Cone, the conversation takes place within the Christian church, and for many years his sources included white theologians. For the Rastas, although they engage the Christian church in conversation and use the Bible as their primary source, the conversation takes place outside the church and in tension with Marcus Garvey's teaching. Further, the Rastas also have a black Christological frame of reference in that the messianic promise of liberation for black people is fulfilled in the black man from Ethiopia, Haile Selassie.

Because Cone and Rastas presuppose Marcus Garvey and his emphasis on "black uplift," I will now probe further Obiagele Lake's assertion that Rastafari is a liberation theology. Exploring issues of race consciousness and black nationalism and seeking to discover ways in which Rastas use Garvey to go beyond Garvey, I turn once again to the father of Rasta theology, Marcus Garvey.

5
Using Garvey to Go beyond Garvey

It is no secret that the unseen hand that guided Rastafari from its initial impulse was that of Jamaican visionary and leader Marcus Mosiah Garvey. His emphasis on Africa as an organizing principle and his insistence that black people view God through the lens of Ethiopia was decisive in shaping Rastafari theology. Even their choice of Haile Selassie as Messiah was credited by the Rastas to Garvey, who was reported to have said on leaving Jamaica: "Look to Africa from which a black king shall arise to deliver his people." Garvey, a son of Jamaican soil, describes the friendship with a white pastor's daughter that led to his discovery that he was not insulated from the darts of racism:

> We romped and were happy children, playmates together. The little white girl whom I liked knew no better than I did myself. We were two innocent fools who never dreamed of a race feeling and problem. As a child I went to school with white boys and girls; like all other Negroes then. I never heard the term used once until I was about fourteen. At fourteen my little white playmate and I parted. Her parents thought the time had come to separate us and draw the color line. They sent her and another sister to Edinburgh, Scotland, and told her that she was never to write or try to get in touch with me, for I was a "nigger."[1]

This was Garvey's first encounter with racism, which was inescapable in the colony. "School-children were taught to accept British rule and to love it. There were pictures of the British sovereign in all schools; the children sang the British national anthem and British songs, and were taught to revere the Governor of the island who represented the British Crown. The Governor himself lived in Kingston in King's House, which was the central point of the official social life of the planters, merchants, and high colonial officials. As such, the life of the colonial ruling class was fundamentally different from that of the ordinary Jamaican."[2]

It was not only in the arts and education that racial tensions were inescapable but in economics as well. Jamaica as a colony grew sugarcane and bananas for export to Great Britain. We grew them only secondarily for ourselves. The produce the natives were allowed to use was usually not good enough for export. In this environment it was difficult not to have a poor image of self. But somehow Garvey made it against the odds, partly due to the influence of Dr. Robert Love, the Pan-Africanist under whose influence Garvey developed a strong love for Africa and for all things black. "Race consciousness," an anticolonial concept, was a constant theme in Love's writings and speeches. It asserted the humanity of a race of people, regardless of class, whom capitalism oppressed, exploited, and branded as inferior.

In this context, racial oppression and class exploitation stemmed from the same source. "Therefore, race consciousness in Love and Garvey was very often both the national cry of a people and also a class cry . . . linked to the common yoke of suffering. Love was an advocate of land reform. He agitated for the distribution of Crown lands to the landless peasantry on terms which would bring their possession within the reach of all."[3] In his newspaper, *Jamaica Advocate,* which brought him into conflict with the colonial powers on the island, Love discussed all aspects of colonial life. He called for the hiring of black people in the colonial bureaucracy and agitated for better health care and education and addressed "the question of black women and their role in society." In November 1896, Love wrote that "the destiny of the Negro race depends upon the elevation of the women of the race. The conditions in which the people of the B.W.I. (British West Indies) are found today [are] due to the fact that no effort has been made to lift the black women up and to put her on the plane that women ought to occupy in society."[4]

Amy Jacques Garvey, the wife of Marcus Garvey, whom I had the pleasure of meeting in 1967, speaks of the influence Love had on her husband. "The first black man to inspire in him leadership was Dr. Love, born in Nassau, Bahamas, educated in England and on the continent. He spent his best years in Jamaica fighting for the uplift of the black masses. He published a paper called *The Advocate.* Courageous and outspoken, he spent all his time and means in this work, and in the practice of medicine, especially among the poor."[5]

As early as 1910 Garvey tried migration as a means of self-improvement. He lived with an uncle in Costa Rica and from there went to Panama. In both places, he was appalled at the conditions under which the peasantry lived and worked. "He left Panama and went to Ecuador, South America, where West Indian labor was being used in tobacco fields and in mining. Again he saw the awful conditions under which they labored—no protection from the British Consul, and no efforts made for their welfare. The same conditions obtained in Nicaragua, Spanish Honduras, Colombia and Venezuela. Sickened with fever, and sick at heart over appeals from his people for help on their behalf, he decided to return to Jamaica in 1911, and try with Government there, as well as to awaken Jamaicans at home to the true conditions of the Spanish mainland."[6] Garvey had an uncanny gift of empathizing with people and allowing their suffering to speak to him. He noted early that the suffering of black people was disproportionate to that of other peoples. On his return to Jamaica, he appealed to the Jamaican government to help Jamaicans abroad, as conditions he observed in those countries were unfavorable for the majority. The colonial government suggested that if conditions were unfavorable abroad, they should return home. It was Garvey's view that economic and social conditions were no better for the poor in Jamaica than in the countries visited.

The people urged Garvey to form an Association for the betterment of Black West Indians at home and abroad. Again money handicapped him, and Government frowned on his efforts. He called the Organization the Universal Negro Improvement Association. The word "Negro" created opposition and prevented help from "better-off Colored people," who felt that Negro was synonymous with low, good-for-nothing. To the few whites it suggested an organized black majority; which they felt would be dangerous to their economic overlordship. These Oppositions were subtle and undermining, so he decided to go to England, and try to enlist the sympathy of black seamen and students from Africa. . . . The year 1912–13 found him in England, and on the European continent, contacting African Seamen and Students, who opened to him new vistas of Africa and Asia. He worked on the *African Times* and *Orient Review*, published in London by Duse Mohammed Ali, an Egyptian Scholar and Traveler. From him he learned much of Africa's ancient history, topography, mineral potential and labor conditions of semi-slavery and serfdom. All this suffering in order to mine and produce wealth to enrich Europeans, and turn their wheels of industry, thereby providing gainful employment for their peoples, with the attendant educational and cultural facilities.[7]

Garvey was fired by the spirit of black nationalism as he asked questions such as: "Where were black people's factories to provide employment for their people? Why should black people always walk hat in hand begging white men for jobs?" In response to these questions, Garvey formulated the aims and objectives of his movement: "To establish a Universal Confraternity among the race; to promote the spirit of pride and love; to reclaim the fallen; to administer to and assist the needy; to assist in civilizing the tribes of Africa; to assist in the development of independent Negro communities; to establish a central nation for the race, where they will be given the opportunity to develop themselves; . . . to establish Universities, Colleges, Academies and Schools for racial education and culture of the people; to improve the general condition of Negroes everywhere."[8]

With these goals and objectives informing his Universal Negro Improvement Association (UNIA), coupled with his untiring work for racial uplift both in Jamaica (to which he returned from England in 1914) and later in Harlem, New York, it should not surprise us that Garvey saw the elevation of Haile Selassie as emperor of Ethiopia as a positive movement in racial uplift. On November 8, 1930, Garvey published an article expressing hope and praise for the new emperor in his Jamaican newspaper *The Blackman*.

Last Sunday, a great ceremony took place at Addis Ababa, the capital of Abyssinia. It was the coronation of the new Emperor of Ethiopia—Ras Tafari. From reports and expectations, the scene was one of great splendor, and will long be remembered by those who were present. Several of the leading nations of Europe sent representatives to the coronation, thereby paying their respects to a rising Negro nation that is destined to play a great part in future history of the world. Abyssinia is the land of the blacks and we are glad to learn that even though Europeans have been trying to impress the Abyssinians that they are not belonging to the Negro race, they have learned the retort that they are, and they are proud to be so. Ras Tafari has traveled to Europe and America and is therefore no stranger to European hypocrisy and methods; he, therefore, must be regarded as a kind of modern Emperor, and from what we understand and know of him, he intends to introduce modern methods and systems into his country. Already he has started to recruit from different sections of the world competent men in different branches of science to help to develop his country to the position that she should occupy among the nations of the world. From what we have heard and what we do know, he is ready and willing to extend the hand of invitation to any Negro who desires to settle in his kingdom. . . . The Psalmist prophesied that Princes would come out of Egypt and Ethiopia would stretch forth her hands unto God. We have no doubt that the time is now come. Ethiopia is really now stretching forth her hands. The great kingdom of the East has been hidden for many centuries, but gradually she is rising to take a leading place in the world and it is for us of the Negro race to assist in every way to hold up the hand of Emperor Ras Tafari.[9]

There are a number of emphases worth noting in this important article commending the new emperor of Ethiopia. The first thing that strikes me is that Garvey refers to the emperor as Ras Tafari, not as Haile Selassie. The significance of this for me is that this reference could be the origin of the name Rasta or Rastafari. Why not the people of Selassie I? I believe it would be significant to Rastas that Garvey, their supreme prophet, so referred to him. The other thing that strikes me as a theologian is that Garvey provides biblical warrants to undergird the uniqueness of the event that occurred. This was not just another African being crowned king; the hope of the race resided in this event, and the Scriptures so attested. Ethiopia would be the center for the freeing of black people throughout the world. As noted, this was a critical and pivotal text for Rastas as they sought to make theological and political sense of Ras Tafari's elevation to king in Ethiopia. I believe it is widely acknowledged that if Garvey had not linked the coronation of Ras Tafari to Psalm 68:31, there is every reason to believe that the Rastas would not have made the connection. Garvey's prophecy not only helped the Rastas make the connection between Haile Selassie and African redemption, but it provided legitimacy.

However, we are reminded that Garvey did not regard Haile Selassie as God. In a profound sense, we can say that the Rastas used Garvey to go beyond Garvey. The Rastas, in focusing the hopes of the entire race in Haile Selassie, were able not only to give rise to black consciousness and black power throughout Jamaica and the Caribbean but also to fashion a black liberation theology. As noted, their understanding of "I-and-I consciousness"—the basis of which is something akin to Martin Buber's "I-and-Thou" relationship—is posited on an intersubjectivity between the Rasta and the man-God Haile Selassie. This "I-and-I consciousness" became the basis for an awakening of consciousness, a new way of viewing reality no longer through the eyes of the colonial overlord or through a Eurocentric lens but as an attempt to hammer out the relationship of the individual in relationship to Africa. Rastas were able to use the Christian Scriptures and hymns to underscore their theology and cosmology.

It was this unwillingness to regard Haile Selassie as divine that gave Garvey the freedom to criticize Selassie's handling of Ethiopia's war with Italy in 1935. For Garvey, Haile Selassie was the emperor of Ethiopia and not God. We should not forget that Garvey grew up Methodist and saw himself as firmly anchored in the Christian tradition, so criticizing the king of Ethiopia was not off-limits. In one of his critiques, Garvey pointed out that Haile Selassie was not a modern leader who prepared his country for modern warfare. Garvey observed that the king exhibited a penchant for feasting, fasting, and prayer while the enemies of Ethiopia were building up armaments of the most destructive kind as their way of securing the peace. Garvey admonished Haile Selassie that it was an error for Ethiopia to use the Coptic Church to seek to pull God into the war with Italy as God refused to take sides, allowing the stronger side to prevail.[10]

Rupert Lewis indicates that in the formative years of the movement Garvey vehemently disagreed with Leonard Howell's claim for the divinity of Haile Selassie.

> Not surprisingly, Garvey's attitude toward Haile Selassie was bitterly criticized by his opponents, as well as by some of his supporters, in correspondence and articles to *Plain Talk*. Some of the opposition to Garvey derived from the view that the emperor was a descendant of King Solomon and therefore untouchable. The power of the Hebrew Bible record was often invoked in the interpretation of the Emperor's ancient lineage. Others felt that Garvey's criticisms were simply unfair. No doubt exists that Garvey lost support among his followers as a result of his criticisms. However, his work and his reputation after his death caused him to become a prophet to Rastafarians and a national hero in Jamaican society.[11]

It is worth noting that while Garveyism was a broad social movement that included many sectors of Jamaican society, Rastafari was primarily a movement among the underclass in Jamaican society. Certainly in its formative years no middle-class blacks belonged to the movement. Rastafari was a community for the disinherited. Even when Hinds and others had their King of King's Missions, membership was among the outcasts and the disinherited. The inclusion of the middle class in Rastafari came with the rise of the black power movement in the 1960s, coupled with the issuance of the University Report and the active leadership among the poor by Walter Rodney.

Another important distinction that must be made between Garvey and Rasta concerns their views on ganja, which is used both as sacrament and socially by Rastas. An editorial that appeared in Garvey's newspaper *New Jamaica* on August 13, 1932, makes very clear Garvey's position regarding the holy herb.

> Ganja is a dangerous weed. It has been pronounced so by responsible authorities. The smoking of it does a great deal of harm or injury to the smoker; we understand it has the same effect on the subject as opium does. Every day we hear of cases of ganja sellers being brought before the Court—fines, small and heavy, have been inflicted with the object of destroying the trade, but yet it grows. The other day a man was found in possession of ninety pounds of ganja. This was enough deadly weed to destroy a thousand men. That our people are being destroyed by the use of ganja there is absolutely no doubt. We have come in contact with young men and middle aged men who have become a menace to society through the smoking of ganja. Sometimes they perform in such a crazy manner as to frighten us. Aren't we playing with the danger by not more severely putting it down? Most of the people who smoke ganja do so as a means of getting themselves in such a state or condition as to forget their troubles and worries—troubles and worries brought upon them by the bad conditions that exist in the country. . . . It would be good that more serious steps be taken to suppress this ganja habit. . . . Between ganja and fanatical religion, we are developing a large population of half-crazy people who may not only injure themselves but injure us. Some will do it in the name of the "lord" and others do it under the influence of the evil weed.[12]

Garvey's position means conflict with those who practiced the ritual and religious use of ganja. He had very harsh words for those who traded in ganja. But in spite of his stance on ganja, his prophetic and Ethiopianist vision provided a crucial inspiration for Rastafari. It is an interesting fact that warrants further investigation that in spite of Garvey's fundamental opposition to the primary beliefs of Rastafari, they hail him as their prophet and mentor. In the meantime, we must be clear that while Garvey may be credited with providing the inspiration for the ideological thrust of the movement in regard to repatriation and the centrality of blackness in their beliefs, there are many ways in which Rastafari differs from the Garvey movement. One difference I have not discussed is the structure of the movement Garvey led, which was rigorously centralized and institutionalized through the UNIA (Universal Negro Improvement Association). The Rastas resist any attempt at institutionalizing or centralizing leadership. There is autonomy of local leadership. While there is no pope or moderator, they nonetheless defer to elders, especially those who have been with the movement for a long time. I cannot imagine anyone overruling Mortimo Planno, one of the elders in the movement who was a part of the delegation to Africa to study the feasibility of repatriation and who personally met with Haile Selassie when he visited Jamaica in 1966. While there is no centralized system that accounts for how decisions are made, there is a practical wisdom that ensues from the community of elders. This was also my experience in my visit to the Bobo community. In both the teaching from the temple and the reasoning session after the worship experience, it was clear that although unacknowledged, there was a hierarchy of leadership in the local setting. There is no one person who may speak for all Rastas, yet when they meet, leadership emerges.

The converse was true with Garveyism. The structure was clear with Garveyism as it drew support from middle-class communities. "The Garvey movement, by contrast was, multi-class: teachers, journalists, small business people, black industrial workers in the United States, and sugar plantation and banana workers in Cuba and the Caribbean, most of whom were peasants. Each of these groups brought to the Garvey movement their view of the world, their distinct interests, and their common experiences of racial oppression."[13] The multiclass composition of the Garvey movement gave it a built-in capacity for conflict. A case in point was when the Rastas objected to Garvey's critique of Haile Selassie's leadership style during Ethiopia's war with Italy in 1935. Garvey is also on record for criticizing the early religious practices in Revivalism and the obeah practices that were present in early Rastafari. His candid criticism of ganja smoking placed him on a collision course with Rastafari, yet his stature in Jamaican culture as national hero and mentor of Bob Marley, the primary evangelist of modern Rastafari, secured Garvey's place in the movement.

We should not forget that Garvey made these claims in colonial Jamaica, where the symbol of ultimate power was the British Crown. In this regard, Garvey warned Ras Tafari not to allow Europe to separate Ethiopia from the rest of Africa. And perhaps most strongly of all, Garvey insisted that the new king should set about building a modern state.

If the central question of black liberation theology is where we stand in relation to Africa, there is no doubt that Garvey at least provided the inspiration for the Rastas. Garvey expressed with exquisite beauty a commitment to African redemption: "No one knows when the hour of Africa's redemption cometh. It is in the wind. It is coming. One day, like a storm it will be here." Or Garvey could appeal to his God: "Oh God help the Black man and rescue him from outrage!" And again: "We have gradually won our way back into the confidence of the God of Africa, and he shall speak with the voice of thunder, that shall shake the pillars of a corrupt and unjust world and once more restore Ethiopia to her ancient glory."[14]

It is quite clear that Garvey and the Rasta movement were about the uplift of Jamaicans and black people throughout the world. Both wanted this to occur through the agency of black people. Wherever Garvey went he bemoaned the plight and predicament of black people and insisted that the winds of freedom accompanied by thunder and lightning were signaling that change was imminent. Garvey, however, was a pragmatist and felt he could help the change occur by creating the Universal Negro Improvement Association with chapters in strategic locations. Garvey wanted to locate businesses black people owned that would help ease unemployment among the black masses. And he sought to practice what he preached by investing in a ship, the *Black Star Liner*.

The Rastas, on the other hand, were visionaries. They had a vision of a transformed Jamaica that would occur through the agency of Haile Selassie, who as the returned Messiah would transform Babylon. Rex Nettleford, in his *Mirror, Mirror,* suggests that this millenarian expectation began to change in the 1960s as Rastas began to take responsibility for their social location and work for social change. But even if one grants that the emphasis began to change in the 1960s with the University Report, Rastas began to learn that all Jamaica was not organized against them, and Jamaica's independence in 1962 provided a modicum of hope. Even so, it is still the case in Jamaica that there is an overarching eschatology that guides the movement. Jah will work through the Rasta man and woman. But it is nonetheless Jah's work.

The incidents of the late 1950's climaxed almost thirty years of waiting since Garvey's prophetic utterance was translated into an apocalyptic foretelling of the salvation of blacks and the fate of the white world. During those years nothing constructive had been done to facilitate the passage to Africa or the downfall of white society. The extent to which expectations of the cataclysm were sustained is measurable by the 15,000 followers of Henry who bought tickets [for repatriation to Africa]. Presumably the personnel of the movement had changed over the span, but the vision of a redeemed Africa had certainly not dimmed in the imaginations of the new recruits. To them, the African redemption was as attainable and inevitable as it had been to the first believers.[15]

Although there was much openness to the idea of social transformation, Rastas had to come to grips with the reality that Babylon was not transformed and Africa's redemption had not transpired. This reality kept alive their faith in the ontological necessity of Haile Selassie as the miseries and evil they encountered in Babylon called for supernatural help. It was widely rumored by the Rastas that during the emperor's visit in 1966 he said they should liberate Jamaica before they repatriate to Ethiopia. With this in mind, Rastas sought to hold together the notions of liberation and repatriation. This meant, among other things, that while they would hold on to their vision of Africa, they would work for the transformation of Jamaica. One can detect this double emphasis in the movement as it pressed forward into the latter part of the twentieth century. In a profound sense, repatriation meant liberation. One's relationship to Africa meant one would work for change among brothers and sisters in one's social location.

> The University Report and the mission to Africa had given the cult some semblance of legitimacy and although migration negotiations collapsed, the possibility of a physical break with Jamaica was supported by the growing numbers of emigrants, many of whom traveled to England. Added to these, was the emergent popularity of American black power replete with its "black is beautiful" slogan, clenched fist insignia and Afro-hair styles, imploring black people to recognize their African heritage. Together, they blended to produce a fresh nucleus of interest in the Rastafarian movement, and it was of this nucleus that the electrons and protons of the latest phase were born.[16]

There can be no denying that Rastafari has given Jamaican society a trans-formative religious practice. In the Jamaican context that was marked by white supremacy ideology and practices, Rastas seized the power of self-definition and began to raise critical questions concerning the power of self-identification of the poor. Jamaica, which for over three hundred years was a colony of Great Britain, very naturally found itself ordering its values according to British ideals.

Color, for example, which determined where one went to school, who owned the business, and who wrote school and church literature, was taken for granted. We did not stop to consciously think about how color functioned in the society in both secular and religious terms. With the legacy of the Native Baptists, followed by the Revivalists, whose practices the early Rastas incorporated, this began to change. Building on the work of Marcus Garvey and yet departing from Garvey's vision in important areas, the Rastas asked profound questions about the kind of people Ja-maicans had decided to become and what that implied. The Rastas, as they looked at Jamaican society from the perspective of the underclass, con-cluded that criticism of Jamaican society needed to begin with criticism of the church. They judged the church to be part of the Babylonian establish-ment that was organized against the poor. It did not help when, during the Ethiopian-Italian war of 1935, the pope gave his blessing to the Italian armed forces. This confirmed their fears that the church, whether Protes-tant or Catholic, took sides against the poor.

For Rastafari, this meant that the God who these Christians repre-sented did not have the best interests of the poor at heart, and that if the Jamaican underclass—those outside the mainstream who could not afford the canons of respectability demanded by the churches—were to have a modicum of respect and dignity they had to abolish the God of the Chris-tians. The Rastas saw very early that one of the main criteria of a God who would help deliver them from Babylon was that this God would have to become one of them.

In a profound sense, the Rastas foresaw the need for an incarnational theology. God could no longer be a foreigner representing the interests of Europe and North America but had to be black and committed to African redemption. Their gaze focused on Haile Selassie in part because Jamaica had a strong Ethiopic tradition perhaps going back as far as 1784, when George Liele called his church the Ethiopian Baptist Church, and continu-ing until Marcus Garvey adopted the Ethiopian national anthem as the theme song of the UNIA. It was not inconceivable that the Rastas would look to Africa in general and to Ethiopia in particular for their emancipator and god. Was Africa not the home of black people and all people of African descent? For three hundred years Jamaicans and people of African descent had looked to Europe and the United States of America. What benefit did they derive but a culture of dependence in both socioeconomic and religious terms?

In Jamaica, we looked to England for three hundred years for our laws, our educational system, our religious liturgies, and in many respects for our God. Rastas seized the power to choose their God and in the light of Psalm 68:31 began to look to Africa for help. Further, it was reported that Garvey on one occasion when leaving Jamaica enjoined his followers to look to Africa from where a black king would arise who would lead his people out of bondage. There was a confluence of reasons why they would look to Africa and not to the established churches of Europe or North America. This was a very anticolonial act—indeed, an act of resistance—as it occurred in Jamaica, which the British government ruled supreme and which was replete with pictures of the British monarch in most public buildings, including educational institutions.

During the formative years of the movement, the cardinal beliefs of Rastafari were laid with Leonard Howell, Archibald Dunkley, Robert Hinds, and teacher Joseph Nathaniel Hibbert—all of whom subscribed to the divinity of their new God, the black man from Ethiopia. Indeed, God had become one of them. Their new God raised the ontological question of all Jamaica: Where do you stand in relation to Africa? The majority of Jamaicans were clear about their response. They rejected Africa—only a handful of Jamaicans sided with the Rastas. Even Marcus Garvey, who in many ways broached this question before the Rastas, had some openness to middle-class values and provided room for a multiclass response to this question. One of Garvey's responses was to run for political office in Jamaica, thereby seeking through Jamaican political institutions to correct the intractable problems of Jamaica. Garvey felt that liberation was a possibility in Jamaica through political institutions, and of course the church was one such institution even if in the end he opted for a nondenominational church. It is quite clear that for Garvey the church could serve as an instrument of liberation.

The Rastas, however, looked outside the church and outside the political institutions. They argued that the system was corrupt and that repatriation and liberation was the answer. I would like to press the claim that any responsible view of repatriation must include liberation. In the concept of liberation, I include the valuing of the self in the light of one's vision of God. In this case, liberation has to do with the image of God articulated by the Rastas. To speak of God as black in a society in which the symbols of power are European or North American is an expression of black pride and dignity. So for Rastas the blackness of God not only ensures the dignity and sanctity of the black underclass but it also serves as a symbol of black empowerment as Rastas connect emphasis on the "I-and-I consciousness" to the blackness of their God. This connection to the divinity of God makes divinity available to Rastas. As I have indicated, the notion of "I-and-I consciousness" is a movement from the human subject to the divine and vice versa. It is a model of intersubjectivity in which Rastas are able to share in the divine life and claim son-ship and daughter-ship with God.

One of the important things about this move is its methodical significance for Rasta hermeneutics. To posit the divinity of Haile Selassie and to claim that he is God returned to deliver black people is to begin from the divine pole. It is to begin with God and—as the Rastas did particularly in the formative years—to see liberation in only divine terms. That is, Babylon was so evil and hopeless that God had to remove them from the scene through divine intervention. This theology then had a distinctly millenarian focus: God would intervene and bring forth the new era of justice and peace. Human agency had to take the backseat. But as the theology evolved to include "I-and-I consciousness," in which human life becomes infused and suffused with the life of the divine, Rastas began to identify themselves and to see their mission in a new way. They are no longer merely waiting for the in-breaking of the divine in the fullness of time to deliver them. They are now beginning to claim Jamaica as home even as they look toward the promised land of Ethiopia. Their view of eschatology is no longer merely futuristic as they wait for Jah to take them out of Babylon, but as they sing about the vision of the end time this vision impels them to work for change in the here and now. The vision of seeing self within the divine life reminds Rastas that not only is God on their side but they now have divine agency. In truth, they are Gods.

For the Rastas, new possibilities loom large on the horizon as they differentiate between the now and the not-yet and the ways in which the end of history breaks into the midst of history in new and transformative ways. This new vision of their inclusion in the divine life through "I-and-I consciousness" does not soften their assessment of the evils of Babylon. This does not mean that Rastas begin to make peace with Babylon, but it means change is possible because of divine agency. This is another way of saying that Rastas do not have to wait for Ethiopia to experience the meaning of liberation but as they work for the changing and building of institutions of justice and peace making in Babylon, they begin to change the face of Babylon.

This, I believe, is one of the effects of music as a tool for social change. Through music, Rastas begin to move beyond the "I-and-I consciousness," which at its best is still steeped in individualism. This undoubtedly is one of the characteristics of Babylon that is so insidious and subtle that the Rastas do not recognize its potential for setting brother against brother and sister against sister. The weakness of their emphasis on intersubjectivity is their attempt to experience God and each other individually. There is not yet in Rastafari the richness of the African concept of community.

Here we can reflect on East African theologian John Mbiti's claim that the cardinal doctrine of African anthropology is "I am because we are and it is because we are that I am." At its best, the Rastas seem to say, "Because Jah is I am." It is a belief still focused on the individual, and perhaps this is one reason why Rastas have not been able to take on institutions and posit a plan for social and economic change in Babylon. Garvey's theme of Africans uniting did not take hold of the Rastas. They latched onto black pride and black dignity but have not gone far enough. I believe that the way forward is for Rastas to take a fresh look at Garvey's plan for social change; perhaps it will help them move from the individual to the collective. The individual may begin to find self not only in the life of the black man from Ethiopia but in the light of the black community. However, one of the positive attributes of the Rastas' focus on the individual is that it forces us to deal with the body.

The Body in Rasta Theology

I cannot emphasize too much the signal contribution Rastas have made to Jamaican cosmology in their emphasis on the body. The Rastas have forced us to openly consider issues of shame and guilt that we were prone to disguise and through conscience relegate to the realm of unimportance. One of the issues that Rastas force us to talk about concerns the reality that the body for several hundred years was literally owned by the master. The master had the right to flog, sell, and brutalize at will the body of Afro-Jamaicans because Afro-Jamaicans were considered chattel that the slave owner could dispose of as he saw fit. In much of our literature, we do not address this aspect of the body—the sense that the black man and the black woman have never really owned their bodies. We get a sense today of what this must have been like when we examine the present penal system, in which prisoners are not free in relation to their own bodies. In many prison systems, inmates surrender their bodies to the system. They are told when to eat, when to retire, when to work, when to play, and they are punished as the jailer sees fit.

The situation was even worse for women as many were considered the plaything of the master, who would rape and abuse them according to his whim. In the United States, it was even more gruesome as lynchings were very common in the South. What is ironic is that many missionaries who condoned slavery or felt impotent to affect the system of slavery for good taught a separation of body and soul. They preached that the soul belonged to God while the body belonged to the master. The missionaries often did not make a separation between the saving of the soul and the brutalizing of the body. What a profound difference it would make if the church recognized that both body and soul belonged to God.

An interesting observation notes that enslaved Jamaicans practiced an embodied religion as they realized the body belonged to God. That was one reason why they became impatient with bondage and continually rebelled for freedom. The maroons of Jamaica are examples of slaves who fled to the hills and fought the British in guerrilla warfare until the British signed a treaty acknowledging their right to freedom. I do not need to recount the stories of Sam Sharp or Paul Bogle, leaders of rebellions in Jamaica who demanded freedom not only for their souls but also for their bodies. Another point to remember in Jamaican spirituality is that the body has always been passionately involved in religion. In a plethora of Jamaican practices, Jamaicans would dance, clap, stomp their feet, and in some cases fall into trancelike experiences. Food was also essential and served as an invitation to fellowship. They also rebelled against white supremacy and racism and sexism of many kinds.

While a good percentage of Jamaicans refused to acknowledge the importance of the body in attempts to talk about God and as a way to affirm life, the Rastas have been at the forefront in broaching the critical question of where Jamaicans stand in relation to Africa. There are at least two reasons why many Jamaicans refuse to focus on body ethics or to see the body and its needs as central in attempts to talk about spirituality. One, I believe, is they feel the history of slavery that raises the question places them in a position to re-live the shame. There is a shaming that takes place when we recall and recount this history, which in many ways was a history of shame for both the oppressed and the oppressors. One source of the shaming is that we have to face the uncomfortable fact that Africans sold Africans into slavery. I recall visiting Ghana in July 2000 and hearing a stirring lecture by an eminent female professor of history who pointed out that greed was the cause for slavery. Africans sold Africans, and Europeans traded in human cargo for profit. I recall asking her how the children and great-grand-children of these Africans feel knowing that our parents sold us into slavery. Talk about black bodies and slavery raises the uncomfortable issue of shame.

Another reason we tend not to talk about our bodies and their relationship to slavery is based on an interpretation of the Pauline Epistles. Many churches in Jamaica teach that the body is flesh and as such is prone to fleshly things like lust, fornication, avarice, envy, and corruption and that what is to be strenuously sought after is the fruit of the spirit. The flesh is seen as something to suppress, to control, and to discipline, while the fruits of the spirit are love, peace, joy, and so on. This prevalent interpretation of Paul tends to rein in a high anthropology that elevates body ethics. This is somewhat unfortunate because in a poor country where issues of health care, child nutrition, and care for the elderly are crucial, attention to the importance of body ethics could prove liberating.

The truth is that one reason Rastas press for repatriation is because they dare to remember. The retrieval of the past is the guide to the present and the future. Rastas would sing that Afro-Jamaicans are nothing if they forget their past. There are negative and positive uses of the past, but Rastas dwell on the positive. John Mbiti illustrates this in *African Religions and Philosophy* as he highlights two Swahili words that refer to the force of the present and the past in East African understanding of time. According to Mbiti, *Sasa* points to the present that is always returning to the *Zamani* period in which the ancestors live, those who have died and gone on before. When one dies in African cosmology, one does not go to an unknown future but rather one returns to the Zamani period to join the ancestors. It seems to me that there is some relevance here for Rasta cosmology. In that repatriation is a return to Ethiopia, a return to blackness where one may be at peace with Haile Selassie.

Rastas are life-affirming and do not want to talk about spirituality apart from bodily existence. They are not eager to talk about joining the ancestors in the afterlife. Indeed, one of the critiques they have of Christianity is that Christians make too much of life after death and not enough of life before death. Rastas do not seem to show too much interest in the ancestors who are dead or living dead. They prefer to affirm life and freedom in the here and now.

It is equally important to note that Rastas see the self as being in organic unity with the natural world. They take Genesis 2:15 seriously: "And the Lord God took man and put him in the Garden of Eden to dress it and keep it." They take seriously the invitation to care for Mother Earth and the sense that the earth belongs to Jah. Rastas are concerned that in Babylon the cosmic order is alienated from people because of abuse and oppression. Humankind is part of the natural history of creation and the created order. Rastas do not use chemicals or pesticides or any substance that is not natural. The natural environment has its own claim on humanity and is to be respected in its own right. Rastas do not see the environment as a means to an end but as an end in itself. Babylon's vision of the created order or the natural world is narrow and limited as in Babylon the order of the day is exploitation. For Rastas, the dignity of humanity is tied up with preserving and maintaining the dignity of the natural order. We cannot preserve the dignity of humanity when we destroy the unity of body and the natural order. Rastas are able to see the beauty and organic unity of the natural order because their eyes have been profoundly opened through their new consciousness made possible through "I-and-I consciousness." They can see the dignity and the unity of the created order.

As noted earlier, the Bible, especially the Old Testament and apocalyptic books like Revelation, is the primary source for Rastas' view of life and their understanding of cosmology. They view much of the alienation between humanity and earth as humanity's rejection of naturalness. Father Joseph Owens captures the centrality of the organic unity between the earth and people:

> In professing to be people devoted to nature and the good earth, the Rastafarians reject the western civilization which has divorced itself from the true sources of life for too long and has worshipped instead all types of artificiality. Nature is a basic concept in the Rastafarian creed, one that helped to explain other key doctrines, such as repatriation, the use of ganja, and the growing of locks and beards, the humanity of God, and the "churchly" nature of the human body, to name a few. Africa, for instance, is for the brethren the place where nature is still relatively unspoiled, where the white man has not brought his artificial foods and medicines and machines. The Rasta man here in the West is striving to return to the natural state of affairs represented symbolically and actually by Africa. . . . The Rastafarian is a man who deals with the ways of nature, not the foolish ways of the white man, which are exhausted with war-making and profit-making: "Waging war and running business is wickedness.

Our heart comes on to the things that come naturally. That's why I say we are all naturalists, for the thing that comes naturally is where we the greatest." The Black nation is closest to nature of all people on earth and has no desire to be separated from it. The common people are especially intimate with nature since they are free from middle-class existence which tends to alienate people from nature.[17]

Rastas are bearers of a new hope in history. In the midst of a culture that fosters dissolution between people and their natural environment, they dare to dream of an organic unity. Rastas want to end the division between people and their natural world. They dream not only of communion with Jah through "I-and-I consciousness" but also of communion with nature. Rastas participate in nature as they tend the garden and refuse to despoil Mother Earth. Rastas seize the power of definition as they refuse to allow Babylon to define them. Their cry exudes from the earth. It is a cry of justice for the poor. It is a cry of justice for the earth. The dream is of a just society in which there is a reverence for the earth. It is a dream with others. Rasta would often set up their communes in the hills away from the exploitative practices of the city. And as is to be expected, many of these communes in the hills, in which the dwellings blend in with nature, were cooperative ventures. Mother Earth provided for all the needs of the Rastas. Here goods were shared and work was done in common. Communalism and collective work ruled the day.

Social and Economic Justice

Even Rastas will have to admit they live in society and cannot extricate themselves from it however much they try. The preoccupation with a foreign God even if this God is black provides a theological basis for repatriation. One of the unintended consequences of Rastas' focus on repatriation is that they do not give enough attention to their social environment. Rex Nettleford states the problem:

In focusing attention on the need for Jamaican blacks to assume economic as well as political control of their country, the phenomenon of Black power can lay some of the strongest claims to relevance. Jamaicans did seek the political Kingdom first but all things have not followed in the interest of the blacks and so many are now stronger in the view that *economic independence is a necessary pre-condition of any real political independence.*... There is a universal outrage

Using Garvey to Go beyond Garvey

at the control of our destiny by foreign exploiters and this is to be found among a wide cross-section of Jamaicans. . . . Over one hundred commercial businesses are controlled says the information sheet by "four white families." In most cases they are outright owners.[18]

Nettleford reminds us that the three major industries in Jamaica—sugar, tourism, and bauxite—are all owned by foreigners. It is extremely difficult for Jamaicans to effect reform in these industries when they are not owners but rather must come, in Garvey's expression, "with hat in hand begging for jobs." One of the sad realities in Jamaica is that foreigners own and control too much property and too many industries.

Another reason for the seeming lack of interest in owning and controlling our own industries is that we associate these industries with our oppression. Rastas, for example, feel that these industries are the engines of capitalism and exploitation and so withdraw in ascetic style to their communes. "Sugar remains a special problem to Jamaica. After all it did bring slavery and indentureship, the plantation system and colonial dependence. It now brings little return in terms of living wage for the vast majority of workers."[19] Sugar continues to be a symbol of servitude in Jamaica. A part of the problem is the inability to find a comparable substitute in a setting in which many of the jobs for working-class Jamaicans, especially in the rural parishes, are still drawn from the sugar plantation.

Similarly, in the tourist industry most of the hotels are owned by foreigners, and the cycle of dependency continues. This means that the fortunes of Jamaica are tied to how other countries perceive us and that the money made in Jamaica is often sent abroad to build other economies. The dilemma in Jamaica is that the local dollar is not accepted abroad to purchase medicine, raw materials, and resources important to our well-being. The accepted currency is the U.S. dollar, which is earned by entertaining tourists who have no interest in our indigenous symbols or in the development of indigenous resources. It is a sad fact that the primary beneficiaries of the tourist industry are not the local people but the mega-corporations that often exploit the people and their resources. The locals resort to selling their culture and pandering to the whims and fancies of the tourist. This approach to our resources does not spell liberation but self-depreciation and alienation. We must believe that emancipation and liberation do not have to come from outside. The answer is not outside of us. It is we who "must emancipate ourselves from mental slavery."

The same is even more true of the bauxite industry. "The distrust of North America comes out strongest, however, in attitudes to the bauxite-alumina industry. . . . For many Jamaicans see this as the 'colonial industry' *par excellence*, controlled as it is from multi-national bases situated outside of the country. They know that decision-making does not rest with Jamaicans and seldom with white functionaries who reside in the island. The subtle discriminatory practices against native Jamaicans in the matter of appointments and job responsibilities are abhorred."[20] It is clear that the Jamaicans discussed are not working-class Jamaicans but rather privileged, middle-class Jamaicans. Even those Jamaicans are often excluded as the jobs that go with responsibilities of leadership are reserved for foreigners from the United States and Europe. It seems to me that in this climate the attitude of withdrawal and disinterest does not advance liberation in Jamaican society.

The problem so far with the Rasta response to social and economic inequities is the perpetual cycle of dependency. The Rastas, informed by many years of colonial history and a sense of the omnipotence of mega-corporations, write off Jamaica as Babylon, a country in collusion with the international capitalist system. "That system consists of central (metropolitan) economies, like the United States of America, which extract surpluses from the peripheral (Third World) economies such like Jamaica. Surplus extraction derives from ownership of Third World resources, from the 'unequal exchange' in trade, from interest charged on loans, from management services provided, and from royalties and fees charged for technology. Together, these constitute a substantial drain on the productive potential of Third World countries."[21]

In their study of the Jamaican economy since political independence in 1962, Beckford and Witter reason that multinational corporations in collusion with the International Monetary Fund and the World Bank provide the institutional mechanisms that effect transfers of surplus. In fact, some of the surplus reinvested in the local economy increases the economic power of foreign capital and enhances the political power of the dependent country. "Thus capitalism on a world scale simultaneously generates economic growth (development) of central metropolitan economies and economic retardation (underdevelopment) of the peripheral economies. The two results are linked. They stem from the nature of capitalism as a world system."[22] Beckford and Witter's attempt to link development and underdevelopment in a capitalist system is similar to the unholy union of master and slave. They feed off each other and the only way to dissolve this unholy union is to provide an alternative approach that means the decimation of this relationship. The dilemma that we face in Jamaica—and that the Rastas are aware of and in response to which they throw their hands up in the air in a gesture of despair—is that in a small country like Jamaica with 2.5 million people, the problems seem intractable. The model of development that the country embraces is one with a built-in negative that places Jamaica on the course to underdevelopment. A part of the problem is that the model adopted is not indigenous to Jamaica and is not geared toward the needs of local people. Beckford and Witter put the problem in perspective:

> The Jamaican economy depends on the central economies of the United States of America, Western Europe (chiefly the United Kingdom), Canada and Japan for trade, finance, technology and management. Most of Jamaica's wealth is owned by capitalists in the United States of America and the United Kingdom. As a result, the Jamaican economy is disjointed. The national economy is weak and underdeveloped because land and capital are concentrated in the export economy which is, moreover, predominantly under foreign control. Labor is concentrated in the national economy where land and capital are in limited supply. In these circumstances, under-employment is endemic. And foreign capital benefits from massive surpluses as a result of the fact that the reserve army of labor allows capitalists to keep wages relatively low.[23]

The problems, as Beckford and Witter see them in Jamaican society, are that the contradictions are institutionalized in the structure of the economy. "On close examination, we find that the Jamaican economy consists of a functionally disconnected national economy which has grown up as an appendage of, and in the interests of, a foreign-oriented and dominated export economy. And the common theme that runs through the two aspects of the Jamaican economy is the exploitation of labor by property."[24]

One of the problems to which Beckford and Witter allude is that in a context such as the Jamaican economy, which is geared toward outsiders or exports, the indigenous population ends up with a rather low view of themselves. In Jamaica we depended on surplus to survive whether we are talking about bananas or sugar. We were always trying to meet export quotas and in many instances when we did not, there were no surpluses, and we were often deprived of basic necessities. Our quality of life never went beyond survival. The masses of Jamaicans were not able to dream of thriving—that is, to move toward self-determination and a life with dignity in social and economic terms. Another aspect of the dilemma was that we were always producing for the consumption of white people in North America and Europe. And there was no fair exchange. We watched the prices of their goods increase while the prices of our exports decreased. "Given the high rate of inflation and the low rate of interest, the real savings of peasants and workers over time are negative; so that the net effect is a subsidy to the profits of the capitalist class. In general, our resources are not fully utilized for the benefit of the people. Instead, they are largely exploited by foreign capitalists and the small client class of Jamaican capitalists."[25]

The central contradiction that exacerbates and gives credence to the other problems relates to production ownership and the role of the working class to provide cheap labor for merchants and landowners. An indication of the magnitude of the problem is that our exports are tied to advanced capitalist countries in North America and Europe. "They are tied through the use of imported employment, technology, raw materials, foreign finance and foreign markets. This is the case, to one degree or another, for bauxite and alumina, sugar, tourism and manufacturing. And the majority share of the financial system—commercial banks, insurance companies, etc.,—is foreign-owned. It operates to facilitate a certain skewed pattern of production. It means that our people and our resources are exploited through high prices for what we buy and low prices for what we sell."[26] The other side of the dilemma is that not only are the producers in the local economy devalued since they do not receive fair compensation and prices for goods produced while they seem to pay an inordinate price for goods imported, but there is also an even more basic problem—the local industries like bauxite and tourism are disconnected from the national economy. In Jamaica, we ship the raw material for the production of bauxite to the United States for production so the local people do not benefit from the production of alumina. Think of the availability of jobs if the local population was trained to produce bauxite.

In a profound sense the same is true of the hotel industry. The masses of Jamaicans are poor people who do not have access to the tourist hotels. Most of these hotels have guards trained to keep poor people out. Too much of the produce that these hotels use is imported from the United States so that little local labor is used. Hotels should be required to use local produce, whether we are talking about chicken, vegetables, or local supplies.

However, we must also acknowledge signs of hope, as not all of the national economy depends on overseas markets:

There are numerous small businesses, a few large manufacturers and hundreds of thousands of small peasants who utilize local raw materials in the production of goods for local consumption. Add to that the myriad of petty trading and hustling activities (legal and illegal) without which the masses of our unemployed could not survive. The growth of production in the national economy has been stifled largely through land ownership of our resources by the foreign capitalists. Land and finance are not available to the small peasant farmer who, therefore, cannot produce sufficient food to feed the nation. And why? Because land and finance are monopolized by the agrarian capitalists, the foreign monopolies, such as bauxite companies and the banks. Furthermore, the tools and fertilizers needed by the farmer, if he could get the land and finance, are imported at high prices.[27]

Small businesses have been the hope of Jamaica. Through them, we have been able to build many institutions and educate families. The Rastas fit nicely in this category because their artistic work and farming have modeled self-sufficiency and resourcefulness. That aside, the small businessperson is hampered as access to capital is limited and is forced to purchase supplies at exorbitant prices. Because of this, the profit margins are minimal. I could not imagine Jamaica making it through some of its difficult periods such as the early 1970s without the role and contributions of the market women (the "higglers," as we call them). "The creativity of our people, born out of struggle for survival, has allowed them to exist on the margins of the productive economy, by selling their services, engaging in petty trading of consumer goods, and hustling of all sorts. These activities sometimes cut across the frontiers of legality; but, even so, they must be squarely faced as genuine economic activities."[28]

An important aspect of what I have been saying is that independent Jamaica has not delivered on its promise to provide a society in which economic power is shifted to the masses. In a sense, we have seen the shift in political power as the masses of black people are able to exercise their right to vote and to assume political office at all levels. But this is not to be overstated. In many instances, the state forms alliances with foreign capital and works against the best interest of the peasants and working classes. "The present Jamaican state is decisively in the service of the propertied rather than the property-less class. There has been a strategy of subsidizing and protecting big capital-foreign and local. . . . Since the thrust of government policy has hardly been toward small business and small farmers, workers and unemployed, those aspects dealing with the national economy are highly underdeveloped. Legislation protecting the small businessman and the small farmer from exploitative prices, unfair trading practices, onerous loan terms, and competition with big capital is yet to be written."[29]

One response of Jamaica was the growth of Rastafari. It was anchored in the notion that a spiritual response was needed to social and economic problems. At the end of the 1960s and early 1970s, there were many young people who identified with the Rastafari community as the blackness of the God of Ethiopia called into question the white values perpetuated by the Christian church and society. While there were many in the church who highlighted the death of Jesus, Rastas saw themselves as life-affirming and focused on an ideology of presence in that they articulated a theology of presence and life rather than death. "Jah in his blackness negated the whiteness of Jesus; in his living he negated the death of Jesus by Crucifixion. He was the symbol of resistance to the white Christian church, in which the power to oppress black people, was thought to reside. In the bondage and oppression of the Hebrews in Egypt, they saw their own bondage and oppression in this latter day Babylon. And just as the Bible spoke of the return of Israel from exile to their homeland, so too the Rastafari saw repatriation to Ethiopia/Africa as the escape from Babylon."[30]

Rastas viewed Christianity as the teachings of the white oppressors and reinterpreted it in a way that made it appealing to the unemployed as well as alienated youth. For Rastas, Haile Selassie was the second coming of the Messiah. The Rastas replaced a European Messiah with an African Messiah. Haile Selassie became the symbol of black resistance in a culture that marginalized blackness. As Rastas analyze the sociopolitical and cultural realities that impinge on their lives, they confront them with a holy reverence for the dignity of life and the importance of intersubjective relationships.

In Rastafari, a sense of subjectivity, selfhood and community defies the kind of objectification and depersonalization that occurs in the context of domination and oppression. The language of self-expression and self-reference, used in terms of relationship, bears this out effectively. The expression "I and I" is very significant in this regard; it links a vibrant hope to a clearly perceived destiny of freedom, justice, righteousness and peace. The thrust of the Rastafarian messianic ideology puts it in tension with the present "Babylon" order,

which is undesirable and unacceptable since it represents and subsists on the denial of the human rights and freedom of Africans. . . .
Babylon constitutes oppression and exploitation of the black race in
general and is therefore an evil system. Rastas have a very strong
expectation of a new order of existence in a radically new setting. In
this new environment, current wrongs and wickedness perpetuated
against Rastafarians will be corrected.[31]

One of the contributions that Rastas have made to anticolonial resistance in the Caribbean in general and Jamaica in particular is their penchant to exegete not only their texts, biblical and otherwise, but also the
context in which they find themselves. Rastas also read the sociological
text and press for human dignity and the liberation of African culture from
captivity. They bring a "hermeneutic of suspicion" not only to the reading
of written texts but to the sociological text. For example, when one listens
to Rastas' discussion of the evils of Babylon and their unwillingness to
coexist with this evil, one readily accepts repatriation to Ethiopia as the
answer to the inequities and injustices in Babylon. But as one listens to
reggae songs such as "I Shot the Sheriff" or "Crazy Baldheads," one discovers that liberation is included in repatriation as oppressive social systems must be chanted down. Babylon, like Jericho, must fall, and the
Rasta man or woman will not rest until this happens. For example, in the
Burnin' album, the Rasta man chants: "I hear the words of the Rasta man /
Babylon you throne gone down, gone down / Babylon you throne gone
down." It is clear that for the Rasta man Babylon will not stand.

There is also a sense of moral outrage as Rastas refuse to coexist with
oppression and remain silent. You can depend on Rastas, like the prophets
of the Old Testament, to dramatize their displeasure in the face of evil.
One way to understand Rasta existence is that their presence is a form of
resistance to the attempts of colonialism and neocolonialism to subjugate
black people.

Toward an Ethical Frame

As admirable as is their penchant for questioning the social context, Rastafari do not have a social theory or an ethic that helps them raise the fundamental questions that affect their quality of life. It must be noted that the
Bible as such does not provide a blueprint for moral action. Hence, an
analysis of life in Babylon is crucial to the vision that Rastas seek to put
forward. I suggest the approach James McClendon takes in his book *Eth-*

ics, where he agrees with Rastafari that talk about human beings, their world, and God must begin with talk about the body. The reality is that we cannot wish our bodies away. We are confronted with the inescapability of its needs at physical, emotional, and spiritual levels. One advantage of beginning with the body is that it brings to the fore issues of poverty and racism that are central for Rastafari. Talk about the body also forces us to talk about sexism and homophobia, which Rastas are not eager to discuss. McClendon further notes that the body raises questions concerning the organic relationship of human beings with Mother Earth. Questions concerning the meaning of creation, why we are on planet earth, and who owns the land emerge for theological attention.

McClendon insists that the body is only the first strand. Talk of the body begs for talk about its social environment. We noted earlier how George Beckford and Michael Witter painted a picture of the social context in modern Jamaica. They illustrate that megacorporations along with the International Monetary Fund and the World Bank had too much to say about the quality of life for average Jamaicans. Although in that setting there were hundreds if not thousands of small businesses chipping away at the oppressive system, they did not turn back the tide of neocolonial oppression. McClendon suggests that there are two concepts that may be helpful as we seek handles to help analyze institutions and social life in societies.

He suggests the concepts of games and practices and directs us to Bernard Suits and his book *The Grasshopper: Games, Life, and Utopia.* Suits defines a game as an activity directed toward bringing about a specific state of affairs, using only means permitted by rules. The chief elements in a game, according to Suits, are the end or the goal of the game, the means allowed, the rules, and the attitude of the players. To play a game fairly requires that all four elements are taken seriously. McClendon explains:

> That a game must have a goal logically prior to the goal of winning
> seems evident; how else would we know what constituted winning a
> race, for example, unless crossing some finish line were designated
> as the goal of the racers? Next, that strictly limited means are to be
> employed seems to be accepted by every game player—else I might
> win the race by cutting across the track's infield, or might reduce my
> golf score by carrying the ball right up to the green rather than hitting
> it there stroke by stroke. From these two, the third necessity, that of
> rules, becomes evident. The rules are not arbitrary additions we
> might very well discard in actual play: It is exactly the rules that con-

stitute tennis as tennis, or bridge as bridge, and without them we would have no notion of which game we were playing.... This brings us to the fourth essential element, the attitude required of players— namely intending to play the game. Without this, an Olympic class runner who just happens to jog along the course of a neighborhood footrace might be supposed to have won the race—but this will not do if the Olympic speedster wasn't even in the race.[32]

We are warned to be cognizant of triflers, spoilsports, and cheats. "Consider Aunt Lucy, who doesn't really want to play checkers, but who to oblige bored nephew Billy sits down at the board and takes a turn moving the pieces on the squares. She is not playing, though, she is *trifling* with the red and black discs, and her failure to play is an exemplary though unattractive lack of the lusory attitude."[33] While the trifler does not really want to play, the spoilsport ignores rules, and the cheat pretends to play by rules. "Triflers recognize rules but not goals, cheats recognize goals but not rules, players recognize both rules and goals and spoilsports recognize neither."[34]

McClendon underscores the importance of rules as they make the game possible in the first place. We cannot play a game without rules. The other important key is that players are those who intend to play the game. Because players intend to play and play by rules, it means that games are always ends and never means. The bottom line is that to become a player one must play the game itself with its goals, means, and rules. "Also, the distinction between 'just playing' and 'playing to win' is a phony one; *playing* is playing to win; there can be no intelligible contrast between those who play 'for the game's sake' and those who merely want victory.... those who do not play to *win* are not players; they are triflers; while those who do not *play* to win are cheats."[35]

The other aspect of games that McClendon underscores as important in asking questions relative to societal context is what he terms the "social context" of the game. Here McClendon intimates that he is not interested in solitary games that do not involve a partner. He feels an important ingredient of a game is being with others: "Most games require partners, opponents, or both. ... In this regard ... his end-means-rules-attitudes definition embraces cooperative as well as contested games. Thus the point of one kind of table tennis may be to keep the celluloid ball in action on the table, rather than forcing the other player to miss a stroke. Still better examples are found in the childhood games of 'playing house' and 'playing cops and robbers,' where cooperative imaginal activity is required of each player exactly in order to keep the game going."[36]

I am grateful that McClendon tempered his competitive approach with a more cooperative one. It seems toward the end that he suggests there are times when one does not have to play to win or one does not have to be competitive. It appears as if he tacks this on at the end because his central concern is that one must intend to play, play by the rules, and play to win. While it is important to know the rules, are there occasions when one knowingly breaks the rules? What if the rules are oppressive and are intended to keep one in one's place?

During slavery and the apprenticeship period in Jamaica, what saved the day was that many Jamaicans who did not make the rules gladly broke them and in many cases paid the ultimate price. The story of Rastafari is one in which a people edged out on the margins of society seized the power of self-definition as they created new rules in language and in religion. I believe McClendon missed the ball in failing to underscore the importance of being a spoilsport at crucial moments in this game called life. The Rastafari in Jamaica have illustrated to us in a fashion reminiscent of the civil rights movement in the United States that it is immoral to play by oppressive rules even if one is invited to play with others. Who, we may ask, decides what the appropriate goals are? When do the means justify the goals? Asking such questions about the main players, the means, rules, and goals may be helpful in evaluating whether the game as played is working toward liberation and in establishing a basis for either playing by or breaking the rules. I recall a song in Jamaica that I believe was sung by the Rasta brethren that went something like this: "To be a winner you do not have to be number one. Just stay in the race." The focus was on cooperation rather than competition. What was central here was an ethic of care. There has been a long tradition of an ethic of care in Jamaican culture. The agrarian nature of the society allowed for cooperation in performing tasks such as groups working together in farming and in construction tasks. I recall seeing, as a child growing up in Jamaica, groups of ten to fifteen men who went from field to field to plant ground produce, till the soil, or reap sugarcane. They would be accompanied by women— many being wives of the workers—who would provide meals. A special feature of these cooperative approaches to farming was the songs they sung. Often someone began, and then the chorus joined in. This was done at construction sites as well. If someone's home needed a roof or some form of repair, the group would take responsibility.

The same applied to saving money. It was a form of cooperative economics in which each member of a group—about twenty persons—would contribute a couple dollars per week, and this was given to a member of the group who was unanimously selected to serve as treasurer. Each person received his/her savings once per year, and this went to some special project such as sending a child to college or providing for a child's wedding. The Rastas tap into this tradition of cooperative economics with their communes in the hills where they live communally, developing an ethic of care, an ethic in which the community shares all things. Their view of land seems to support this penchant for communalism. Claiming that the land belongs to God, they argue that all people have a right to the produce of the land. If Jah owns the land, it means that the neighbor has rights in relation to the land. I will never forget my surprise when I pastored a church in Jamaica. One morning I noted a Rasta man climbing one of my fruit trees without receiving permission. I inquired of him: "What are you doing in my tree? Who told you to climb that tree?" The Rasta man replied: "It's not your tree. The tree belongs to Jah." According to the Rasta, if the land belongs to God, the Rasta has a right to the fruit of the land.

The point of emphasis is that cooperative economics, sharing of resources, and communalism have long been a part of the Jamaican tradition. Certainly one of the weaknesses of McClendon's emphasis on playing the game to win is that someone has to lose. For too long it has been the Rastas and other poor people who have lost. According to the Rastas, they are unwilling to play according to the rules of Babylon and so they begin to create new rules in language, theology, and economics. For example, Rastas began to point out that Babylon plays word games with language and the poor dare not trust their use of language. The following provides one illustration of Rastas' use of language:

> Dem time we neber use the term baldhead, or how man woulda she now, baldtail. Dem is man I-n I call *raas* plucky. For even within de Youth Black Faith is Comb and Locks mix up together before we step to de House of Boanerges. De culture was still developing up and dreadlocks was not compultry at dat time as a Rasta. And in those time not so much man use *chalice*. Is *cutchie* use in dem time. We don'e call it *chalice*, we call it "hot rod." A pure *cutchie* I-n I use dem time. Coming up the lineridge we step to *chalice*.[37]

Certainly, one way in which Rastas differentiate themselves from Babylon is in making decisions about how language is used. Their experimentation with language facilitates the development of a vocabulary that takes their social context seriously. For example, Rastas insist that to use the word "oppress" is to miss the mark as there is nothing "up" about oppression. Therefore Rastafari speak instead of "downpression." The same rule applies for understanding, which Rastas speak of as "overstanding."

Practices

Earlier we looked at games as a theoretical construct to help analyze social reality. We observed the vulnerability of James McClendon's analysis of the lifestyle and customs of Rastafari. I now turn to *Practices* as a means to unravel the purview of social reality. At the very onset we are told by McClendon that there are striking similarities between games and practices. First, they are both end-means activities. In games there is an intentional end such as cooperation, playing to win, or playing for fun. Practices also have their own internal goals—such as holding the friendship together, the practice of marriage, or the practice of wellness. Second, it is important to note that just not any way of pursuing these ends will suffice for either games or practices. "Thus the gamessmith must create games whose means are neither too hard nor too easy and obvious, while similarly, real-life practices must develop means of reaching their goals that are sufficiently stable and sufficiently flexible to permit the growth of the practice and the human life it invests."[38] The point is, as difficult as the practice of medicine or religion may be, it should be teachable to the initiate and yet able to change over the years with changing needs and new knowledge. Third, both games and practices should have the means to convert them into rules that make sense. Rules should be appropriate to that activity, even if the rules are unwritten and not formulated. And finally, goals should be clear and achievable. Participants should intend to achieve their goals by the rules prescribed. "Thus, just as it is possible to pick out as non-players those who wander into the ball park and engage in some vaguely athletic activity or other, so must it be possible to distinguish quack doctors, and bogus architects and invalid marriages from the real thing. Possible even if not always easy."[39] But what if one could achieve the goals of marriage, medicine, or cricket without the rules of practice?

What if we could all have health without doctors, merely by wishing it. . . . Or what about family love without anyone taking the costly path of marriage? In the game case, we would say the "runner" had not really won because he [or she] had not run the *race*. What of these other practices? Surely, no one would object on moral grounds to health by fiat, or for that matter to the providential abolition of disease? Yet, on the other hand, an entirely effortless world would seem to omit something that is valuable in itself even apart from the usual goals of practices just mentioned—namely the value of the practices themselves. Unlike games, the "obstacles" in a (nongame) practice may be set by circumstances alone. Life, we say, is worth living, and part of what we mean is that the struggles entailed by such a world as this are worthwhile independent of the ultimate rest that will come when all is over. Yet the kind of struggle we have in mind here may be, not difficulty for difficulty's sake, but exercises that are part and parcel of practices such as those just described.[40]

The key here is that practices occur in the real world, not in one imagined by us. In the real world, we set goals, make rules, and engage in practices in spite of the obstacles. Frederick Douglass said, "we should not expect crops without tilling the soil." We cannot expect to achieve our goals without participating, without practicing. The story of black people in the Diaspora is the story of confronting and overcoming obstacles. Caribbean theologian Kortright Davis speaks of a black story that is common to African-American and Caribbean peoples.

According to Davis, story becomes a way of chronicling achievements of ancestry. It is the means whereby succeeding generations can be sure to emulate their parents and at the same time cultivate the will to succeed. The black story is anchored in Africa and is the "attempt by Caribbean and African American people to transform the meaning of slavery and oppression, poverty and dependence, failure and weakness, into powerful signs of promise, achievement, fulfillment, and historical emancipation. . . . Who would dare deny the historical facts of racism today? Racism was conceived in Europe, incubated in the Caribbean, baptized in America, ordained in North Atlantic trade, and canonized in Southern Africa. So the Caribbean and Americas are a major spiritual center of the Black Story."[41]

One of the practices against which practices of the poor must be directed is racism. It is a practice that is imbedded in Caribbean society and supported by the powerful practices of the rich neighbor to the north—the United States. It is manifested in the cultural alienation of Caribbean peoples in relation to things Caribbean as we often prefer and believe the foreign is better. I recall singing "Lord wash me until I am whiter than snow" as a child. Whiteness symbolized the negation of everything Caribbean and black. It meant a preference for things foreign.

This fascination with foreign things made Caribbean Christians look to Europe and North America for images of God. The image of the white God became the fountainhead of our understanding of self, world, and religion. The Rastas saw this dilemma clearly. If the cycle of dependence is to be broken, then the white God in the Caribbean had to be abolished. As long as Caribbean people accepted a white God as the ontological basis of their reality, the rejection of self and the internalization of oppression were unavoidable. Following in the tradition of Marcus Garvey and Alexander Bedward, who taught that God should be seen through the lens of Africa, the Rastas look to the black king from Ethiopia and claim him as their God. If Davis is correct in assessing that the black story has its roots in Africa and finds incarnations in North America and the Caribbean, then it becomes logical that the liberation and emancipation of that story also needs to be rooted in Africa. This, undoubtedly, is the strength of the Rasta position in claiming their God as an African. They resolve the ontological problem of God's whiteness and begin to answer the question of where Caribbean people stand in relation to Africa.

The Rastas' claim posits a reversal of values in the Jamaican context in which everything good and beautiful is related to Europe and whiteness, and everything problematic and undesirable is related to blackness and Africa. In the Caribbean, we are accustomed to associating problems of ignorance, poverty, and diseases such as HIV/AIDS with Africa. And our estimate of blackness is not much different—hence Caribbean people often speak of themselves as "colored" for fear of being associated with blackness, which is a synonym for backwardness. So for the Rastas to find God in what is despised and rejected (Africa and blackness) is for them to begin to turn the world upside down. For so long we were taught to rid ourselves of blackness and to pray for the salvation of the heathen in backward Africa. Then we learned from the Rastas that God is black and African.

Have the Rastas broken the rules of the game? Have they invented new rules? How do we address their practice? The Rastas seem to help us understand that we cannot free ourselves with practices that are anchored in the narrative of others. As we begin to take our own story seriously, we begin to value self and discover that we are made in the divine image of blackness.

In *Black Theology and Black Power*, liberation theologian James Cone suggests that the critical and important question that confronts black people in an absurd world is, "How should I respond to a world which defines me as a non-person?" Absurdity, according to Cone, is black people being awakened to the reality of their beautiful black selves being made in the image of God, yet discovering the contradiction between who they are essentially and how the dominant society defines them. Absurdity is understanding what is versus what ought to be. The way forward is for the practice of black power to confront this existential absurdity. Therefore, the question to ponder is what then is black power?

> Black power, in short, is an *attitude*, an inward affirmation of the essential worth of blackness. It means that the black man will not be poisoned by the stereotypes that others have of him, but will affirm from the depths of his soul: "get used to me, I am not getting used to anyone." And "if the white man challenges my humanity, I will impose my whole weight as a man on his life and show him that I am not that 'sho good eatin' that he persists in imagining. This is Black power, the power of the black person to say Yes to his own 'black being,' and to make the other accept him or be prepared for a struggle."[42]

The challenge, according to Cone, is that whenever the black person tries to relate as a person he/she is confronted with the demand to respond as a thing. In such a world, the enduring question is, how should I respond? Should I respond as I know myself or as the world defines me? The choice is clear. Either the black person accepts the estimate of self assigned by the dominant culture or he/she rebels. "From this standpoint the response of Black Power is like Camus's view of the rebel. One who embraces Black Power does not despair and take suicide as an out, nor does he appeal to another world in order to relieve the pains of this one. Rather, *he fights back with the whole of his being*. . . . The man of Black Power will not rest until the oppressor recognizes him for what he is—a man. He further knows that this campaign for human dignity, freedom is not a gift but a right worth dying for."[43]

I would like to pursue further a discussion of Cone's understanding of the form and position of black power as a practice in black communities in the United States since, according to Caribbean theologian Kortright Davis, both Caribbean and North American black people originate in the same story. Concerning the relevance of black power models in Jamaica, I would ask whether Rastafari is one form of the practice of black power.

Caribbean theologian Davis believes that the black story provides a chronicling of the common struggle of black people against suffering that has been imposed from without by the oppressor class: "The Black Story is much more than the underside of Western history. It is not so much the retelling of the story from the Black perspective; neither is it merely the attempt to bring into open and full recognition the story of a people whose existence was historically undermined." The black story is "little kids, enveloped and almost crushed by an insidious fantasy that was reinforced daily by the most powerful society on the face of the earth. . . . We had to come to know in some fundamental way that no matter what the power of wealth relationships in this society may be, we were not invented by American white people and we did not stand on this earth at their sufferance. One good way to start was to understand that before the European invasion of Africa five centuries ago, the people from whom we got the contours of our lips and the curl in our hair walked their land in their way and arranged their lives according to their lights."[44] Cone agrees with Davis that the story of black people was cradled in suffering.

> In black religion, story is thought of in two ways. First, there is the story of the people as a whole. This story goes back to the memories of Africa and the experiences of being taken into slavery in North America. It includes the strivings of the people to survive the ordeal of servitude and retain a measure of togetherness in the struggle. But even when slavery was declared illegal, our struggle did not end. . . . The black story moves to the second level, that of *personal* story. Personal story is accounts of individual triumphs in struggle.[45]

Ultimately, if we listen to Cone or Davis, the story of black people is the struggle to refuse to allow white structures to be determinative of black existence. The meaning of black life does not depend on the structures of Babylon. Black power becomes protest against the tricksters of Babylon and their attempt to thwart the lives of black people. In the *Exodus* album, Bob Marley encapsulates a working definition of black power:

> Open your eyes and look within
> Are you satisfied with the life you are living?
> We know where we're going
> We know where we're from.
> We're leaving Babylon

We're going to our father's land
Exodus!
Movement of Jah people[46]

The refusal of black people to accept blackness as the point of departure for talk about humanity, God, and the world is for black people to accept black self-hatred. To reject blackness as the organizing principle of his/her world is to begin to accept the story of others as normative. "Any careful assessment of the place of the Black man in America must conclude that Black self-hatred is the worst aspect of the legacy of slavery. 'The worst crime the white man has committed,' writes Malcolm X, 'has been to teach us to hate ourselves.'" During slavery, black people were treated as animals and were systematically taught that such treatment was due them because of their blackness. "When slavery was abolished, the Negro had been stripped of his culture and left with this heritage: an oppressed black man in a white man's world."[47] These are exactly the sentiments of the Rastas. They are in exile in the white man's land, and it is Jah's will that they be repatriated to their home. And so the Rastas sing "By the rivers of Babylon, where we sat down when we remembered Zion." Rastas assert that their existence in Jamaica is one of exile in Babylon, and that the longing for Zion is the longing to return to Africa.

Black people confronted with systematic oppression in Babylon basically have two possible responses: one is accommodation, and the other is protest. Accommodation has been variously referred to as integration or assimilation. Often when integration is suggested what is meant is assimilation, since those in power have no intention of relinquishing power. "The Negro also had to recognize that one hundred years after emancipation he lived on a lonely island of economic insecurity in the midst of a vast ocean of material prosperity. Negroes are still at the bottom of the economic ladder. They live within two concentric circles of segregation. One imprisons them because of color, while the other confines them within a separate culture of poverty. . . . When he seeks opportunity, he is told, in effect, to lift himself by his own bootstraps, advice which does not take into account the fact that he is barefoot."[48] The problem with integration is that it presupposes equality—it assumes both parties come to the table as equals forgetting that some people are shoeless. It presupposes that those who have power are willing to give up power so that the meeting of minds and hearts at the table is one among equals. Experience has taught that people with power do not willingly share it. Because of the imbalance of power, oppressed groups have accommodated the status quo in order to survive. Needless to say, accommodation has been most damaging to op-pressed people because it means a denial of their identity as human be-ings with a right to human dignity and justice in race relations. "As with the black African who had to become a 'Frenchman' in order to be ac-cepted, so to be an American, the black man must strive to become 'white.' To the extent that he does, he is considered 'well adjusted'—one who has 'risen above the race question.' . . . At the present time, integration as a solution to the race problem demands that the Negro foreswear his iden-tity as a Negro. . . . They [black people] live in a society in which to be unconditionally 'American' is to be white, and to be black is a misfor-tune."[49]

Without the ability to participate in the body politic in a way that makes it possible for black people to engage in justice making in their communi-ties, there is a danger that black people will remain a permanent under-class. "The goal of Black self-determination and black self-identity—Black Power—is full participation in the decision making process affecting the lives of Black people, and recognition of the virtues in themselves as black people."[50]

The practice of black power raises the question of the relationship be-tween black power and love. Cone reminds us that this was an issue in the civil rights movement. Black power emerged because black people be-came disenchanted with Martin Luther King Jr.'s demand to love the en-emy. "'Martin King,' says one black power advocate, 'was trying to get us to love the white folks before we learn to love ourselves, and that ain't no good.' . . . While most Black Power advocates do not prescribe hatred (only a small minority), few, it must be admitted, would suggest love as the black man's appropriate response to white oppression. Most seem to feel like Malcolm X 'It is not possible to love a man whose chief purpose in life is to humiliate you and still be what is considered a normal human being.'"[51] Cone, who writes from a Christian perspective, struggles with how love may be understood from the perspective of Jesus Christ. He observes that while questions are raised about a love directed to some and not others, the central question is how we understand God's love directed toward black people.

I find it intriguing that when one compares the scene of oppression in the United States among black church people with that of the Rastas as it pertains to black power, the Rastas appear to have fewer hang-ups con-cerning identity and love for others. Reading Cone inspires in me the idea that a part of the problem black people in the United States have as they seek to relate love to the practice of black power is the struggle with double consciousness. They have a fundamental struggle with two-ness. Many black people feel they can love themselves only if they love white people. This means that love for the black person in the United States has to come through white people. The presumed frame of reference is always the op-pressor. The Rastas are clear that accommodation to the oppressor is not an option; they see protest as separation. Theoretically, they renounce the practices of Babylon and see no conflict in loving self because they have obliterated a white frame of reference. The Rastas are clear that God has become a black man, and that through "I-and-I consciousness" they par-ticipate in the divine life. The Rastas do not understand their identity as being made accessible through whiteness or as a consequence of Baby-lonian captivity.

Their identity is fashioned in the context of a "hermeneutic of return." This hermeneutic of return is anchored in Africa and sees as its central question, "Where do you stand in relation to Africa?" It is interesting that in Cone's articulation of a philosophy of black power, he does not see the relationship of African-Americans to Africa as a central question, which, mentioned or not, seems to be the relationship of black Americans to whiteness. Here I believe Cone is unduly influenced by W.E.B. Du Bois, who does not present the relationship of black people to Africa as a central question in his *Souls of Black Folk*.

Walter Rodney

Between 1962 and 1972, there was a move to consider black power as an option by the Jamaican middle-class intelligentsia due to their disillusion-ment with the new independent government. Much of the middle-class intelligentsia felt the government had not done enough in regard to issues of poverty and cultural identity.

> This radicalization crystallized into the Jamaican version of the Black Power movement. These radical intellectuals, some of whom faced the brunt of British racism as they trained in the corridors of Oxford and Cambridge, found a ready critique of Jamaican society and a more acceptable view of life in the ideology of Rastafari. One of these intellectuals, Walter Rodney, who was a Black Power activist ... gives this appraisal of Rastafari: "It was to the Rastafarian movement and its predecessors that Africa was our spiritual homeland and our 'so-journ' in Jamaica should be used to develop her traditions and civili-zation as far as was possible in 'Babylon' that is Jamaica. That was the

only way in which Black men could find themselves. In our epoch the Rastafari have represented the leading force of this expression of Black consciousness. They have rejected this philistine white West Indian society. They have sought their cultural and spiritual roots in Ethiopia and Africa."[52]

Rodney's observations signal the discussion of Rastafari ideas pertaining to black power among the Jamaican middle-class intelligentsia. The black middle-class intellectuals had come to agree with Rastafari that if Jamaica were to move forward in a way that valued its cultural identity, then Jamaica had to view Africa as the root of its national identity. It was widely acknowledged that after the release of the University Report a rapprochement ensued between Rastafari and the Jamaican intelligentsia, particularly at the University of the West Indies. "With this acknowledgement of Rastafari's social significance, the progressive elements of the Jamaican intelligentsia soon developed social and intellectual exchanges with Rastas. These exchanges resulted in the forging of alliances between the Rastas and the Black Power Movement. Walter Rodney himself epitomized this exchange and the resulting alliance. The very title of his book, *Groundings with My Brothers,* is a testament to his involvement with the Rastafarian movement."[53]

It is believed that the term "groundings" is an attempt to recall the Rasta activity of "reasoning" often referred to by the Rastas as "groundation." Therefore "groundings," as Rodney understood the term, was an attempt to sit with Rasta brethren in a reasoning session. I had the good fortune of being a student at a local theological seminary in Kingston, Jamaica, at the same time Walter Rodney attended the University of the West Indies as an undergraduate student. After graduate studies at the School of Oriental and African Studies in London, Rodney taught for a year in Africa before returning to Jamaica to teach at his alma mater. It was widely known throughout Kingston in the latter part of the 1960s that Rodney would visit Rasta yards to teach concerning the connections between African history and liberation. He was also at pains to clear up any misconceptions the brethren had concerning Ethiopian history. A historian himself, Rodney taught that there were powerful connections between African history and liberation struggle:

One of the major dilemmas inherent in the attempt by black people to break through the cultural aspects of white imperialism is posed by the use of historical knowledge as a weapon in our struggle. . . . The white man has already implanted numerous historical myths in the minds of black people; and those have to be uprooted, since they can act as a drag on revolutionary activity in the present epoch. Under these circumstances it is necessary to direct our historical activity in the light of two basic principles. Firstly, the effort must be directed solely towards freeing and mobilizing black minds. There must be no performances to impress whites, for those whites who find themselves beside us on the firing line will be there for reasons far more profound than their exposure to African history. Secondly, the acquired knowledge of African history must be seen as directly relevant but secondary to the concrete tactics and strategy which are necessary for our liberation.[54]

Walter Rodney made an explicit connection between Rastafari and the freeing of black minds. Rastas taught that the minds of black people had been colonized and needed to be set free by the awakening of an African consciousness. As Rodney affirms Rasta ideology he affirms African history as a servant for the liberation project of black people. It is interesting that although like Marcus Garvey before him, Rodney sought to emancipate the minds of black people, he did not attempt to launch a mass movement or to convert the masses. He simply went from yard to yard patiently teaching the connection between African history and liberation. It should not surprise us then that his work among Rastas seemed so threatening to the government that in 1968 the government declared him "persona non grata . . . as part of the suppression of Black Power, among people associated with the Rastafarian movement."[55]

But Rodney completed his job. He was able to give confidence to many middle-class young people that it was fine for them to identify with Africa and Rastafari. This opened the door for the emergence of one of the new groups to emerge within Rastafari, the Twelve Tribes of Israel.

> Robert Hill, one of those who sought to establish *Abeng* [a newspaper sympathetic to Rastafari ideas] described Twelve Tribes as middle class drop-outs who converted to Rastafari and formed a tight, closely knit sect under the leadership of a man called Gad. The Twelve Tribes of Israel centralized the worship of Haile Selassie and repatriation as their beliefs, stressing the need to read the Bible. This organization achieved notoriety and membership following the adherence to the Twelve Tribes' beliefs of prominent cultural reggae artists; and the Twelve Tribes was one group which took the promotion of reggae seriously.[56]

Edmonds points out that the publication of *Abeng* was an important signal of the coming together of middle-class intellectuals and Rastas. Those associated with the publication of this newspaper included university professors, students, and several persons who later became prominent politicians. The purpose of this newspaper, which was formed in response to the banishment of Walter Rodney from the island, was to critique the social and political life of Jamaica. *"Abeng* declared solidarity with pop singers who were critical of the society, highlighted the marriage between Rastafarian ideas and reggae music, gave prominence to issues of race, class, Black Nationalism, and the plight of the poor, employed Rastafari lingo liberally, and focused explicitly on issues of particular relevance to Rastas."[57]

The genius of Rastafari during this period was its capacity to bring together the working-class poor, who identified with the "folk ethos" of Rastafari, and now the middle class, who facilitated the accommodation of the wider society to Rastafari beliefs. During the late sixties, I taught at a high school in Montego Bay, Jamaica, and I recall many male students wearing their hair high against school regulations and using the Rastafari term "I and I." The principal would often punish students because of their "Rasta ways."

> Even before the alliance of Rastafari and radical intellectuals, Rastafari was gaining ground in the consciousness of the poor and the young throughout the society. . . . Rastas had found ways to impose their transcendental framework of reality on the surrounding environment. By the late sixties . . . there was much more widespread embrace of Rastafarian attitudes, ideals and even practices. . . . Examples of the diffusion of Rastafari in the wider society include the popularity of "long and carefully unkempt hair," the donning of multicolored clothing believed to be African, defiance of "ganja laws," firm and fervent affirmation of Africa and blackness, condemnation of neo-colonialism, repeated calls for an end to police brutality against the poor, criticisms of the white orientation of the society, and a reevaluation of colonial history.[58]

For the first time since Marcus Garvey, middle-class Jamaica began to take sides with Africa. Through dress, hairstyle, in many cases ganja smoking, and the new acquired forms of speech, they began to question the colonial heritage. An independent Jamaica began to listen to Rastafari and question the efficacy of the colonial model that elevated whiteness and denigrated Africa and things Jamaican. Walter Rodney was an important key in forging the link between Rastafari and the middle class in Jamaica. Rodney was able to do this as a middle-class intellectual himself who had won the respect of both Rastafari and middle-class intellectuals. What I find compelling about Rodney's model of "practices," or praxis, is that he spent much time in the trenches with Rastafari. He visited their yards and communes and was able to relate his teaching of African history to the historical project, but Rodney was not a wild romantic who wanted to convert the black masses to Rastafari. He observed that the way forward was to educate the masses, and this included a special role for the middle class. Rodney puts it this way: "though Jamaican freedom fighters will read some African history in the course of preparing for hostilities; the struggle of the masses will not wait until the mass of black people reaches an advanced stage."[59]

Rodney was clear that teaching African or Ethiopian history would not be enough to prepare the working poor to link history with the liberation project for Jamaica. According to Rodney, Europe had a head start of some three hundred years in which it planted colonial myths in the hearts and minds of black people, and an uprooting of those myths was now required for the freeing and mobilizing of the mind for liberation. What was required was helping the new middle class prepare for the new challenge of critically evaluating the society. This requires cognizance of what is right and what is wrong with the society and willingness to facilitate change. The liberation project that is joined to history does not seek to recite history but chooses decisive moments of that history as lenses through which vistas of the new humanity are seen, a humanity that is at peace with Africa and blackness.

This took many forms in an independent Jamaica. For many middle-class Jamaicans, the practice of black power meant wearing African dress as a way of making a statement that one's racial consciousness was alive and one was aware that he/she belonged to the African race. For many others, it had to do with hairstyles or wearing dashikis. Popular in Jamaica in the 1970s and 1980s was the wearing of large Afro hairstyles, especially among middle-class black women, who felt it important to make a race-conscious statement by displaying their unwillingness to straighten or curl the hair. Many middle-class Jamaicans felt that this was a statement in favor of Africa and related it at the same time to the Rasta teaching about the natural style. One reason Rastas gave for wearing the dreadlocks and not adding salt to their diet was that true Africans were "natural" people.

They allowed their hair to grow naturally and trusted nature to add the essentials to foods. The Jamaican cultural critic and close observer of Rastafari Rex Nettleford wonders out loud whether or not middle-class Jamaicans were in danger of confusing symbols of poverty with cultural symbols.

> The so-called Afro hair style now popular among American black women has also found its place among black power advocates as well as among others who are either in the fashion or have discovered the style's flattering potential. The Rastafarians had gone much further two or three decades before wearing their hair in long and matted braids. They also adopted sandals and knitted woolen caps and sashes of red, green and gold—colors of the flag of Ethiopia. Like some of them, many Black Power advocates mistake the form for the substance and betray much misunderstanding in what Africa is about. The late Tom Mboya's article written for the *New York Times* magazine was reprinted in the Jamaican leading newspaper. In this he revealed that New World blacks would find it extremely difficult to become Africans. "Some think," he wrote, "that to identify with Africa one should wear a shaggy beard or a piece of cloth on one's head or a cheap garment on one's body. . . . An African walks barefoot or wears sandals made of old tires not because it is his culture but because he lives in poverty. . . . White people have often confused the symbols of our poverty with our culture. I would hope that black people would not make the same error."[60]

Rex Nettleford acknowledges that many Jamaicans are guilty of this confusion and need to understand that the culture of the black peoples of Africa is something much more profound. Nettleford joins with Rodney in calling for the teaching of African culture and history as one way of advancing African-ness in Jamaica. An emphasis on the teaching of African history and culture would highlight as essential to African culture the importance of the extended family ties and the codes governing relations between the young and old. Also important for understanding African history and culture are the importance of mutual responsibility and a sense of communal activities, humor, belief in a supreme being, and the importance of ceremonies celebrating birth, death, and marriage.

Rex Nettleford uses Rodney to go beyond Rodney in suggesting that superficial estimates of African history must be left behind as the study of African history explores the ground and goals of family and religion in

African tradition. We must also suggest that the practice of black power in Jamaica as it relates history to the liberation project must examine the ways in which kinship networks were formed and maintained, how the community raised and socialized children, how they carved worldviews and fashioned a rich and expressive culture that reflected the uninhibited imagination and provided the means to articulate their hopes and hurts, their dreams and doubts.

Nettleford also raises the issue of whether or not it is enough to focus on African history. In a sense, the tendency of black power advocates in Jamaica to focus on African history is a response to the call of Rastafari to forsake Babylon and think of Africa as the spiritual home for black people. African history as the way of building black awareness in a culture and country that regards Africa as backward and uncivilized is an attempt at countercultural critique. It is an attempt to place over against the dominant culture another way of viewing the world. The same applies when black power advocates and Rastafari enjoin a discourse with the Christian church.

The church in Jamaica has not engaged African history in any sustained way. In theological schools throughout the Caribbean, it is mentioned in passing that some of the great church leaders of the early Christian church like St. Augustine, Origen, Tertullian, and others are from Africa, but no attempt is made to study the social settings in which these people worked and were formed. The challenge to engage meaningfully with African history, therefore, is an important contribution by Rastafari and black power advocates not only to the wider culture but also to the church. This challenge is extended to the Christian church at another level. The Rastas further claim—and many black power advocates are sympathetic to the claim—that God is an African. Jamaicans, about 95 percent of whom are of African ancestry, have been conditioned by colonial theology to view God as having European features. It is no exaggeration to say that most Jamaican church people, if asked to describe their understanding of what God looks like, would describe a European male. This of course was part of the slave theology systematically taught during slavery and buttressed with colonial symbols of power. Pictures that could be seen in most Christian homes of Jesus and his family were all European, and since we were taught that sin was black, the devil was black, and blackness was ugly and African, it is not surprising that Christian Jamaica would be hesitant to locate God or their Christ in Africa.

It was therefore extremely difficult for middle-class Jamaica or even for working-class Jamaica to accept Rastafari's locating God in Africa and pressing for an incarnational theology that posits the blackness of God. Add to this the sense of self-hate that has been the lot of most colonial peoples, and it becomes understandable why God or the Christ could not look like us or be like us. God would have to be the other, since the other was the symbol of freedom. For many years, ever since slavery, blackness has been the symbol of bondage, and whiteness the symbol of freedom. To be born black was to be a slave, and to be born white was to be free. Even in an independent Jamaica, this association of whiteness with privilege and freedom continues. It should not be surprising then that Rasta theology as it pertains to who God is and what God looks like would be an extremely hard sell. A black God would not have access to power as a white God would. It even goes further than this. Black Jamaicans perceive white people being united in a way that black people are not. The self-hate that has been the mother's milk of slavery makes us devalue ourselves and allows us to boast one of the highest black-on-black crime rates in the world. The time has come for us to stop and ask why we kill each other in such large numbers and why violence is part and parcel of our way of life. The church teaches that the way out of this malaise is through the guidance of the white and Europeanized Christ. It is no wonder that some continue to sing in our churches in a land where many have never seen snow, "Lord wash me until I am whiter than snow." The bottom line is that we want to look like God since we are made in God's image. We want to be white.

Professor Nettleford's critique is also far-reaching as he begins to ask if even the study of the history of ordinary Africans—not just the history of African kings and philosophers—offers enough as resource for the liberation project. Granted that our roots are in Africa, but are we not Jamaicans or Caribbean people? Why should Caribbean people not combine the study of African history with Caribbean history? How well do Jamaican people know Jamaican history, and in what sense could this history serve as a resource for the liberation of Jamaica? Prior to the engagement of Rastafari with middle-class intellectuals in Jamaica, this was not a major concern as the focus was repatriation narrowly conceived and defined. The feeling was that Rastas in particular and poor people in general were exiles in the white man's land. As the conversation ensued with the black power intellectuals, the notion began to surface that African study in general and Ethiopian study in particular needs to be in the service of freeing and mobilizing the minds of Jamaican black people. There began to emerge a commitment for the people of Jamaica to Jamaica. African history must be in the service of Jamaican people, but Nettleford takes it a step further:

Using Garvey to Go beyond Garvey

Their emphasis on African History even at the expense of West Indian and Jamaican History betrays a basic dilemma. It is what Mboya called *the contradiction between black nationalism and, in this case, Jamaican nationalism.* It is a contradiction because complete identification with Africa (or countries of Africa) is difficult in a world of nation states. Yet it is reasonable for New World blacks to be concerned with the reconstruction of an African past that can serve their interests of identity wherever they may find themselves. Their very identity, wherever they are, is thwarted by an attitude born of the very assumption by a ruling white ethos that the blacks have no past beyond slavery and degradation. African achievement therefore has a place not so much for the sake of the past but for the present and the future. . . . Black power militants may well exploit the creative potential of their black brothers in the West for they are the very expression of this continuing expression of cross-fertilization. One God, one aim, one destiny in some things perhaps but not in all and to further deprive the black man of the agony of individual choice may be to deprive him of his humanity.[61]

The liberation project must not only include African history as resource but must also consider Caribbean and Jamaican history. Nettleford has placed his finger on an important reality that is a relic of our long history as a colonial subject—the characteristic of forgetting ourselves and diminishing the importance of our own story. It is important to consider African history as that has been an important part of who we are. In our Caribbean high schools, we were forced to study European and North American histories, which provided us an important view of the world and allowed those of us who migrated to Europe or to North America to compete. However, we knew nothing about Africa.

Rastas and black power advocates have sought to correct this gap in our identities, but they have not gone far enough. While we have discovered the other in Africa, we have not found the brother and sister at home. The critical question raised by Rastafari—"Where do you stand in relationship to Africa?"—is not yet enough. Africa must also include home; as painful as it is, Africa must include Babylon. I believe we begin to see a move in this direction when we listen to Rasta poetics articulated in reggae music. In what Bob Marley considered his greatest song, "No Woman No Cry," he wails:

No woman no cry
Cause I remember when we use to sit

In a government yard in Trench town
Observing the hypocrites
Mingle with the good people we meet
Good friend we have
Oh, good friends we have lost along the way.
In this great future
You can't forget your past
So dry your tears, I say.[62]

To forget the history of our social locations is to forget friends and families. This is one reason that women have not received their rightful place in our story. Part of the problem is that we have focused so much on the macrostory that we have neglected the microstory. The challenge is to see how our histories relate and what questions they ask. The other problem I have with focusing on African history at the expense of Jamaican history concerns God and Rastas' depiction of God as Ethiopian. I am grateful to the Rastas for bringing God a little closer. The God I grew up with and was introduced to in the church was European. So it was timely and helpful to meet a God who knows something about my distant past and knows something about my ancestors. In the same vein in which Nettleford asks if the study of African history may be coupled with Jamaican history, I wonder if God would come all the way and be Jamaican.

The problem with a God who is totally African is that God runs the risk of being a foreigner and therefore a stranger to the Jamaican situation. According to Rasta theology, Jah is not really interested in liberating Baby-lon as Jah will take Rastas and poor people out of Babylon. I have not discovered in Rasta theology any commitment of Jah to work for the libera-tion of Jamaica. While Rastas are stuck in exile awaiting Jah's arrival, they work for a measure of transformation in Babylon.

The advantage of the Rastas linking God to Africa and Ethiopia is that it protects the transcendence of Jah. After all, in some African myths the African deity receded from the earth because God was tired of the sound of fufu mortars or of people begging all the time. The sky that was once close to the earth receded from the earth. The Rastas got an important part cor-rect. It is important for God to be in Africa (heaven). It protects God's transcendence. But God also needs to be near, "since we will be forever loving Jah." It is only a God who is near who can save us. Perhaps then God is Afro-Jamaican. If we are made in God's image, then this is logical. To speak of God as Afro-Jamaican would preserve God's transcendence and would make Jah "God with us." The notion of God's immanence would begin to shift the way Rastas view Babylon. Babylon would no longer be intractable and perceived beyond salvation. The nearness of God would place Babylon within the purview of salvation. Hence liberation would be conceived and understood within repatriation. Jah would become one of us and no longer a stranger.

Hope for the Practice of Black Power

I noted that one of the practical results of black intellectuals' relationship with Rastafari was the emergence of the black power movement in Jamaica and the opening of the door for the black middle class to enter and converse with Rastafari. Walter Rodney linked the study of African history to the liberation project in Jamaica. Rex Nettleford took the project a little further as he indicated that it is not enough to relate African history to the liberation project in Jamaica but that true liberation also entails the study and appropriation of Caribbean/Jamaican history for the liberation of structures that imprison and diminish the quality of life of Jamaican people. This also has implications for my discussion of God's transcendence and nearness. Now I must examine the practice of black power as a liberative construct.

Kortright Davis suggests four hurdles we must work through in the Caribbean if in spite of our history of slavery and oppression we would create a just society in which the dignity of all people is affirmed. The first hurdle we must overcome is that of poverty. Our first hope is liberation from the stifling effects of poverty. Hope is more than wishing things will be different but is also the struggle to effect change. The new middle class will have to learn from the Rastas in this instance because they are trapped in the ways of Babylon. It is well known that Jamaicans, caught up in the culture of consumerism and pandering to the market economy, live way beyond their means. "Where a society chooses to adopt an economic model that promotes capital to a position of pre-eminence, there should be no real surprise at the resulting escalation in crime, the blatant disregard for human life, and recklessness of every imaginable sort. . . . In smaller and lesser developed economies such as those of the Caribbean, the consequences of the market driven economy are further aggravated by the scarcity of resources, the instability of the national currency, and labor unrests. These factors are quite the opposite of those which are necessary for growth in the productive sector. Where these persist, businesses fail . . . and layoffs become common features."[63] The people of Jamaica may need to learn from the imaginative creativity and determination of the Rastas, who do not seek to make Jamaica a wealthy country after the model of more developed countries like the United States. Rather, they seek to survive with dignity by planting and growing their own food and sustaining self through small businesses. The important fact here is that children and poor people should not suffer for lack of basic resources. "The emancipatory goal, therefore, is not to create a wealthy region but, rather, to enable the people to move from absolute poverty to relative poverty, from economic decay and despair through resource depletion to economic growth in resource exploitation."[64]

The second hurdle is dependency, which is closely related to economic poverty. Because of the small size of our island and the lack of basic economic resources coupled with the legacy of colonialism, we have been trained to look to England to provide our needs. This has not changed with the advent of political independence in 1962. The truth is that with political independence we did not achieve economic independence. Through slavery and the ensuing history of colonialism, we were taught to believe that we were not resourceful and that someone else had the answer to our problem. The Rastas, in turning their backs on the economic structure of Jamaica, calling it evil and corrupt, have not been caught in the spiral of economic dependency. Although they are poor, they look to themselves and to each other to get them out of this mindset.

It has worked for many Rastas who entered into the music industry and developed their own style of music. Others have explored the artistic world and have made much progress there. The Rastas have modeled for us that the answer to our woes does not exist outside of us but within us. It is only as we look to each other and to self that we will throw off the yoke of dependency and put on the virtues of independence and interdependence. The primary reality that must be broken if the practice of black power is to become pervasive among our people is the cycle of dependency and denial. There is danger that the spirits of our people are being colonized as poverty and the attitude of dependency are being institutionalized. These evils have their roots in the history of domination and colonization that took root in Jamaica during slavery and over three hundred years of British colonialism. The structure of domination expresses itself through dependence of many Caribbean islands on the International Monetary Fund, which dictates the monetary and financial policy of many islands. There is in Jamaica and many islands the belief that if help comes and if it is to be liberative, then it must come from outside. We are accustomed to looking to the United States, Great Britain, Germany, and even Japan. We even look to Africa for God (according to the Rastas), but we refuse to look to ourselves. What is needed, it seems to me, is a decolonizing of the mind.

We need to acknowledge that deep within the innermost recesses of the Caribbean mind is the notion that the foreign is better even if this results in alienation from our history and our roots. Our spirits are in danger of being colonized. This negative attitude to self has been a part of the legacy of the colonial church and colonial powers. Unfortunately, this cycle of dependence on foreign capital and investments is systemic and emblematic of our way of life. We need to begin to understand that emancipation and liberation do not have to come from outside or above but rather must come from among our people. It is as we turn to each other and become self-reliant that we discover the breach in the cycle of dependency. The people must believe in themselves through I-and-I consciousness and affirm that truth is given in the birth of our communities. We must determine our futures, be clear about our priorities, and find the courage of the Rastas to articulate these truths.

Cultural Alienation

Kortright Davis suggests that in the Caribbean, cultural alienation is more insidious and deadly than poverty and dependency. He views cultural alienation as the basis of most of our problems regarding self-acceptance and self-love.

> Cultural alienation has perhaps been more devastating than either poverty or dependency. The official policy of divide and rule was relentlessly pursued by the colonial overlords and rigidly woven into the fabric of colonial social life. It encouraged Caribbean people to become mutually contemptuous and accept patterns of self-contempt, sometimes as a means of social progress or acceptance by others. That which was foreign was good; that which was local was not good. So people were alienated from each other by inducement. They were also alienated from their natural cultural endowment (race, color, language, belief systems, relationships, preferences, entertainment and leisure, work schedules, family mores, personal aspirations) and from the rightful corridors of power, influence, opportunity, and social access.[65]

The Rastas have sought a reversal of cultural alienation by affirming the dignity of self-expression whether in terms of their beliefs or in terms of their creation of a language that speaks to their own identity. It seems to me that the area in which this alienation has been most severe is in terms of the loss of our native languages, which was a part of the enslavement process. It is well known that in the deculturation process that occurred during slavery, enslaved persons were forbidden to speak their native languages or to refer to themselves by their African names. In the process of enslavement, the master stripped African peoples of their languages and with the force of whipping and brutal punishments enforced their adopting the English language as their mother tongue. With the loss of language that ensued, African peoples were in danger of losing and in fact did lose their culture. With the loss of culture came the loss of self and with the loss of self, the loss of who we are. The oppressor class imposed their language and culture. They taught us and we believed that our blackness was a curse and their whiteness was a blessing. With the loss of language came the loss of our memory of Africa. On one of my first visits to Africa in search of self, I was seated at the breakfast table with my African family host when the family began to speak their African language. I was reminded that my beautiful African language was stolen from me by the oppressor as I heard words, beautiful African words, that I could not understand as I had lost the language.

It is precisely here, I believe, that Rastas have made their greatest contribution to the culture. They regard the English language as the language of the oppressors and as much as possible seek to avoid using it. They identify their language by the term "Dread Talk." "The feature that most identifies Dread Talk today, however, is neither the biblical turn of phrase nor the punning per se but the 'I-ance,' what Nettleford calls the 'battery of I-words.' Next, he describes the 'small but pointedly relevant lexicon of normative descriptive word-symbols.' It is in these categories that the stance of protest, of revolt in words is evident."[66] For the Rastas words have power to be enacted. As they were for Old Testament prophets, words are sign events for Rastas. Therefore they are not used lightly. "To the Rastas, words are seals of the mind, words have power and they must not be abused but rather used with awareness. . . . The Rastas have always resented English as the language of colonialism and have developed their own [language] based on its bastardization."[67] Pollard acknowledges that the Rastas do not view their "doctoring" of the language as bastardization but as "stepping up" the language or taking out of the language the unfortunate double meaning often associated with words of the English language. Here is a Rasta man's recollection of how Rasta moved from using the language of the oppressor to the evolution of Dread Talk. The founder of this commune, I-rice, recollects:

> We exile ourselves to the hills where there is no noise, no bus, no pollution. Is a different meditation reach yuh there. Ya see, only a Bible and mi rod I tek to de hill. Eventually now, we guh into ourselves—into de "higher mountains" as wha Moses did do for his meditation—in search of de Creator. And de Creator speak to I-n-I through the spirit and fix a new tongue in the latter days which is de I-*tesvar* I-*yound See-knots-see*-I, I-*yah- Yinghi*-I . . . *One Yantifull I yound!* Those are words dat Headful I-on and I create even up to *I-rie I tes*. We started dat at Wareika Hill . . . it never come from nowhere else. Well, after a time now we had to leave Wareika Hill to penetrate all dem *I- tesvar I-ses I yasta y-oo-I I yantifull-I* into Back-o-Wall to form a group. Dat was de *I-gelic House*.[68]

For the Rastas, the ultimate signifier of their alienation from Africa and blackness was being required to use the language of Babylon. The creation of their own language was an expression of protest against Babylon and all that it represented. The change of language was the ultimate protest for Rastafari against the impositions of Babylon. It is no surprise to note that as a colony of Britain, Jamaica imported Great Britain's educational system, adopting and replicating it in Jamaica without any consideration for the social location of Jamaicans. The same is true of the worship experience in many of our mainline churches. To attempt to change the language handed down by the oppressor class is to lash out against a system that imposed its way of life on a subject people. It is intriguing to note that Rasta is no longer merely the language of Rasta communities but through reggae music—which has taken Jamaica by storm from the 1970s to the present—Dread Talk has now become commonplace among middle-class Jamaicans, especially the young. "Clearly the movement's contributions to Jamaican society are remarkable. The net effect has been Rastafarianization of Jamaica and while certain phrases and expressions have evolved from Rasta youth, their distribution in the general population is widespread. . . . And Rasta has become a unit of Jamaican man. In the talk of the young people, 'Yes Rasta' is frequently heard where 'Yes man' was used before."[69]

The key for Rastas is that unless people have an opportunity to learn about their own heroes and heroines, which in effect means learning about themselves in their own language, education is of no avail. One Rasta says: "the education that them is trying to give the people is going to fail. You know why I say, and why I know, that it is going to fail? Only the Rasta alone sees that now, yet that Rasta see that a long time: you cannot give a man a education without you give it to *him* with him language and *him* nationality. Otherwise him is still dunce."[70] The Rastas are insistent that education must take seriously who people are, their history, geography, religion, culture. If not, they are alienated from their own cultural heritage.

With the creation of their own language, Rastas have not only protested against the education offered them through the schools as culturally alienating but also have seized the power of definition. Through their own language, they have the power to define their own reality on their own terms. For example, God for Rastas is "Jah," and they refer to the unjust system in which they live in Jamaica as "Babylon." Marijuana is the "holy herb," and Rastas consider themselves divine because of their relationship to the black Messiah Haile Selassie. They refer to this unique relationship with Haile Selassie as "I-and-I consciousness." It is this "I-and-I consciousness" that is the key to understanding Rasta identity, a relationship that explains their rebirth and new status as sons and daughters of Jah.

Imitation

Imitation has been and is the main problem Rastas have with fellow Jamaicans—being children of Babylon and imitating Babylonian ways. For the Rastas, "Babylonian captivity" signals the selling out of the values that are intrinsic to Jamaica and a frenzied attempt to imitate European and North American ways. Rastas insist on finding their own voice rather than parroting the voice of the "downpressor." The bottom line for Rastas is that they must be true to themselves and their heritage as African roots are affirmed as the basis of integrity. In his *Survival* album Bob Marley sums up the ethos of Rastafari as it relates to imitation:

> We refuse to be
> What you wanted us to be
> We are what we are
> That's the way its going to be
> You can't educate I.[71]

With the Rastas we must pray, "Jah lead us not into imitation." The Rastas have given us clues concerning the practice of black power. We noted that black power Jamaican-style takes seriously the role of African history in the liberation project. The liberation project must take seriously the extended family, rituals of births, marriages, and deaths, how communities are formed, economic cooperation rather than competition, and most centrally the reality that God is a black man from Ethiopia. We also observed that Rastas gave us clues, especially through the Twelve Tribes, that African history had to include Jamaican history. To take a people seriously we must talk about them in the context of their existential history—their history of suffering and exploitation as well as their history of dreams and aspirations. It is in this context that the practice of black power in Jamaica could take on existential issues like poverty, political dependency, cultural alienation, and the penchant for imitation because it is not enough in the practice of black power to separate liberation and repatriation. As repatriation is seen to include liberation, Africa and Jamaica are conjoined as heaven and earth are joined. I argued that the Rastas were/are correct to locate God in Africa because Africa is the symbol of heaven, and the notion of heaven protects God's transcendence. However, a God who is transcendent and not immanent cannot save or liberate Jamaica from its "Babylonian captivity." This is one of the weaknesses in Rastafari theology that might be compensated for if the Rastas engaged African spirit more, which is crucial in the study of African cosmology.

To continue the Rastas' focus on Jah as God, I suggest it would be more liberative to speak of God as an Afro-Jamaican than as African. The Rastas, in speaking of God as African, protect the transcendence of God as they point to the universality of God. Rastas highlight God's availability to all humanity since Africa is the home of humankind. It is widely accepted in the scientific world that humanity originated in Africa, connecting Africa with God as Africa places God at the service of humanity. What is missing is the specificity of the Jamaican situation. The incarnation teaches us that God is not only African but Afro-Jamaican. That is, Jamaicans can take on the issues of poverty, political dependence, cultural alienation, and the struggle for integrity against imitation because God is with us showing us the way out of oppression. The practice of black power becomes the movement of Jah's people toward liberation. Exodus!

I must now consider the meaning of resurrection as we look at the music of Rastafari.

6
{ Reggae and Rastafari

Reggae music became the means and the method through which Rastafari theology and ideology were universalized. In a profound sense, reggae became the equivalent of a resurrection ethic for Rastafari. Reggae was the means through which Rastafari transcended its local environs, taking Rastafari teaching and practices from their local Jamaican habitat and placing them on the world stage. There is also a sense in which reggae transcends Rastafari in that when one mentions Jamaica, reggae is often the first thing that comes to mind.

Consummate artist Robert Nesta Marley, often referred to as Bob Marley, is widely known as the father of reggae. Through Marley, reggae emerges as a black cultural art form, giving expressive power to black voices that were long silenced on the margins of Jamaican society. Reggae and Rastafari emerged in similar social settings. Rastafari came on the Jamaican scene because of the impoverished conditions in which many working-class Jamaicans had to live. Coupled with the harsh social and economic conditions that confronted Jamaicans was the fact that their lives were determined and governed by the policies of Great Britain, for which Jamaica was a colonial outpost for over three hundred years. Don Taylor, a close associate of Bob Marley, gives us a glimpse into the world that shaped the early Marley: "Trench Town and the rest of West Kingston were beginning to show a flare-up of the ghetto problem which had started to become noticeable in the early fifties: there were large tracts of waste land crammed with makeshift houses of the itinerant rural squatters who captured every square inch of living space, as they moved from country to town. The shacks were built cheek-by-jowl and somehow the politicians thought the way to solve the problem was to bulldoze them all down and build large and concrete structures. . . . This was where Bob ended up, in the area the country would later call Concrete Jungle."[1] The harsh reality in this world where Marley grew up is that unemployment was rife and "idleness" was a form of existence that characterized the lifestyle of the masses: "Many idle days were spent by the majority of young ghetto dwellers in a world without regular work and opportunities. A world where the only escape seemed to be in the learning of a trade for the boys and the cleaning of white people's houses for the girls, or in migration to 'foreign' by first the mother and finally the family."[2]

Reggae, like Rastafari, emerged in a context in which ghetto life is woven into a "black popular narrative." Through music the poor and marginalized find their voice and are able to acknowledge and celebrate their identities. Reggae, born in a context in which the first artists were seen as social outcasts, turned to a religious faith that was itself outside the mainstream, Rastafari. The reggae artist became committed to the main themes in Rastafari: "Rastafarianism, whose roots are in Africa, in Jah, Haile Selassie, the Emperor of Ethiopia. The themes of their message are rooted in the despair of dispossession, their hope is in Africa or diasporan solution. As a result, their messages emerge as ideology of social change."[3]

As Bob Marley came into the consciousness of being a Rasta, he began to spend more time with Mortimo Planno, who is regarded by Jamaicans as the foremost authority on Rastafari. Planno took Marley under his tutelage and became the primary inspiration for Marley's journey to Rastafari. "Planno took Bob through the stages of Rastafarianism, taking him to the settlements deep in the interior of the country where he learnt about the groundation ceremonies, and the all-night convocations which meant feasting on coconut meat, rice and peas (ital cooking). It was here that he listened to the chants of the traditional Bongo Man and the humba and Nyabinghi chants, while hundreds of Rastas sat on their haunches passing the chillum pipe."[4] The relationship between Planno and Marley was so all-embracing that on his public declaration as a Rasta, Marley chose to sing a song whose title Planno had given to him. "Over a molasses-slow Nyabinghi drum track, Bob chanted: 'Haile Selassie is the Chapel, power of the trinity, conquering lion of the tribe of Judah, He's the only King of Kings.'"[5]

As reggae emerged it was characterized by a community ethos. It is difficult prior to 1972 to ascribe authorship to many songs as many were created by the original Wailers, Peter Tosh, Bunny Livingston, and Bob Marley, a group with a cooperative approach to writing and producing songs. "While Bob strummed and brooded, Perry would croak out catch-phrases and doggerel, trying to find the right lyrics to match the sputter-ing, bumpity Afro-style percussion tracks that the Barretts were experi-menting with. Perry was a witty and imaginative lyricist who contributed immeasurably to the great records the Wailers made with him. As to who actually wrote the songs (Bob or Scratch-Peter's and Bunny's songs are unmistakably their own), confusion still reigns. Most likely they were writ-ten by both men and the band, improvising in the studio."[6]

The verbal spontaneity of the group with their commitment to improvi-sation is attributed to the shaping of reggae lyrics prior to 1972. One of the central themes that emerges in reggae lyrics is that of exodus and exile. This theme is set within the context of the present system referred to by Rastas as Babylon, which represents exploitation, bondage of all forms including the oppression characterized by the slave trade and the Middle Passage, and the neocolonial system of oppression that confronts poor people in Jamaica expressed in police brutality, economic oppression, and racism. One of the goals of reggae is to chant down these walls of oppres-sion that support this Babylonian system.

"In contrast to 'Babylon' there is 'Zion,' Ethiopia, or Africa generally, which Marley calls 'our father's land' (in 'Exodus'), to which Jah is guiding his people in a new exodus/return/repatriation, led by various prophetic figures. 'Give us another brother Moses' sings Marley in 'Exodus.'"[7] The Christian church is among the institutions identified as a part of the Baby-lonian structure and represents an area from which people need to be liberated. In his *Red X* tapes, which Peter Tosh recorded as his autobio-graphical reflections, he calls attention to the many levels of oppression experienced in the Christian church during his youth and his gratitude that Rastafari offered an alternative reality and vision.

Then they started to teach me of the devil, and Satan, and hell. They teach me of the Christians. But they made sure that they teach me that Jesus, the son of God, was a white man. When I ask why am I black, they say I was born in sin and shaped in iniquity. One of the main songs they used to sing in church that make me sick, is "Lord, Wash Me and I Shall Be Whiter Than Snow."

In my search I heard of the name "God." I go to church and they say God made me in his own likeness and image. If I make a doll in my image it is quite obvious that the doll must look like me. Yet still I am faced with the ignorance, lost in fantasy, seeking to find the reality in what they taught me in this religion, of God.[8]

Reggae artist Peter Tosh reminds us that one of the central questions for the reggae lyricist is not only, as in Rastafari, "Where do you stand in relation to Africa?" but also "How does one recover the lost self?" How does one recover the beautiful black self created by Jah? Bob Marley provides an answer in his album *Redemption Song*:

Emancipate yourself from mental slavery
None but our selves can free our minds
Have no fear for atomic energy
Cause none a them can stop the time.

In the *Exodus* album, Marley opines that oppressed Jamaicans must open their eyes and examine whether or not they are satisfied with the life they are living in Babylon. They need to know where they are going and where they are coming from. The truth is they are leaving Babylon and going to the father's land.[9]

Marley calls for "Exodus," the movement of Jah's people. In the same vein we are told by reggae singers that knowledge of self does not originate from the books we read but rather from participating in community. Chuck D, the lead singer of Public Enemy Number 1, unfolds three vital elements of sustaining and creating black community: education, economics, and enforcement. These elements, he states, are an integral part of the mission of rap and reggae. "During my years of crisscrossing throughout major and minor cities in America I've developed a theory with regard to the black community. I call my theory the 'Plantation Theory.' The Plantation Theory states that black people don't really have communities; what we have are clusters of plantations. A community is an environment that has control over the three E's: education, economics and enforcement. Without control of these vital aspects of our existence, we're like robots existing in an environment with no real control."[10] Bob Marley supports Chuck D's basic thesis that black people dare not trust the system to teach or to educate the masses of poor people. It is important that black people resist the system and educate themselves. "We refuse to be what you wanted us to be. We are what we are. That's the way it's going to be. You can't educate I, for no 'equal opportunity.' Talking about my freedom, people, freedom and liberty."[11]

Reggae and rap contribute uniquely to the education of black people by interpreting black life through music. The key here, as Marley points out, is that recovery of the lost self is needed to make it in this society. The critical issue is, "What do we do to recover our black selves?" We must open our eyes and look within and learn who we are ourselves for ourselves. What is required in community building is education from a black perspective. Marley indicates in "Redemption Song" that education offered by the dominant culture is education by the "Babylon system" which deceives the people and produces thieves and murderers. Marley likens the Babylon system to a vampire that sucks the blood of children and poor people. Babylon feigns that the building of churches and universities is for the uplift of the people, but the truth is that these institutions produce thieves and murderers. Reggae must speak truth to the people. The Babylon system sucks the blood of sufferers.[12]

What is needed is education that tells the children the truth about themselves. At the beginning of this chapter, I noted that Peter Tosh observed that the Jamaican church refused to tell him the truth about himself—the truth that he was black and beautiful, and that he was made in the image of God. In the Christian church, he was taught that God was white and that as a black man he needed to be "washed until he was whiter than snow." We also get in the lyrics of Bunny Wailer this sense of being sinned against by the dominant culture as he indicates the importance of an alternate consciousness in the struggle for survival in Babylon. According to Bunny Wailer, it is a mark of Babylon to lead people astray, and survival in Jamaica necessitates that oppressed Jamaicans cultivate an oppositional identity based on following their own minds.[13]

The truth must be found in black symbols, heroes and "sheroes," and black communities. Education from the black perspective is required. Underlying this assertion that education must take the black community seriously is the belief that black people's understanding of self must be shaped by conversations with blacks like Marcus Mosiah Garvey and Zora Neale Hurston rather than by the exploits of European explorers. The critical question that Chuck D and Bob Marley help us raise concerns the economic and political consequences of the recovery of the black self in the context of the black community. Earlier I noted that Peter Tosh saw a commitment to the black self and the black God as demanding a critical attitude toward the church. Tosh, Marley, and Chuck D now question the sense in which the return to the black self constitutes a criticism of society.

Chuck D informs us that "the original purpose of education wasn't just to prepare for a job, but to prepare young minds to meaningfully contribute to society. Schooling in its original plan was for the white man, only, to send their sons, only, to school to create a business for the family, or to enhance the business that the father already had. America was so one-sided, sexist, and racist that they didn't even include their women or daughters in the school program."[14] He suggests another way in which education needs to take place in the black community—black people must learn to be family to each other. He observes that this does not happen in sufficient numbers for black people in the Diaspora. In this regard he is hopeful that black people will learn from Jewish, Italian, and Korean families, who create opportunities for their communities through family businesses. It is not enough for black people to get an education and then get a job to work for someone else. What is needed is the creation of black businesses that provide employment for other members of the black community. In *Where Do We Go from Here,* Martin Luther King Jr. echoes Chuck D: "The economic highway to power has few entry lanes for Negroes. Nothing so vividly reveals the crushing impact of discrimination and the heritage of exclusion as the limited dimensions of Negro business in the most powerful economy in the world. America's industrial production is half of the world's total, and within it the production of Negro business is so small that it can scarcely be measured in any definable scale. Yet in relation to the Negro community the value of the Negro business should not be underestimated. In the internal life of the Negro society it provides a degree of stability."[15]

Martin Luther King Jr. and Chuck D emphasize the importance of black-owned business in the black community. Both underscore the need to look beyond white society to provide jobs for black people. The music industry could be a place to start since there are many black people who have made important inroads in this industry both in Jamaica and in the United States. The Rastafari echo similar sentiments, although the language is different. Simply, responsible black people cannot depend on Babylon to provide them with either education or economic opportunity as the system of Babylon is arrayed against them. Martin Luther King Jr. cautions that racism in America makes it unwise and imprudent for black people to trust an economic system that has excluded them.

> The Negro also has to recognize that one hundred years after emancipation [w]e lived on a lonely island of economic insecurity in the midst of the vast ocean of material prosperity. Negroes are still at the bottom of the economic ladder. They live within two concentric

circles of segregation. One imprisons them on the basis of color, while the other confines them within a separate culture of poverty. The average Negro is born into want and deprivation [and] struggle[s] to escape . . . circumstances. . . . hindered by color discrimination . . . [he or she] is deprived of normal education and normal social and economic opportunities. When he [or she] seeks opportunity, he [or she] is told, in effect, to lift [themselves] by [their] own boot straps, advice which does not take into account the fact that he [or she] is barefoot.[16]

Reggae artists want to pay particular attention to concrete problems that confront them in Jamaica. While on the one hand there is a sense of fidelity to Rastafari beliefs, the divinity of Haile Selassie, and repatriation to Ethiopia, they nonetheless are committed to social change in Jamaica. In this sense, liberation is understood within the context of repatriation. This is clearly expressed as they highlight themes of economic despair and frustration with life in Babylon. Yet theirs is a theology of hope as the answer is an African one. As sinister and final as Babylon appears to be, reggae begins to craft a theology of hope grounded in biblical imagery that through music, Babylon, like the walls of Jericho, will fall. "Love to see when you move to the rhythm. . . . It remind I of the days in Jericho. When we trodding down Jericho walls. These are the days when we'll trod through Babylon, Gonna trod until Babylon falls."[17] It may seem simplistic for Rastas to believe that the simple act of singing will threaten the system of Babylon sufficiently to effect transformation, but they observe it was simply walking around the walls of Jericho and chanting that brought the wall down. "So feel this drumbeat, as it beats within. Playing a rhythm, resisting against the system."[18]

Often reggae music calls on the hearers—even listeners in Babylon—to rebel against the system that has consigned them to death or in other ways seems to render them invisible. In a speech by Haile Selassie that became the basis for Marley's song titled "War," Haile Selassie stated:

Until the philosophy which holds one race superior and another inferior is finally and permanently discredited and abandoned; until there are no longer first class and second class citizens of any nation; until the basic human rights are equally guaranteed to all without regard to race; until that day, the dream of lasting peace, world citizenship and the rule of international morality will remain a fleeting illusion to be pursued but never attained; And until the ignoble and unhappy regimes that hold our brothers in Angola, in Mozambique, and in South Africa in sub-human bondage, have been toppled and destroyed; until that day the African continent will not know peace; we Africans will fight, if necessary, And we know that we shall win as we are confident in the victory of good over evil.[19]

Marley saw this as an opportunity to promote the positive contributions of Haile Selassie at a time when, due to information concerning the 1975 revolution in Ethiopia, the confidence of the Rasta movement was shaken. At the same time, "Marley was astute enough to promote the positive contributions of Haile Selassie on the anti-colonial front, while singing a single called 'Jah Lives' to reassert the fact that Rasta had a life beyond Haile Selassie, saying that 'Dread shall be dread and dread again.' . . . Just as the slaves of the Americas had invoked the will of God in their deliverance, Rastafari was looking to a black land and a black God which would help to free them from neo-colonialism. The Jah which Marley and other Rastas sang about was one who had to be willing to join the struggle of black people and bore little resemblance to the autocratic monarch Haile Selassie turned out to be."[20]

Anthony Pinn's *Why Lord?* calls attention to the ways that rap, like reggae, not only seeks to change the system by changing the perspective of victims but also uses black history and black culture as tools to dismantle oppression and point to the dignity and worth of black life. Pinn alludes to the ways in which rap in harmony with reggae points to a legal system that oppresses those who are most in need of protection.[21] It is precisely at this point that Chuck D reminds us that "the movement of Jah's people" (to paraphrase Marley) requires that black people participate in the creation and enforcement of laws. In his view, the uplift of the black community requires the black community to make advances in economics, education, and law enforcement. He also believes that both economics and education must be rooted in black values in the black community. This perspective is in harmony with the Rastas' emphasis on leaving Babylon and recognizing that the Babylon system offers only death and decay. One cannot root economics and education in a system that is on its way out. Now Chuck D posits that this lack of adequate participation means that black bodies are being brutalized and not treated with respect. It means black people are not taking with sufficient seriousness the need for active participation in the black community. The failure to participate means that black people tacitly play a large role in the destruction of their own community and their own people.

Chuck D calls on the black community to look within and see how the failure of involvement could contribute constructively to community destruction. Granted a defiant Bob Marley cries out "I shot the Sheriff" as his musical lyrics call attention to a system arrayed against the poor. He is not yet calling on Rastas or the poor to participate in the system and thereby begin to change the system in favor of the poor. The tough question that Rastas ask at this point is whether Rastas can reject the status quo and participate in it at the same time, especially in an area as sensitive as law enforcement. I am fairly sure that Rastas with one voice answer no.

It would be a sign that Babylon was changing if we had some Rastas participating in the creation and administration of laws and justice in Jamaica. At this point, Rastas would visibly begin to link liberation and repatriation. They would begin to discover that perhaps one way to leave Babylon is to work for the transformation of that evil system. As reggae serves as an instrument of change it would become more than a means of disseminating information about African history and black culture. It would begin to make poor people aware of the role they can play in nation building. The Rastas have not provided leadership in this area as their emphasis is repatriation and not liberation. If Rastas were to see repatriation within the matrix of liberation, the press for social change and transformation in Jamaica's economic, educational, and political life would be more forthcoming.

I agree with many Rastafari scholars—especially Rex Nettleford, who makes a compelling case for this interpretation in *Mirror, Mirror*—that after the publication of the University Report in 1960, as Rastafari discovered that there was a measure of acceptance for their ideas among the Jamaican intelligentsia, they began to see their existence as exiles in Jamaica (Babylon) necessitating the need to work for social change. The importance of repatriation to Africa (heaven) for a group that lived on the periphery of Jamaican society and that was for a very long time regarded by middle-class Jamaicans as nobodies cannot be emphasized too strongly. It is clear that a group that was constantly harassed by the police and found itself at the base of Jamaican society would not want to stay in that society, even if they had some commitment from the society. There was a ray of hope for the Rastas in Jamaican black power as explicated by Walter Rodney, but even here it was African history that was being heralded as a source of liberation, and the Rastas understood the main focus as repatriation. The reggae artists affirmed this posture, and while themes of liberation emerged, they were set within the more strident notes of repatriation.

Chuck D suggests that black religion should contribute to the liberation of black people. Black religion expresses itself in its articulation of black identity and consciousness, and in its refusal to imitate patterns of behavior that will perpetuate the status quo. Black religion, as it seeks to advance the well-being of the black community, must reject status quo economics, politics, and social relations.[22] It is quite clear that Marley's "Redemption Song," which urges "Emancipate yourself from mental slavery," points to the need not only for emancipation from the external oppression found in Babylon but also for liberation from internal bondage and the positing of an alternative consciousness.

Richard J. Middleton, in his article "Identity and Subversion in Babylon," calls attention to reggae's focus on liberation motifs:

> Although concrete and economic oppression—including the threat of nuclear war between superpowers—is very real for Marley, he is aware that without an alternative consciousness with which to resist the "mental slavery" of the ideology *behind* the social and economic reality of oppression, it would be impossible to survive this reality (this "shitstem" or "shituation" as Peter Tosh liked to call it). So in the song "Exodus," where Marley appeals paradigmatically to the biblical memory of both the Exodus and Babylonian exile (superimposing one on the other, as is typical among Rastafarians), he focuses not only on social and economic bondage and liberation, but also on this *inner* bondage (or mental slavery) and calls the listener to self-awareness and spiritual liberation.[23]

It is clear that reggae lyrics not only are a symbol of struggle for inner and outer freedom but become a space where this struggle occurs. As the lyrics "Emancipate yourself from mental slavery" indicate, the struggle is to recover and in some cases discover our beautiful black selves. Reggae music becomes a mode of resistance against all that would encroach on the freedom of the self to affirm blackness. With Rasta artists leading the way, oppressed people in Jamaica begin to sing their way out of bondage. We sing songs of freedom such as "We refuse to be what you wanted us to be," "Open your eyes and look within," "Don't let them fool you or even try to school you," "You preacherman, don't tell me, heaven is under the earth," and "Don't forget your history." To recover our beautiful selves— including our beautiful bodies, of which we are not ashamed—means a retrieval of our Afro-Jamaican history. The history of oppression in the New World and certainly in Jamaica is one in which colonization and the domination of Babylon sought to destroy the self. The alternative consciousness that reggae lyrics posit is one that calls into question the history of violation and dehumanization that sought to tear the community and the self apart. Reggae lyrics seek to help us see ourselves for who we are, and through the recovery of African history they help renew confidence in our beautiful selves. It is no longer Babylon or our status in exile that determines what the people see and perceive but rather the new consciousness as a people now directed by "I-and-I consciousness." The self finds itself in relation to other selves and supremely in relation to Jah. This relationship of the self with other selves and Jah triggers a new social consciousness of our world—an awareness of both the divine and the demonic forces in our world. This means Rastas do not forget who they are and where they stand in the struggle because "There ain't no hiding place from the father of Creation."

It is not enough to name the pain, but we must educate for transformation of the self and the community. Reggae music becomes a strategy of resistance and transformation. It points to the necessity of self-recovery as the self is linked with other selves in an "I-and-I consciousness" and at the same time begins to posit critical consciousness as the way forward. An important focus of this "I-and-I consciousness" that Rastas sing about is the insistence that they are not objects to be manipulated or objects seeking to become subjects. Indeed, they are subjects creating a new language, subjects who are busy shaping their identity and naming their world. Perhaps one of the unintended consequences of reggae music is the ability of the artists to reach the masses with their music.

Soon more and more of Jamaica's top musicians became Rastas, and reggae, the dominant music of Jamaica, became the main vehicle of expression for the Rastafari movement. Its radical ideas were carried by radio into every home, and soon Rastafari permeated the society. Reggae singers like Marley became more than mere entertainers, they became "revolutionary workers" and representatives of Kingston's poor. "Them belly full but we hungry / A hungry mob is an angry mob / A rain a fall but the dirt it tough / A pot a cook but the food no 'nough." Sung with simplicity and the clarity of Marley's skeletal voice, those ideas were easily understood and quickly absorbed by even the most illiterate among the poor. Through music, Marley and other musicians attacked Jamaica's skinocratic system that placed whites at the top, mulattoes in the middle, and blacks nowhere.[24]

Through music, Marley and other singers awakened Jamaica's poor, who were urged to "Get up, stand up for your rights." Through music, the consciousness of the masses was raised in a way like no other medium including Christianity ever did. These musicians had the rare ability to use their lyrics to make the poor keenly aware of their situation as the poor were prodded to organize. This call to consciousness that exploded on the airwaves was presented as a right belonging to every Jamaican. The poor are no longer nobodies but are armed with these "songs of freedom" as they become agents of their own liberation. "Build your penitentiary, we build our schools," Bob Marley wailed in "Crazy Baldhead." Or as Peter Tosh wailed in his *Equal Rights* album, "We gonna stand up for our rights."

Reggae music points to a clear option for the poor and powerless. Jamaicans began to learn and to take seriously that all people including the dispossessed have inalienable rights and have a responsibility to change their world and affirm their dignity. They have a moral obligation to stand up for their rights. Marley captures this in his song "No Woman No Cry." The bottom line is that Jah is on the side of those who weep and are victimized. Jah is the one who stands up for the weak and all who are disabled. In Kingston, where Marley and most of the other singers performed, they would see each day hundreds of women who could find no employment and thousands who were landless and homeless. As far as Babylon is concerned, these people do not exist. The reggae artists cry out on their behalf, and Marley explains that "no one gives Jamaican people a chance, that's why we say the earth is corrupted and everyone has to die and leave we. . . . How long will they pressure we? We are the people who realize the place where they thieved us from, so we say, *Ah,* you took us from there, *ah,* this is what we are. But they still tell us, No, no, this is what you are! This is what you must be. . . . The greatest thing that could happen would never happen, so you could say God has we for a purpose and reason."[25]

Richard J. Middleton indicates the religious themes that he discerns are embedded in the reggae lyrics. Predictably, the central themes are exodus and exile. The central reality of Rastafari is the placement in exile since the first slave ships brought them from "their father's land" to Babylon.

> . . . the present world order as "Babylon," a system of bondage and oppression that represents everything from the West African slave trade to colonial and neocolonial class structure, racism, economic deprivation, police brutality, as well as ideological bondage or "mental slavery." In contrast to "Babylon," there is "Zion," Ethiopia, or Africa generally, which Marley calls "our Father's land" (in Exodus), to which Jah is guiding his people in a new exodus/return/repatria-

tion, led by various prophetic figures. "Give us another brother Moses," sings Marley in *Exodus*.[26]

Themes of exodus and exile are played in reggae lyrics capturing stories of God's deliverance of the Hebrew boys Shadrach, Meshach, and Abednego from the fiery furnace and of David who "with sling and stone" would slay Goliath. The genius of Bob Marley is that he does not leave his audience in ancient history as he re-tells the biblical story but contemporizes the story as he joins the historical with the contemporary and incorporates modern Jamaican heroes such as Paul Bogle and Marcus Garvey.

It is important for Marley that reggae does not neglect the history of the people and that their history is joined with the biblical history. Through reggae, Marley is able to help oppressed Jamaicans fashion their identity as they place their oppressive history in the larger context of the narrative history of the biblical story. This means, among other things, that the oppressive history of Babylon is no longer decisive in shaping the image and identity of oppressed Jamaicans. "That is, it is by the conscious 'indwelling' of a larger story of meaning, a story larger than the individual self, and beyond the confines of the dehumanizing present, that we find meaning for our lives and come to a sense of identity, in a manner that enables us to resist the dehumanization of a world system undergirded by its own large story of meta-narrative. So memory shapes identity."[27]

The appeal to biblical stories and the history of freedom fighters such as Paul Bogle and Marcus Garvey helps the Rastafari community and all the audience in Babylon to whom the music is also addressed to begin to shape an alternative identity based on songs of redemption and stories of protest and resistance. Through songs such as "Exodus, Movement of Jah's People," Rastafari and all who are willing can participate in ancient and contemporary stories as a basis for fashioning their identities. As the people discover their story, they begin to leave Babylon; they begin to recognize that their sojourn in Babylon is temporary as they discover they are meant for Zion. This is certainly another illustration of history in the service of liberation.

Another strategy of liberation in Babylon is the appeal made in reggae lyrics to the doctrine of creation. "The other strategy is by appeal to creation, specifically to God's creational intent from the beginning, which can call into question the status quo, that is, the present unjust order of things. Thus we have Marley's famous song, 'One love.' . . . The power of a creation theology to sustain hope is evident in these lines found in the very center of the song: As it was in the beginning (One love!) So shall it be in the end (One heart!)."[28] The key here is that "as it was in the beginning

Reggae and Rastafari

(One love!) so shall it be in the end (One heart!)" the purpose of creation is revisited. The purpose is one love and one heart. The point here is that the love of God, which constitutes the meaning and purpose of creation, calls the present order of injustice into question. God's love, which is the cause and reason for creation, calls into question the present order of society and presses for reconciliation, the uniting of hearts. "But 'One Love' is even more profound than this. The phrases, 'One Love!' 'One Song!' 'One Heart!' that are repeated throughout the song constitute a reiterated call to reconciliation, even with 'hopeless sinners.' Marley speaks of fighting a spiritual battle (an Armageddon) for the unification of the human race and for reconciliation with God because he does not want anyone to face judgment at the eschaton."[29] The human choice is one love and one heart because "there ain't no hiding place from the father of creation." Marley's creation theology serves as a basis for a theology of hope. There is hope for all creation because God's purpose and plan is one love and one heart and certainly one song. The song is one of exodus, people leaving oppressive traditions and histories and moving to their father's land. The basis of this hope is love, One Love rooted and grounded in God because this love provides hope for the "hopeless sinner." Love's call is identical with reconciliation.

In January 1978, Bob was approached by rival gunmen from the two main political factions in Jamaica, who came to his temporary headquarters in England with a special request. A spontaneous peace truce had broken out in the ghettoes of West Kingston, and to cement this momentous occurrence, a giant musical event called the "One Love Peace Concert" was to be held in Kingston on April 21, the twelfth anniversary of Selassie's visit. The gunmen begged Marley to return to headline the event. He did, and on that evening, under a full moon in a jammed National Stadium, he implored "the two leading people in this land to come on stage and shake hands, to show the people that you love them right, show the people that you're gonna unite!" Leaping in a frenzy, Bob forced right-wing leader Edward Seaga to shake hands in public with the socialist prime minister Michael Manley, a moment that has been immortalized in Jamaican mythology.[30]

Bob Marley was instrumental in making the call to "One Love" the basis for a peace movement in Jamaica. With the coming together of the rival factions in the political parties, new reggae songs such as "The Peace Treaty Special" and "War Is Over" became immediate favorites in Jamaica.

It is worth mentioning that the confrontation between the poor and the police did not immediately disappear. The quality of life among the poor seemed to get worse. Peter Tosh seemed to have captured the irony of both political leaders posing and seeming to advocate for peace when he exclaimed, "Me don' wan' peace . . . me want equality! I am not a politician. I jus' suffah de consequences."[31] Tosh saw through the façade and understood that peace without justice would be short-lived, and that is exactly what seemed to happen as "that September, just five months after the concert, Peter Tosh was stopped by two Kingston policemen as he was coming out of the Skateland dance hall on Half Way Tree Road. Tosh, who was smoking a spliff at the time, suffered a broken right hand, lacerations to the head, and a severely bruised right foot. Nine months after the Peace concert, Claudie Massop and two other JLP stalwarts, Trevor Tinson and Lloyd Nolan, were killed execution-style after a taxi in which they had been riding was stopped."[32]

Marley was aware that a peace concert was not enough and that years of colonial rule and oppression of poor people would not disappear overnight. What in fact the peace concert with its themes of love and peace brought to the fore was the importance of continuing the struggle and the value of using a method and mean—namely reggae—to expose the atrocities meted out to the poor and to articulate a vision of what things could look like in an independent Jamaica.

The year following the peace concert, Bob Marley dedicated an album to children titled *Children Playing in the Streets*. He sang about the plight of Jamaican children born in poverty and diminished by existence in darkness but who continued to search for the light of a new day. "The Wailers held a benefit concert in the National Heroes Arena for Rasta children on September 24, 1979. Bob previewed two songs from his forthcoming *Survival* album. . . . it was plain to the people of Jamaica that Bob was going for broke, openly lending his strenuous support to the struggle for a truly free and independent Jamaica—a struggle which could very well end with the installation of a black, Marxist government in a country that had long been dominated by right-wing colonialist white regimes."[33] With music as his weapon, Marley led a full-scale assault on the forces that kept poor children and their parents in poverty. It was clear to Marley that the forces of Babylon had conspired to keep the poor and downtrodden children oppressed. So in his *Survival* album Marley wailed, "Babylon system is the vampire, sucking the children day by day."

Marley used music to fight for children and those who were locked out of basic rights so often denied to those who struggle to keep body and

183

Reggae and Rastafari

soul together. "Bob seemed to be obsessed with the challenge of bringing together not just the increasingly divided tribes into one unified organization, but the warring political activists whose constant violent confrontations were growing in intensity and viciousness. Bob wanted to demonstrate to the people of Jamaica, and indeed throughout the world, that opposing parties could live together in peace and show respect for each other. 'God never made no difference between black, white, blue, pink or green. People is people, yuh know. That is the message we try to spread.'"[34] Marley's singing career spanned the period from 1961 to 1981. During this time, he was widely recognized as a spokesperson for Rastas and other oppressed groups in Jamaica. There were a number of Rasta women who were invaluable for Marley's success as a reggae performer, namely Rita Marley, Judy Mowatt, and Marcia Griffiths, all gifted singers in their own right.

> Dressed in long African gowns, with their heads wrapped, they toured Europe and North America with Bob Marley, always on stage with a picture of the young Haile Selassie and Marcus Garvey in the background. Bob Marley's music transcended the contradictions implicit in the attitudes of Rasta man, especially Twelve Tribes, towards their women; and this transcendence was epitomized in *No Woman No Cry*. The images of burning log wood, of the tenement yards of Western Kingston, of food of the poor—cornmeal porridge—and the hopes for the future, were expressed with such humility that this song became one of Marley's most successful singles. Throughout his career Marley continued to sing songs of love and tenderness, for, like Che Guevara, he understood that one could not aspire towards changing the world unless one were guided by the principles of love.[35]

Marley spoke from the community of the oppressed as he had been an oppressed youth himself. He was not interested in music for its own sake. Music was a tool for the liberation of oppressed poor people whether in South Africa or in Jamaica. His music gave expression to the experience of those on the margins of society, particularly the urban poor. "At other times, the music articulates 'the oppressive world and environment of the masses,' raises questions about the political and cultural integrity of the status quo, and declares their resolve to have their 'piece of the pie, right here, right now.' The African elements in the music strike responsive chords in the hearts of a people who have struggled for centuries to keep the African presence in their song. The embrace of Jamaican popular music by the masses of the poor is unreserved and enthusiastic."[36]

With the national embrace of reggae, Rastas became bearers of the cultural heritage of Jamaica. Reggae music remembered Africa and used African history as a tool for the liberation of oppressed Jamaica. Learning from the Rastas, reggae artists used their experience of suffering and victimization as the prism through which to criticize Babylon and to work for social change in Jamaica. Marley called on the exploited workers of Jamaica to take matters into their own hands. They were implored to take action to change their own lives. "The task at hand is collecting the survivors of centuries of exploitation, racism, and degeneration—people who . . . are necessarily left out of the mainstream of society. Those survivors are political revolutionaries, and Marley's Reggae invokes them to keep up the fight as the life's work of this generation. The mission of Rasta is to recreate society on a moral basis of equality."[37] No one understood better the heartbeat of the Jamaican people than Bob Marley, who had spent many years as a youth in one of the harshest ghettoes of western Kingston, Trench Town. It is not surprising then that he became a member of the Twelve Tribes. Part of Marley's attraction to the Twelve Tribes was its doctrine and ideology, and part was that it originated in Trench Town. Many middle-class Jamaicans joined this Rasta group because of Marley's affiliation with it. The central teachings of the Twelve Tribes are:

> The principal dogma . . . proclaimed that the human race was divided into twelve scattered tribes, each named for one of Jacob's sons, who Jah sent down into Egypt. Each tribe was associated with a certain month of the year, symbolized by a certain color and endowed with a secret blessing. Starting with the month of April, which was the first month of the ancient Egyptian calendar before it was corrupted by the Romans, the canon was: April—Reuben, silver; May—Simeon, gold; June—Levi, purple; July—Judah, brown; August—Issachar, yellow; September—Zebulum, pink; October—Dan, blue; November—Gad, red; December—Asher, gray; January—Naphtali, green; February—Joseph, white; March—Benjamin, black.[38]

Because Marley was born in February, he belonged to the tribe of Joseph. The members of the Twelve Tribes regard themselves as black Hebrews and organically related to the original Hebrews. That is due in part to their careful organizational structure "with a ruling council and a group of alternates consisting of twelve men and twelve women plus one—a pyramidal structure."[39] There were a number of Rastas like Mortimo Planno who complained that the attempt to provide Rastafari structure was undemocratic and went against some of their basic tenets. It is interesting that the Twelve Tribes provided space for middle-class Jamaica and several of the leading reggae singers such as Dennis Brown, Freddie McGregor, and Judy Mowatt and athletes such as Alan Cole and Rupert Hoilett to become members of the Twelve Tribes of Israel. It is therefore not surprising that the Jamaican middle-class found a home in Rastafari.

Perhaps because of this, reggae became synonymous with the best of Jamaican indigenous culture. Even the Jamaican government, which for a long time openly expressed its disdain for Rastafari and reggae, began to embrace reggae. This was a major turnaround for a government that in former years had banned several reggae songs it regarded as dangerous for the social and political ethos of the country. With a middle-class sector of Jamaica participating in the Rasta faith, with its position at the forefront of reggae lyrics, and with the masses of Jamaicans embracing reggae, even the government had to fall in line.

Some scholars contend that both political parties exploited Rastafari and identified with the ethos created by reggae-mania that swept Jamaica in the 1970s and 1980s in order to win popular support. It is not unusual in the United States to see advertisements selling Jamaica as a tourist destination introduced with reggae performers.

> With the national embrace of reggae has come the elevation of Rastas to the status of culture bearers and cultural heroes. Bob Marley, the most famous exponent of reggae music, exemplifies this elevation. ... With Marley's international success, the society came to embrace him as a cultural hero and Reggae music as Jamaica's contribution to the world. Any lingering doubt concerning Marley's status dissipated when he was awarded the Order of Merit, Jamaica's third-highest honor, and was further granted the respect of a state funeral at his premature death. For a man who had made a career of "wailing" against the system and who once sang "mi no have no friend inna high society," these were incredible honors.[40]

The outpouring of affection for the man who taught Jamaica to practice "One Love" and in its search for reconciliation to seek "One Heart" and to sing "One Song" indicates the long way Rastafari and reggae had journeyed to lead Jamaica out of traditions of exploitation and self-abnegation. At Marley's funeral on May 21, 1981, all of Jamaica turned out to pay their last respects. The leaders of both political parties eulogized him as one who did not merely entertain but sought to call Jamaica to its best self:

> According to Seaga, "his music did more than entertain. He translated into music, in a remarkable style, the aspirations, pain and feel-

ing of millions of people throughout the world. As an individual, Bob Marley was the embodiment of discipline and he personified hard work and determination to reach all his goals. He left us with a rich heritage of popular Jamaican music." Manley was equally eloquent: "He is a genius. He is one of those extraordinary figures that . . . comes along perhaps once in a generation; who, starting with a folk art, a folk form, by some inner magic of commitment, sincerity of passion and of just skill, turns it into part of the universal language of the arts of the world."[41]

Millions of Jamaicans who embraced the culture of silence because of severe sufferings and feelings of alienation broke through hopelessness and pain as reggae offered them a voice to express suffering and hope for a better life. Reggae offered oppressed Jamaicans a language that led them out of their lack of awareness of their own suffering and helped create sensitivity to the suffering of others. There are times when suffering numbs one to one's own pain and anguish. This undoubtedly was the situation of many Jamaicans, especially those in western Kingston who lived in Trench Town, about which Marley sings when he wails, "No Woman No Cry." Reggae music could lead the oppressed out of poverty because it presented an alternative to Babylon. Marley views his music as one way of "resisting against the system." Marley points out that "sometimes you have to fight with music."[42] Bunny Wailer, one of the founding members of the Wailers, indicates that the power with which Rastas are able to use music as a weapon comes from Jah: "The Bible says that the singers went before, and the players of instruments followed after . . . so it's a whole spiritual order, where angels sing, and then we carry out that message, so it's something more than just Bob Marley . . . or the Wailers. It's the most High, Ras Tafari."[43]

Perhaps this notion that the power that suffuses the music comes from Jah is one reason reggae music has endured. Jamaicans share this sense of the divine source and focus of music. There is a sense in the populace that Marley's music was the ordained channel through which was expressed the power that critiques the ways of Babylon and at the same time articulates a hope for the future. It is clear that the one gift the oppressor could not steal from the oppressed was their song, whose reach was beyond the oppressor. Or so it was in the beginning of slavery in the New World. Africans stolen from their homes were stripped of many of their cultural traditions and in many instances denuded of their dignity. But the master could not steal from the slave his/her song. Whether the slave worked in the home or in the field, he/she would sing their "songs of freedom." Marley echoes this in his album *Redemption Song,* in which he points out that when black people were sold into slavery, all they ever had were their songs of freedom. This was all they ever needed because the song had salvific power.

What occurred in slavery is repeated in contemporary Jamaica. In present-day Jamaica, or Babylon, the oppressed are buffeted by psychological and sociological oppression that renders them mute and unable to understand their suffering. They often are resigned to live in a state of violence and oppression because of ignorance or because they are numbed by poverty. They lack an awareness of their own suffering and therefore feel no desire to transform their world. In this world of suffering and oppression, many lose their voice. The poor become mute, submissive, and powerless. It is precisely at this point and in this context that the reggae artist cries out in lament, invoking the help of Jah to empower the songs of freedom to point the people out of bondage and toward freedom. The oppressed, as they claim reggae music and discover their own song, begin to press for change internally as they "emancipate themselves from mental slavery" or as they hear the reggae artist wailing "wake up and live." The call embodied in the song is for the poor to wake up from apathy, the sense of being beaten down so badly by the economic and political system that nothing really matters. People often decline to vote when they feel that the political process offers nothing more than replacing one set of devils with another. Why participate? But the song of freedom means that as the people find their voice they "chant down Babylon." They wail against the system; they enter into solidarity as they wail about exodus, the movement of Jah's people from oppression to liberation. Marley understood his music as a "sermon" for freedom. Freedom was not merely the removal of physical chains because Marley indicated that in many instances the chains were removed from people's feet only to be placed in their minds. There are different kinds of chains. Poverty, for example, is one chain that reggae music means to break. Marley would wail, "Them Belly Full But We Hungry." There is a definite hope in reggae music, a hope that is expressed in the amazing album *Exodus*: "We are leaving Babylon, we are going to our father land." This is possible because Jah has come to break the back of "downpression," to wipe away transgression and to set the captive free. The power of the song resides in Jah's decision to make the song live.

Conclusion: Identity and Salvation

The Rastas have been at the forefront of groups in Jamaica that have challenged certain aspects of capitalism, racism, colonialism, and imperialism throughout Jamaican society. Over against these forms of injustice they have proffered an alternative vision of solidarity and social justice that is reflected in their understanding of the self and its relationship to community. There has continued to emerge over the years a tension between their understanding of the individual and the group. A rugged independence of thought and outlook is emblematic of the Rastas' approach to community as the true Rasta refuses to surrender his or her personal identity.

At a conference on religion and poverty in Kingston in July 2003, Tekla Mekfet, a prominent Rasta, addressed the issue of personal power in Rastafari. When asked to speak of his own identity in relationship to Rastafari, he was emphatic that each Rasta possesses the truth and does not need to belong to any group or to follow anyone. "Rastas are not followers," he said. "Each Rasta is divinely guided by Jah. . . . The story of Jesus is a story of deference to the Father. As one makes a house to live in, so Jah made Rastafari to dwell in." According to Tekla Mekfet, because the divine indwells Rastas there is no need for them to look outside of the existential relationship between each Rasta and Jah. The church or religious community is needed by persons who have not responded fully to the divine within. As one occupies a house, so does Jah occupy the heart of the Rasta. Guidance and a sense of "I-and-I consciousness" are realized as Rastas enter into fellowship and conversations and occasions for reasoning with Jah. Although there are Christian believers who share with Rastas the views that God indwells the human heart and that communion with the divine within is essential for guidance and direction, one profound distinction between Christian and Rastafari perspectives is that the Christian makes this claim from within the community called church. Even when the Christian makes the claim that all she or he needs is God from the quiet of the home, the church is presupposed. The Christian sentiment presupposes that in this relationship with the beyond who resides within, the church is a necessity. The converse is the case for Rastas.

The solidarity and unity among Rastas is realized in doctrinal positions, ritual practice, and their identification with the poor. All Rastas affirm the divinity of the black man from Ethiopia, Haile Selassie, and assert the priority of repatriation to Ethiopia. While not all Rastas smoke ganja (as some Rastas are unable to smoke for health reasons) or wear the dreadlocks, they nonetheless recognize the importance of these symbolic gestures for the faith. The refusal to be a follower of anyone, according to Tekla Mekfet, or to belong to any one group is an important area in which Rastafari differentiates itself from the Christian church, where there is a priority of community in relationship to the individual. The Christian's identity is inseparable from the community called church.

There is no such thing as a solitary Christian. One becomes a Christian with others. Rastas argue that the others they require are not necessarily a specific organization or community such as the church. Rather, they find solidarity with the poor or the community of oppressed persons.

One becomes a Rasta in relationship with Jah. This is an aspect of their interpretation of "I-and-I consciousness," the basis for an awakening that occurs in each individual Rasta as she or he experiences a rebirth through an existential relationship with Jah. Although Rastas do not use the Christian metaphor of being "born again," they speak of this awakening that becomes the basis of their identity as "sonship" and "daughtership." The true Rasta is born of God.

In the search for identity, Rastas seek to preserve their distinctiveness over against Babylon. It is important that they are "in the world but not of the world," that their identity is independent. This is certainly one area in which the Christian church in Jamaica could learn from Rastafari. Although Rastas claim they are not owned by any community or organization, it is indisputable that they belong to the community of the disinherited. In their resistance to becoming a community like the church in Jamaica or like the Christian church as they know it, they have become a community of the dispossessed that is constituted of all who protest against the ways of Babylon. Through their lifestyle and refusal to ape the ways of Babylon, they express solidarity with all who are locked out of opportunities for social advancement as they fashion an oppositional identity in relation to Babylonian culture. Rastas voluntarily practice a kind of self-emptying, believing that in the emptying of self they discover a new self. The passage from Luke that asserts that "Whoever seeks to gain his or her life will lose it, but who ever loses his or her life will preserve it" (17:33) has been a cardinal principle for Rastafari. It is by turning their backs on all that is alien to them in Babylon—political conflict, the preoccupation with materialism, and the lifestyle presented by American television and tourists—that they begin to claim an oppositional identity. This is in stark contrast to the prosperity gospel that is sweeping the United States and has come to Jamaica through cable television. Ian Boyne, Jamaican theologian and political reporter, puts the problem in perspective:

> The Christianity which is really "running things" in Jamaica today is the "Bling-bling" Christianity. Through the widespread penetration of cable television and the existence of *Love TV,* Jamaicans are exposed to a brand of North American Christianity which is promoting a very jaundiced view of the gospel. It is called the health and wealth gospel and it teaches that prosperity is a divine right that is promised to every believer. Only those who do not have faith can't pay their rent, send their children to school and pay their utility bills. . . . I remember . . . [an American pastor] saying that when the Bible says people must see your faith, it means they must see your Benz, Rolls Royce, mansion on the hill. "It is tangible things the Lord is talking about, folks. Things that worldly people can see and know that you are blessed," he said to cheering thousands in the gigantic auditorium.[1]

The Rastas help raise pertinent questions such as these for themselves and the Christian church: What does solidarity with the least of these look like? What does it mean to find the courage to be different from the ways of Babylon? What should Christian identity look like, and to whom do we turn for an alternative vision? While established churches tend to enter into solidarity with authority and status figures of law and order in the society, Rastas identify with the least of these. "I sometimes look at the palpably poor people who are sitting in some of these Jamaican congregations shown on television, while the expensively dressed Pastor or Bishop preaches his prosperity Gospel, and I wonder how these people many of whom don't have a bus fare to go home and have to be at church for early service to hide from the landlord and have to depend on church charity for lunch and dinner that Sunday, feel about this. . . . Where is the radical obedience called for in the Gospel? Where is the self-denial, the taking up of the Cross? Where are the hard sayings of Jesus?"[2]

Theologian Boyne is helpful to both Christians and the Rastas in suggesting that what is at stake is not merely the identity of individuals—be they Rastas or Christians—but also the identity of the community, Rastafari or Christian. While Rastas do not focus on the man from Nazareth who died on the cross, they have an outline for a theology of the cross as they focus on the black man from Ethiopia whom they claim is Christ returned. The blackness of this man, imbued with divinity, functions as a cross for all who come in contact with this blackness.

In Jamaica, to embrace blackness is to be marginalized and thereby counted among the Rastas. Because they experience Jamaica as Babylon, they are in exile in their own home. In the context of alienation, they seek to discover their identity. Perhaps because members of the Jamaican church do not have this experience of being in exile in their own home they do not feel the need to search for their identity. According to Boyne, the Jamaican church is in danger of forgetting the crucified Jesus of Nazareth and losing its identity in relationship to the cross.

Rastas' determination to preserve their identity and integrity in the midst of Babylonian exile becomes a criticism of the dominant society and the dominant church. Rastas protest against economic, religious, political, and social institutions they experience as cruel and unjust. In their eagerness to preserve identity, Rastas choose religion over politics as they look toward Jah's victory over the oppressive forces of Babylon. Unlike their forebears of the Native Baptist Church, "Daddy" Sharp and Paul Bogle, who joined political and religious commitment, Rastas tend to separate themselves from organizations and institutions and do not yet consider political and social commitment as a crucial or even necessary way of transforming life in Babylon. Their religious commitment impels them to look to Jah, who with lightning and thunder will destroy Babylon.

This remains the overarching guideline for Rasta theory and practice. This self-distancing from the very participation in Jamaican political life and institutions that is crucial for the political and social health of Jamaica indicates how profoundly the Rastafari have been damaged by and alienated from the conditions they decry in Jamaica. Rastas seem to contend that self-repair and the return of self-esteem to Rastafari necessitate a separation from institutional Jamaican life. Such involvement would signal a new day for Rastas in the creation of societal Jamaican laws through the political system as well as engagement in this enforcement. This, however, is theoretically impossible for Rastas as they see the political realm in Jamaica as a continuation of the colonial way of life.

This distancing from the political and social realms raises the critical question of how deeply African roots and an African way of life are grounded in Rastafari. It is no secret that African cosmology and anthropology do not make the arbitrary distinctions that Rastas make between religious commitment and social and political commitments. For Africans, the religious and political are unified, not separate. This also raises a more difficult question: In what sense is Rastafari an African-derived religion? Is African-ness for Rastafari to be understood primarily in terms of repatriation to Ethiopia and the divinity of Haile Selassie? These are difficult questions; however, we must acknowledge that Rastas participate in the general society, if often informally, through mediums such as Rasta schools, the arts, and business.

At a conference on "Rastafari Global Reasoning" at the University of the West Indies in Kingston, Jamaica, Sister Andrea Davis, one of the Rastafarian facilitators, stated, "Technology can be bought, but culture must be created." This was a definitive focus at the conference. Two panelists "concentrated on turning the business of Rasta, which is being conducted mostly by people outside the movement, into returns for Rastas. Ras Sekou Tafari pointed out that while Rasta items manufactured in Taiwan and other places continue to generate huge revenues, there are Rasta elders dying for want of money to do a simple hernia operation."[3] The view that emerged at the conference was that Rastas need to change their attitude regarding money as many Rastas were hurting for lack of basic amenities including health care and proper housing. Ras Sekou Tafari concluded: "People say money is the root of all evil. If I never have money, how I would have access to come to Jamaica. Money is the root of all business and man needs roots."[4] The consensus of the conference (which I attended) was the immediate need for Rastas to benefit financially from their own culture and stop supporting capitalist exploitation of Rasta culture. Rastas acknowledged that as their identity and culture become commercialized—when, for example, blackness is marketed as a popular hairstyle—this misuse divorces them from their theology. I noted earlier that dreadlocks were intended to inspire *dread* among the brokers of power in the wider society. But such an effect is undercut when Rastafari identity and culture become pawns of the global market, and when the purchase of dreadlocks is thought to confer Rasta identity.

Sister Andrea Davis suggested an approach that would facilitate Rastas benefiting from their own culture—the creation of "a Rastafari Truth Center . . . as well as a Rasta system of education 'because our youth must be anchored in their heritage in order to maintain their identity in the face of cable, travel and tourism.'"[5] The focus on the Truth Center and the press for Rastafari youth to be anchored in their heritage was not yet an attempt to transform Babylon. This inward turn raised the question of how Rastas may benefit from an exploited culture and how to protect their young people from cable, travel, and tourism.

In a context in which Rastas are often viewed as nonpersons and their contributions in the wider society are often seen as inconsequential, the issue of identity becomes pressing. This is why Sister Davis admonished the conference on "Global Reasoning" that Rasta youth must be anchored in their heritage to maintain their identity, which connects with their African heritage, and this, Sister Davis declared, must be taught. This has been a consistent theme over the seventy years of Rastafari. To be a Rasta is to identify one's self in relation to Africa. To be a Rasta is to accept one's African-ness and accept the black man from Ethiopia as Christ returned. To be a Rasta is to be homeless and alien in your own home as the true Rasta looks toward Ethiopia. This tension is never relaxed. Rastas' presence is a criticism of life in Babylon.

Their presence is also a criticism of the church in Jamaica. Rastas complain that Christians have made peace with Babylon and have surrendered to Babylonian captivity. The posture of the Christian church in Jamaica differs quite clearly from that of Rastafari. While Rastas are resigned to allow Babylon to continue in its path of destruction, the Christian church is committed to economic, political, and social transformation. Boyne elaborates:

> There are some sects and others called cults which teach that God is not really concerned about changing the world now. He is simply interested in providing "witness and warning" and in taking out a few of the chosen remnant. But the mainline churches, many in the evangelical movement and the charismatics whose influence in Jamaica is the most decisive today, believe that God is interested in transforming society now and bringing about the Kingdom of God on earth today. . . . Christians must not be separatists and quietists. They must be active change agents in society; they must be the salt of the earth transforming its people, institutions and governments.[6]

The critical question for me is whether or not this bears out in praxis. Rastas view church as one of those unjust institutions in league with Babylon. Through language, symbols, and rituals, they have fashioned an alternative model of identification, liberation, and solidarity. Rastas fear the institutionalizing of their faith, which when co-opted becomes "Babylonian captivity." That is, they fear that their faith will become co-opted in the general culture and become a representation of Babylon.

Critical for the Rastas is their connection between knowledge and salvation, which comes from the knowledge of God's identity. To know God and to respond to God with one's whole life is to be saved. "God came to set the captive free throughout the entire earth. And all who know that he is the high Rastafari then they too shall have access to the tree of life, regardless of what nation, what nationality, what tongue they may be."[7] This claim holds out hope for humankind since all have access to the tree of life. Rastas portend that poor people have a decided advantage since they are forced to look within and confront themselves. According to Rastafari, one finds God when one looks within. Since life in Babylon does not allow time or space for introspection, those held in captivity miss true knowledge as they fail to meet the God within. "Although every person is called to know God, the poor people have a decided advantage in the Rastas' view, since they are forced to look into themselves and confront the basic reality of human existence—and only there can God be found. 'It is only the suffering people can know Jah. There's no time for the rich person to know Jah. He's got his big business and establishment, which is taking all his time. He knows not even how to pray.'"[8]

It is precisely at this point that Rastas make room for persons who need the church, or, more precisely, for those in search of knowledge who have not yet found it. "Those who have already reached true knowledge need not bother with the church: 'The church in Jamaica is for the people who didn't know the King. But I-n-I from long time know the King and doesn't need to join the church.' Another Rasta expressed the same truth when he quoted Paul to the effect that when he was a child, he did the things of a child, but now that he is adult, he puts away the things of a child, namely, organized religion and the 'beliefs' that go with it, for now he has true knowledge."[9] The Rastas are correct in pointing to the limits of organized religion and its preoccupation with beliefs. In this regard, the church needs to become active in joining God in ministries of liberation. Simply stated, we need to spend more time talking about the realm of God and a little less time with organized religion.

Rastas also served us well in making the connection between knowledge and salvation. They seem to indicate God has taken the initiative and freely made known the divine identity in each person's heart. They assert that the knowledge of God is inborn in all people. The Rastas need to go further, however, in placing primacy on salvation rather than on knowledge. Rastas seem to ask, as their sessions in reasoning attest, what *must* I know? This is not the emphasis of Scripture. On the contrary, Scripture directs one to *becoming* and to *doing*. The central questions are: Who must I become and what must I do to be saved? (See Mark 10:17; John 3:3). The sessions in Rasta reasoning seem to focus on truth as intellectual assent rather than truth as sharing in the divine life and identity. In revelation God goes beyond sharing truths about God-self or offering information about the divine self—God gives God-self to us.

With the connection of knowledge and salvation, *who must I become?* is the first question that confronts us in Scripture. We must acknowledge that Rastas seek knowledge of God. They enjoin us to look within because God indwells us as one occupies a house. When the Scriptures speak of the knowledge of God, they point to the saving knowledge of God—the freeing knowledge of God from Babylonian captivity, the esteeming knowledge of God that makes us whole, that gives peace with blackness and fulfills us in relation to God and others.

The second question—*what must I do to be saved?*—critiques Rastafari theology as this theology presupposes God will transform Babylon in God's own time. A part of the problem, theologically, is that Rastas have not come to the awareness that God not only reveals God's saving knowledge in their hearts but God also reveals God's will. The awareness of this divine knowledge prompts us to ask *what must I become?* The awareness of the divine will impels us to ponder what I must *do* to be saved.

The first response is that our salvation is tied up with others. Rastas need to become cognizant of the enormous endeavors required to release women from the shackles of subjugation and second-class citizenship within Rastafari. Salvation within Rastafari must be inclusive of men and women. One ideological basis for Rastafari's neglect of women is their lack of attention toward the question of salvation. It seems to me that it becomes important for Rastas to assert that the relationship with Jah who indwells their hearts allows them to view the world, including their relationship with women, from a different place. This new place from which they view the world is certainly not Babylon. It is "Zion," or "Ethiopia," the place in Rasta theology where the ways and practices of Babylon have no currency. This new vantage point means that they cannot relate to others, be they men or women, along the traditional lines of Babylon. In Babylon, it is fashionable for masters to keep slaves and for men to lord authority over women. This new spiritual location gives or should give a new posture and a new angle of vision from which Rastas observe or recognize each other. This new place should provide the impetus for Rastas to be inwardly free and outwardly committed to the liberation of Jamaica. It is precisely at this point that we begin to discover, whether as Christians or Rastas, that our salvation is inextricably linked. Here we begin to hope for a new Jamaica as we work in making this a reality in our time.

Rastas' preoccupation with knowledge for knowledge's sake has not expanded their search for identity. There has been a tendency to identify Rasta primarily in terms of maleness and secondarily in terms of femaleness. *What must I do to be saved?* Join Jah in Jah's saving work as you empower women to take their rightful place in Rastafari. Needless to say this critique of Rastafari also can be applied to the Christian church in Jamaica. The church needs to be free from excessive concern with self, from paralyzing fears and the necessity to justify self before others. Whether Rasta or Christian, we need to be free to share ourselves with each other in love, to seek others' good as well as our own. This means we must take the next step and identify with the oppressed and anxious as we participate in causes that seek justice and peace.

Rastas must also partner in salvific participation with active sharing in the liberation of Jamaica—joining liberation with repatriation. If Rastas would struggle with *what Jah is up to in the world,* they might begin to provide answers for their own participation in making Jamaica a more human place. As Rastas continue to struggle with the question of who they have become, the journey should not stop there. They must go on to ask what actions are consistent with their new identity and what actions least violate their integrity. Rastas love to interpret what is going on in the world. Their challenge is to change the world. The challenge that confronted the trailblazers of Rastafari in the nineteenth century as they used the Native Baptist Church as a trade union organization and a center for political strategy still faces Rastafari in the twenty-first century. The challenge that faced our forebears after emancipation was how to translate the newly won freedom into a new society in which the peasantry would have basic human rights accorded them. The challenge was revisited in 1938 as the country erupted in political turmoil in the search for the enfranchisement of the people with the right to vote and to determine their political destiny. This quest for political freedom and economic security came full circle in 1962 when Jamaica gained independence from Great Britain. Then Jamaica through its political and civic leaders promised the people freedom from the ravages of poverty, crime, and disease. In the twenty-first century, as the population of the unemployed, the homeless, and the indigent continues to grow, it is clear Jamaica has not delivered on this promise. The forfeiture of the promise of liberation at our national independence in 1962 raises afresh for us as a central question: What is Jah up to in Jamaica? The challenge is to join Jah. Perhaps the Rastas could lead a new exodus out of crime, poverty, disease, and traditions that diminish the human spirit. Together with the Rastas we join Jah, we exult, "Exodus, movement of Jah's people!"

Glossary

Babylon: A Rasta term used to denote the oppressive colonial conditions that characterize Jamaica and the Western world.

Bedwardism: Beliefs and practices of Alexander Bedward, a revivalist preacher in the 1890s and early twentieth century.

Bobo: Led by Prince Emmanuel Edwards, this group of Rastas continues to live as a community outside of Kingston.

Chalice: Name for pipe used in the ceremonial smoking of ganja.

Chillum Pipe: Pipe used for the smoking of ganja. The practice was derived from the East Indian culture.

Churchical: The opposite of "political," refers to the development of religious consciousness.

Convince: Afro-Jamaican religious group.

Downpression: Rasta word for "oppression."

Dreadlocks: Matted hair that became a symbol of Rastafari in the 1940s.

Dungle: Rasta community located in the inner-city ghetto.

Duppy: Spirit of the dead that has power to scare or harm.

Ganja: Rasta term for marijuana.

Grounding, Groundation: The coming together of Rastas for discussion that usually includes smoking of ganja.

House of Nyabinghi: An informal annual assembly of elders who plan activities and are available to settle conflicts.

"I-and-I": An expression used in place of the first-person singular or plural. It points to the harmony between the human and the divine in Rasta consciousness.

Ital: A term for "natural," especially with regard to foods and their relationship with the environment.

Jah: Rasta term for God, often used in reference to Haile Selassie.

Jah Rastafari: Reference to Haile Selassie as God.

King of King's People: Early designation of Rastafari.

Kumina: Afro-Jamaican religious expression.

Livity: Rasta lifestyle based on adherence to strict dietary customs and respect for the environment.

Maroons: Escaped slaves and their descendants who own communities independent of the plantocracy.

Myal: African-derived religious expression that provided a basis for the Native Baptist and the Revivalist movement in Jamaica.

Nyabinghi: The term was first used to mean "death to white oppressors"; it is also used for dances at special events.

Obeah: The practice of using fetishes, oils, and other substances for individual ends.

Pinnacle: A commune established by the founder of Rastafari, Leonard Howell, on an abandoned plantation.

Ras Tafari: Term for Prince Tafari, crowned Emperor Haile Selassie I, in November 1930.

Reasonings: Gatherings for informal discussion accompanied by the smoking of ganja.

Reggae: Jamaican music popularized by Bob Marley.

Repatriation: The belief that all black people should return to Africa or, more specifically, to Ethiopia.

Sistren: A term for Rastafari women.

Twelve Tribes: Middle-class Rastafari community headed by Prophet Gad.

Youth Black Faith: Rastafari community founded in 1949 to purge Rastafari of revivalist and obeah practices.

Notes

Chapter 1. Rastafari Theology

1. Hill, "Dread History," 43–44.
2. Edmonds, *Rastafari*, 37.
3. Patterson, *The Children of Sisyphus*, 48–49.
4. Barrett, *Soul-Force*, 64–65.
5. M. G. Lewis, *Journal of a West Indian Proprietor*, 126.
6. Ibid.
7. Barrett, *Soul-Force*, 66–67.
8. Lawson, *Religion and Race*, 25.
9. George Blythe quoted in Dianne Stewart, "The Evolution of African–Derived Religions in Jamaica," 40.
10. Curtin, *Two Jamaicas*, 33.
11. Ibid. The practice of having class leaders still occurs in Jamaica. Some years ago when I pastored a congregation in rural Jamaica, several of my deacons functioned as class leaders. They would conduct funerals, discipline wayward members, and christen babies. The truth is that they had much more power than I had in relation to the congregation.
12. Ibid., 33–34.
13. Ibid., 34.
14. Robert J. Stewart, *Religion and Society in Post-Emancipation Jamaica*, 124–25.
15. Lawson, *Religion and Race*, 31.
16. Robert J. Stewart, *Religion and Society in Post-Emancipation Jamaica*, 123.
17. Ibid., 129.
18. Bennett and Sherlock, *The Story of the Jamaican People*, 212.
19. Ibid., 213.
20. Ibid., 214.

21. Ibid.

22. Curtin, *Two Jamaicas*, 86.

23. Bennett and Sherlock, *The Story of the Jamaican People*, 216.

24. Hinton, *Memoirs of William Knibb*, 118.

25. Munroe and Robotham, *Struggles of the Jamaican People*, 16.

26. Bennett and Sherlock, *The Story of the Jamaican People*, 226–27.

27. Phillippo, *Jamaica: Its Past and Present State*, 169.

28. Ibid., 171, 175.

29. Curtin, *Two Jamaicas*, 101.

30. Ibid., 106.

31. Ibid., 158.

32. Ibid., 160.

33. Ibid., 158.

34. Ibid., 169–70.

35. Ibid., 174.

36. Robert J. Stewart, *Religion and Society in Post-Emancipation Jamaica*, 75.

37. Ibid., 77.

38. Ibid., 101.

39. Russell, "Reactions of the Baptist Missionary Society," 600.

40. Bennett and Sherlock, *The Story of the Jamaican People*, 260.

41. Barrett, *Soul-Force*, 115.

42. Raboteau, *Slave Religion*, 28.

43. Beckwith, *Black Roadways*, 168.

44. Ibid., 347.

45. Rupert Lewis, *Marcus Garvey*, 35.

46. Ibid., 38.

47. Amy Jacques Garvey, ed., *Philosophy and Opinions of Marcus Garvey*, 1:121.

48. Jubulani Tafari, "The Rastafari: Successors of Marcus Garvey," 11.

49. Barrett, *Soul-Force*, 130.

50. Bennett and Sherlock, *The Story of the Jamaican People*, 295.

51. Barrett, *Soul-Force*, 135–36.

52. Bennett and Sherlock, *The Story of the Jamaican People*, 301.

53. Amy Jacques Garvey, *Philosophy and Opinions of Marcus Garvey*, 1:24.

54. Ibid., 1:44.

55. Amy Jacques Garvey, *Garvey and Garveyism*, 134.

56. Ibid.

57. Wilmore, *Black Religion and Black Radicalism*, 208.

58. Rupert Lewis, *Marcus Garvey*, 89.

59. Ibid., 90.

60. Ibid.

61. Ibid., 91.

62. Ibid., 172.

63. William F. Lewis, *Soul Rebels*, 5.

64. Sunshine, *The Caribbean: Survival, Struggle, and Sovereignty,* 41.

Chapter 2. The Social Context

1. William Lewis, *Soul Rebels,* 5.
2. Ibid., 5–6.
3. Sunshine, *The Caribbean: Survival, Struggle, and Sovereignty,* 38.
4. Burton, *Afro-Creole,* 123, 125.
5. Ibid., 125.
6. Nettleford, *Mirror, Mirror: Identity, Race, and Protest in Jamaica,* 47–48.
7. Lake, *Rastafari Women,* 37.
8. Burton, *Afro-Creole,* 126.
9. Bennett and Sherlock, *The Story of the Jamaican People,* 396.
10. Williams, "The Seven Principles of Rastafari," 16–22.
11. Ibid., 17.
12. Ibid., 18.
13. Burton, *Afro-Creole,* 129–30.
14. The Rastas give special significance to the King James Version of the Bible, but they do not accord all Scriptures equal weight. Particular significance is given to the Old Testament and apocalyptic passages in the New Testament.
15. Scott, *The Sons of Sheba's Race,* 22.
16. Williams, "The Seven Principles of Rastafari," 20.
17. Ibid., 21.
18. Lake, *Rastafari Women,* 59.
19. Ibid., 61.
20. Rowe, "Gender and Family Relations in Rastafari," 73.
21. Ibid., 75.
22. Ibid.
23. Ibid., 77.
24. Ibid., 79.
25. Ibid., 80.
26. Rowe, "The Woman in Rastafari," 141.
27. Brathwaite, *The Development of Creole Society in Jamaica 1770–1820,* 167.

Chapter 3. The Origins of Rastafari

1. Barrett, *Soul-Force,* 157–58.
2. Chevannes, *Rastafari Roots and Ideology,* 122.
3. Ibid.
4. Ibid.
5. Barrett, *The Rastafarians,* 88.
6. Chevannes, *Rastafari Roots and Ideology,* 123–24.
7. Barrett, *The Rastafarians,* 87.
8. Simpson, "Personal Reflections on Rastafari in West Kingston in the Early 1950s," 223.

9. Chevannes, *Rastafari Roots and Ideology*, 125.

10. Ibid., 126.

11. Ibid.

12. Ibid., 127.

13. Ibid., 128.

14. Owens, *Dread: The Rastafarians of Jamaica*, 80.

15. Murrell, Spencer, and McFarlane, eds., *Chanting Down Babylon*, 327.

16. Owens, *Dread: The Rastafarians of Jamaica*, 37.

17. Barrett, *The Rastafarians*, 80–81.

18. Chevannes, *Rastafari and Other African-Caribbean Worldviews*, 9.

19. Owens, *Dread: The Rastafarians of Jamaica*, 91–92.

20. Hill, "Dread History," 43–44.

21. Owens, *Dread: The Rastafarians of Jamaica*, 98.

22. Barrett, *The Rastafarians*, 119.

23. Owens, *Dread: The Rastafarians of Jamaica*, 39–40.

24. Ibid., 41–42.

25. Cashmore, *Rastaman*, 173.

26. Barrett, *The Rastafarians*, 104–5.

27. Chevannes, *Rastafari and Other African-Caribbean Worldviews*, 27–28.

28. Nettleford, *Mirror Mirror: Identity, Race, and Protest in Jamaica*, 43–44.

29. Bennett and Sherlock, *The Story of the Jamaican People*, 398.

30. Nettleford, *Mirror, Mirror: Identity, Race, and Protest in Jamaica*, 44.

31. Ibid., 45.

32. Edmonds, *Rastafari*, 85.

33. Ibid., 85.

34. Ibid., 86.

35. Ibid., 87.

36. Nettleford, *Mirror, Mirror: Identity, Race, and Protest in Jamaica*, 64–65.

37. Ibid., 65.

38. Nettleford, "Discourse on Rastafarian Reality," 315.

39. Campbell, *Rasta and Resistance*, 115.

40. Owens, *Dread: The Rastafarians of Jamaica*, 63.

41. Wilmore, *Black Religion and Black Radicalism*, 202–3.

42. Angell, *Bishop Henry McNeal Turner and African-American Religion in the South*, 261.

43. Paget Henry quoted in Gordon, *Existence in Black*, 161.

44. Owens, *Dread: The Rastafarians of Jamaica*, 47.

Chapter 4. Organization and Ethos

1. Chevannes, "New Approach to Rastafari," in *Rastafari and Other African-Caribbean Worldviews*, ed. Chevannes, 33.

2. Ibid., 29.

3. In his chapter on "Roots Christianity," William David Spencer suggests that

Rastas will have to deal with Trinity and by implication spirit because the name of their Messiah, Haile Selassie, means "power of the Trinity." I believe this is a rather abstract way of getting at Trinity and spirit. The Rastas are more practical people. See William David Spencer, *Dread Jesus*, 125–30.

4. Edmonds, "The Structure and Ethos of Rastafari," 350.

5. Ibid., 351.

6. Ibid.

7. Cashmore, *Rastaman*, 128.

8. Owens, *Dread: The Rastafarians of Jamaica*, 144.

9. Ibid., 145.

10. Ibid., 146.

11. Ibid., 148.

12. Chevannes, *Rastafari and Other African-Caribbean Worldviews*, 60.

13. Owens, *Dread: The Rastafarians of Jamaica*, 140–41.

14. Chevannes, *Rastafari and Other African-Caribbean Worldviews*, 145.

15. Edmonds, *Rastafari*, 60.

16. Owens, *Dread: The Rastafarians of Jamaica*, 160.

17. Edmonds, "The Structure and Ethos of Rastafari," 355.

18. Bilby, "The Holy Herb: Notes on the Background of Cannabis in Jamaica," 73.

19. Ibid., 74.

20. Owens, *Dread: The Rastafarians of Jamaica*, 162.

21. Ibid., 163.

22. Chevannes, "The Origin of the Dreadlocks," in *Rastafari and Other African-Caribbean Worldviews*, ed. Chevannes, 78.

23. Ibid., 79.

24. Owens, *Dread: The Rastafarians of Jamaica*, 164.

25. Ibid., 165.

26. Campbell, *Rasta and Resistance*, 106–7.

27. Ibid., 108–9.

28. Chevannes, *Rastafari Roots and Ideology*, 146.

29. Murrell and Burchell, "Rastafari's Messianic Ideology and Caribbean Theology of Liberation," 392.

30. Campbell, *Rasta and Resistance*, 96.

31. Ibid., 99–100.

32. Ibid., 100.

33. Owens, *Dread: The Rastafarians of Jamaica*, 154.

34. Chevannes, *Rastafari and Other African-Caribbean Worldviews*, 101.

35. Chevannes, *Rastafari Roots and Ideology*, 158.

36. Campbell, *Rasta and Resistance*, 94.

37. Ibid., 95.

38. Edmonds, *Rastafari*, 58–59.

39. Owens, *Dread: The Rastafarians of Jamaica*, 155.

40. Ibid.

41. Lake, *Rastafari Women*, 109.

42. Chevannes, *Rastafari Roots and Ideology*, 176–77.

43. Lake, *Rastafari Women*, 95.

44. Ibid.

45. See Grant, "CH 661: Theology of the Black Church," research paper, Candler School of Theology, Pitts Theology Library, Emory University, Atlanta, 16–18.

46. Lake, *Rastafari Women*, 3–4.

47. Cone, *Black Theology and Black Power*, 31–32.

Chapter 5. Using Garvey to Go beyond Garvey

1. Garvey quoted in Rupert Lewis, *Marcus Garvey*, 20–21.

2. Ibid., 22.

3. Ibid., 27.

4. Ibid., 28.

5. Amy Jacques Garvey, *Garvey and Garveyism*, 7.

6. Ibid., 8.

7. Ibid., 9.

8. Ibid., 11–12.

9. Rupert Lewis, "Marcus Garvey and the Early Rastafarians: Continuity and Discontinuity," 145–46.

10. Ibid., 150–51.

11. Ibid., 151.

12. Ibid., 152–53.

13. Ibid., 153.

14. Cashmore, *Rastaman*, 23–24.

15. Ibid., 29.

16. Ibid., 33.

17. Owens, *Dread: The Rastafarians of Jamaica*, 148–49.

18. Nettleford, *Mirror, Mirror: Identity, Race, and Protest in Jamaica*, 137–38.

19. Ibid., 142.

20. Ibid., 143.

21. Beckford and Witter, *Small Garden, Bitter Weed*, 79.

22. Ibid.

23. Ibid., 79–80.

24. Ibid., 80.

25. Ibid.

26. Ibid., 81.

27. Ibid., 81–82.

28. Ibid., 82.

29. Ibid., 83.

30. Ibid., 76.

31. Murrell and Burchell, "Rastafari's Messianic Ideology and Caribbean Theology of Liberation," 392.

32. McClendon, *Ethics*, 163–64.

33. Ibid., 164.

34. Ibid.

35. Ibid., 165.

36. Ibid., 166.

37. Chevannes, *Rastafari and Other African-Caribbean Worldviews*, 161.

38. McClendon, *Ethics*, 167.

39. Ibid., 167.

40. Ibid., 168.

41. Davis, *Emancipation Still Comin'*, 118.

42. Cone, *Black Theology and Black Power*, 8.

43. Ibid., 12.

44. Davis, *Emancipation Still Comin'*, 118–19.

45. Cone, *God of the Oppressed*, 105.

46. Cooper, *Noises in the Blood*, 122.

47. Malcolm X quoted in Cone, *Black Theology and Black Power*, 18.

48. King, *Why We Can't Wait*, quoted in *A Testament of Hope*, ed. Washington, 524.

49. Carmichael and Hamilton, *Black Power*, 31–32.

50. Ibid., 47.

51. Cone, *Black Theology and Black Power*, 48.

52. Edmonds, *Rastafari*, 88.

53. Ibid.

54. Rodney quoted in Campbell, *Rasta and Resistance*, 128–29.

55. Edmonds, *Rastafari*, 89.

56. Campbell, *Rasta and Resistance*, 132.

57. Edmonds, *Rastafari*, 89.

58. Ibid.

59. Rodney quoted in Campbell, *Rasta and Resistance*, 133.

60. Nettleford, *Mirror, Mirror*, 151.

61. Ibid., 154, 156.

62. Cooper, *Noises in the Blood*, 130.

63. Redwood, *Pastoral Care in a Market Economy*, 2.

64. Davis, *Emancipation Still Comin'*, 80.

65. Ibid., 83.

66. Pollard, *Dread Talk*, 26–27.

67. Ibid., 27.

68. Homiak, "Dub History: Soundings on Rastafari Livity and Language."

69. Pollard, *Dread Talk*, 35.

70. Owens, *Dread: The Rastafarians of Jamaica*, 184.

71. Cooper, *Noises in the Blood*, 123.

Chapter 6. Reggae and Rastafari

1. Taylor and Henry, *Marley and Me*, 23–24.

2. Ibid., 24.

3. Cooper, *Noises in the Blood*, 120–21.

4. Taylor and Henry, *Marley and Me*, 26–27.

5. Steffens, "Bob Marley: Rasta Warrior," 257.

6. Cooper, *Noises in the Blood*, 119.

7. Middleton, "Identity and Subversion in Babylon," 189.

8. Ibid., 185.

9. Ibid., 186.

10. Chuck D, *Fight the Power*, 31.

11. Middleton, "Identity and Subversion in Babylon," 187.

12. Cooper, *Noises in the Blood*, 123.

13. Middleton, "Identity and Subversion in Babylon," 186.

14. Chuck D, *Fight the Power*, 36.

15. King quoted in Washington, *A Testament of Hope*, 600.

16. King quoted ibid., 524.

17. Steffens, "Bob Marley: Rasta Warrior," 263.

18. Middleton, "Identity and Subversion in Babylon," 187.

19. Selassie quoted in Campbell, *Rasta and Resistance*, 142.

20. Ibid., 143.

21. Pinn, *Why Lord?* 131.

22. Ibid.

23. Middleton, "Identity and Subversion in Babylon," 186.

24. Pulis, "Up-Full Sounds: Language, Identity and the Worldview of Rastas," 52.

25. Goldman, "Uptown Ghetto Living," 46.

26. Middleton, "Identity and Subversion in Babylon," 188.

27. Ibid., 190.

28. Ibid., 191.

29. Ibid.

30. Steffens, "Bob Marley: Rasta Warrior," 260.

31. Tosh quoted in White, *Catch a Fire*, 301.

32. Ibid.

33. Ibid., 303.

34. Marley quoted in Taylor and Henry, *Marley and Me*, 94.

35. Campbell, *Rasta and Resistance*, 141.

36. Edmonds, *Rastafari*, 111.

37. Fergusson, "So Much Things to Say: The Journey of Bob Marley," 56.

38. White, *Catch a Fire*, 279.

39. Ibid., 280.

40. Edmonds, *Rastafari*, 112–13.

41. Ibid., 113.

42. Marley quoted in Goldman, "Uptown Ghetto Living," 40.

43. Wailer quoted in Steffens, "Bob Marley: Rasta Warrior," 253.

Conclusion. Identity and Salvation

1. Boyne, "'Bling-Bling,' Christianity Runs Things," *Sunday Gleaner*, July 20, 2003.

Notes

2. Ibid.

3. Cooke, "Panel Discusses Making Rasta Business Rasta Returns," *Star,* July 18, 2003.

4. Ibid.

5. Ibid.

6. Boyne, "'Bling-Bling,' Christianity Runs Things," *Sunday Gleaner,* July 20, 2003.

7. Owens, *Dread: The Rastafarians of Jamaica,* 172.

8. Ibid., 173.

9. Ibid., 173–74.

Bibliography

Alleyne, Mervyn. *Roots of Jamaican Culture*. London: Pluto Press, 1988.

Angell, Stephen Ward. *Bishop Henry McNeal Turner and African-American Religion in the South*. Knoxville: University of Tennessee Press, 1992.

Augier, Roy, Rex Nettleford, and M. G. Smith. *Report on Rastafari Movement in Kingston, Jamaica*. Kingston: Institute of Social and Economic Research, 1960.

Barrett, Leonard E. *The Rastafarians*. Boston: Beacon Press, 1997.

————. *Soul-Force*. Garden City, N.Y.: Anchor Press/Doubleday, 1974.

Beckford, George, and Michael Witter. *Small Garden, Bitter Weed*. Kingston: University of the West Indies Press, 1991.

Beckwith, Martha Warren. *Black Roadways*. New York: Negro University Press, 1929.

Bennett, Hazel, and Phillip Sherlock. *The Story of the Jamaican People*. Kingston: Ian Randle Publishers, 1998.

Bilby, Kenneth. "The Holy Herb: Notes on the Background of Cannabis in Jamaica." In *Caribbean Quarterly* Rastafari Monograph 2000, 67–81. Kingston: University of the West Indies, 2000.

Bishton, Derek. *Blackheart Man: A Journey into Rasta*. London: Chatto and Windus, 1986.

Brathwaite, Edward. *The Development of Creole Society in Jamaica 1770–1820*. Oxford: Clarendon Press, 1971.

Burton, Richard D. E. *Afro-Creole*. Ithaca, N.Y.: Cornell University Press, 1997.

Campbell, Horace. *Rasta and Resistance*. Trenton, N.J.: Africa World Press, 1987.

Carmichael, Stokely, and Charles V. Hamilton. *Black Power*. New York: Random House, 1967.

Cashmore, Ernest. *Rastaman: The Rastafarian Movement in England*. London: George Allen and Unwin, 1979.

Chang, Kevin O., and Wayne Chen. *Reggae Routes*. Kingston: Ian Randle Publishers, 1998.

Chevannes, Barry, ed. *Rastafari and Other African-Caribbean Worldviews*. London: Macmillan, 1995.

———. *Rastafari Roots and Ideology*. Syracuse, N.Y.: Syracuse University Press, 1995.

Chuck D and Jah Yusuf. *Fight the Power*. New York: Bantam Doubleday Dell Publishing Group, 1997.

Cone, James. *Black Theology and Black Power*. New York: Seabury Press, 1969.

———. *A Black Theology of Liberation*. Philadelphia and New York: Lippincott, 1970.

———. *God of the Oppressed*. New York: Seabury Press, 1975.

Cooper, Carolyn. *Noises in the Blood*. London: Macmillan Education, 1993.

Curtin, Philip D. *Two Jamaicas*. New York: Atheneum Press, 1970.

Davis, Kortright. *Emancipation Still Comin'*. Maryknoll, N.Y.: Orbis, 1990.

Edmonds, Ennis Barrington. *Rastafari*. New York: Oxford University Press, 2003.

———. "The Structure and Ethos of Rastafari." In *Chanting Down Babylon*, ed. Nathaniel Samuel Murrell, William David Spencer, and Adrian Anthony McFarlane. Philadelphia: Temple University Press, 1998.

Fergusson, Isaac. "So Much Things to Say: The Journey of Bob Marley." In *Reggae, Rasta, Revolution*, ed. Chris Potash. New York: Schirmer, 1997.

Garvey, Amy Jacques. *Garvey and Garveyism*. Kingston: United Printers, 1963.

———, ed. *Philosophy and Opinions of Marcus Garvey*. Vol. 1. New York: Atheneum, 1974.

Goldman, Vivien. "Uptown Ghetto Living: Bob Marley in His Own Backyard." In *Reggae, Rasta, Revolution*, ed. Chris Potash. New York: Schirmer, 1997.

Gossai, Hemchand, and Nathaniel S. Murrell, eds. *Religion, Culture, and Tradition in the Caribbean*. New York: St. Martin's Press, 2000.

Grant, E. Velma. "CH 661: Theology of the Black Church." Research paper. Pitts Theology Library, Emory University, Atlanta, 2003.

Henry, Paget. "Rastafarianism and the Reality of Dread." In *Existence in Black*, ed. Lewis R. Gordon. New York: Routledge, 1997.

Hill, Robert A. "Dread History: Leonard P. Howell and Millenarian Visions in Early Rastafarian Religions in Jamaica." *Epoché: Journal of the History of Religions at UCLA* 9 (1981):31–70.

Hinton, John Howard. *Memoirs of William Knibb*. London: Houlston and Stoneman, 1847.

Homiak, John P. "Dub History: Soundings on Rastafari Livity and Language." In *Rastafari and Other African-Caribbean Worldviews*, ed. Barry Chevannes. London: Macmillan, 1995.

Johnson-Hill, Jack A. *I-Sight the World of Rastafari*. Lanham, Md.: Scarecrow Press, 1995.

King, Martin Luther, Jr. *Why We Can't Wait*. New York: Harper and Row, 1963.

————. *Where Do We Go from Here: Chaos or Community.* New York: Harper and Row, 1967.

Lake, Obiagele. *Rastafari Women: Subordination in the Midst of Liberation Theology.* Durham, N.C.: Carolina Academic Press, 1998.

Lawson, Winston. *Religion and Race.* New York: Peter Lang, 1996.

Lewis, M. G. *Journal of a West Indian Proprietor.* Boston and New York: Houghton Mifflin, 1929.

Lewis, Rupert. *Marcus Garvey.* Trenton, N.J.: Africa World Press, 1998.

————. "Marcus Garvey and the Early Rastafarians: Continuity and Discontinuity." In *Chanting Down Babylon,* ed. Nathaniel Samuel Murrell, William David Spencer, and Adrian Anthony McFarlane. Philadelphia: Temple University Press, 1998.

Lewis, William F. *Soul Rebels.* Prospect Heights, Ill.: Waveland Press, 1993.

Mack, Douglas R. *From Babylon to Rastafari.* Jamaica and Trinidad: Research Associates School Times Publication, 1999.

Mbiti, John S. *African Religions and Philosophy.* 2nd rev. and enl. ed. Portsmouth, N.H.: Heinemann, 1990.

McClendon, James Wm., Jr. *Ethics.* Nashville: Abingdon Press, 1986.

Middleton, Richard J. "Identity and Subversion in Babylon." In *Religion, Culture, and Tradition in the Caribbean,* ed. Hemchand Gossai and Nathaniel Samuel Murrell. New York: St. Martin's Press, 2000.

Morrish, Ivor. *Obeah, Christ, and Rastaman.* Greenwood, S.C: Attic Press, 1992.

Mosely, Leonard. *Haile Selassie: The Conquering Lion.* London: Weidenfeld and Nicolson, 1964.

Munroe, Trevor, and Don Robotham. *Struggles of the Jamaican People.* Kingston: E. P. Printery, 1977.

Murrell, Nathaniel S., and Taylor K. Burchell. "Rastafari's Messianic Ideology and Caribbean Theology of Liberation." In *Chanting Down Babylon,* ed. Nathaniel Samuel Murrell, William David Spencer, and Adrian Anthony McFarlane. Philadelphia: Temple University Press, 1998.

Murrell, Nathaniel S., William David Spencer, and Adrian Anthony McFarlane, eds. *Chanting Down Babylon.* Philadelphia: Temple University Press, 1998.

Nettleford, Rex. "Discourse on Rastafarian Reality." In *Chanting Down Babylon,* ed. Nathaniel Samuel Murrell, William David Spencer, and Adrian Anthony McFarlane. Philadelphia: Temple University Press, 1998.

————. *Mirror, Mirror: Identity, Race, and Protest in Jamaica.* Kingston: LMH Publishing, 2001.

Owens, Joseph. *Dread: The Rastafarians of Jamaica.* Kingston: Sangster's Publishing, 1975.

Patterson, Orlando. *The Children of Sisyphus.* London: Heinemann, 1964.

Phillippo, James M. *Jamaica: Its Past and Present State.* London: Unwin Brothers, 1843.

Pinn, Anthony B. *Why Lord?* New York: Continuum, 1999.

Pollard, Velma. *Dread Talk*. Kingston: Canoe Press/University of the West Indies, 1995.

Potash, Chris, ed. *Reggae, Rasta, Revolution: Jamaican Music from Ska to Dub*. New York: Schirmer Books, 1997.

Prahlad, Anand S. *Reggae Wisdom*. Jackson: University Press of Mississippi, 2001.

Pulis, John W. "Up-Full Sounds: Language, Identity and the Worldview of Rastas." In *Reggae, Rasta, Revolution*, ed. Chris Potash. New York: Schirmer, 1997.

Raboteau, Albert. *Slave Religion*. New York: Oxford University Press, 1978.

Rodney, Walter. *Groundings with My Brothers*. London: Bogle L'Ouverture Press, 1969.

Rowe, Maureen. "Gender and Family Relations in Rastafari: A Personal Perspective." In *Chanting Down Babylon*, ed. Nathaniel Samuel Murrell, William David Spencer, and Adrian Anthony McFarlane. Philadelphia: Temple University Press, 1998.

———. "The Woman in Rastafari." In *Caribbean Quarterly* Rastafari Monograph 2000, 140–49. Kingston: University of the West Indies.

Russell, Horace O. "The Reactions of the Baptist Missionary Society and the Jamaican Baptist Union to the Morant Bay Rebellion of 1865." *Journal of Church and State* 35 (summer 1993):593–603.

Scott, William, R. *The Sons of Sheba's Race*. Bloomington and Indianapolis: Indiana University Press, 1993.

Simpson, George Eaton. "Personal Reflections on Rastafari in West Kingston in the Early 1950s." In *Chanting Down Babylon*, ed. Nathaniel Samuel Murrell, William David Spencer, and Adrian Anthony McFarlane. Philadelphia: Temple University Press, 1998.

Spencer, William David. *Dread Jesus*. London: SPCK, 1999.

Steffens, Roger. "Bob Marley: Rasta Warrior." In *Chanting Down Babylon*, ed. Nathaniel Samuel Murrell, William David Spencer, and Adrian Anthony McFarlane. Philadelphia: Temple University Press, 1998.

Stewart, Dianne Marie Burrowes. "The Evolution of African-Derived Religions in Jamaica: Toward a Caribbean Theology of Collective Memory." Ph.D. diss. Union Theological Seminary, New York, 1997.

Stewart, Robert J. *Religion and Society in Post-Emancipation Jamaica*. Knoxville: University of Tennessee Press, 1992.

Suits, Bernard. *The Grasshopper: Games, Life, and Utopia*. Toronto: University of Toronto Press, 1978.

Sunshine, Catherine. *The Caribbean: Survival, Struggle, and Sovereignty*. Washington: EPICA Press, 1996.

Tafari, Jubulani. "The Rastafari: Successors of Marcus Garvey." In *Caribbean Quarterly* Rastafari Monograph 2000, 1–15. Kingston: University of the West Indies, 2000.

Taylor, Don, and Mike Henry. *Marley and Me*. Kingston: Kingston Publishers, 1994.

Washington, James, ed. *A Testament of Hope*. New York: Harper and Row, 1986.

White, Timothy. *Catch a Fire*. London: Omnibus Press, 1983.

Williams, Ishon Ras. "The Seven Principles of Rastafari." In *Caribbean Quarterly* Rastafari Monograph 2000, 16–22. Kingston: University of the West Indies, 2000.

Wilmore, Gayraud. *Black Religion and Black Radicalism*. New York: Doubleday, 1972.

Index

Game: practices and, 145; as theoretical construct to analyze social reality, 141–43

Ganja: association of with violence, 101–2; Bible and, xv; chalice and, 97–98; East Indian community and, 99–100; essential nature of person and, 100, 101; Garvey on, 122; as illegal, 98–99, 100–101, 102–3; importance of, 62; in Jamaican society, 99; Pinnacle community and, 61; reasoning and, 98, 99; smoking of as religious ritual, 96–98

Garden, view of, 92

Garvey, Amy Jacques, 117

Garvey, Marcus Mosiah: Africa and, 43–44; appeal of, 35; Bedward and, 30; black nationalism and, 119; black religious groups and, 35–36; on ganja, 122; on God, 33–34; Jamaican people and, 40; liberation theology and, 124; Love and, 117–18; middle class and, 36–37; migration of, 118; political context of, 123–24; political office and, 127; as prophet, 2, 45, 69, 122–23; racial discrimination and, 31, 116–17; Rastafarians and, 39; repatriation and, 30–31, 48; Selassie and, 36–37, 45, 119–21; teachings of, 32–33, 82–83

Garveyism: Howell and, 60–61; Rastafarians and, 36; as social movement, 121, 123

Genesis 49:10, 70–71

Gibb, George, 10

Gibb, Thomas, 86

God: as African, 147, 161; as foreigner, 3–4; identity of, 103, 195–98; as Jamaican, 161–62; love of, 73–74; search for, 70; Selassie as, 41–42; views of, 33–34. *See also* Blackness of God

God-talk, 104, 126–29

Gordon, Robert, 23–24

Grant, Velma, 112–13

The Grasshopper: Games, Life, and Utopia (Suits), 141

Griffiths, Marcia, 184

Groundings, 158

Groundings with My Brothers (Rodney), 158

Hairstyles, 156–57. *See also* Dreadlocks

Health care, 18–19

Henry, Claudius, 45–46, 76

Henry, Paget, 83

Henry, Roman, 30

Herbal healing, 96

Herschell, Victor, 25

Hibbert, Joseph N., 40, 63–64

Hill, Frank, 76

Hill, Robert: on Howell, 1–2; on Rastafari origins, xvi; on Selassie, 70; on Twelve Tribes of Israel, 154

Hinds, Robert: arrest of, 104; Earlington and, 64; Garvey and, 40; George VI and, 42; King of King's Mission, 65–67; Selassie and, 41, 74

History: focus on African at expense of Jamaican, 159–61; of people, and biblical, 181

Hoilett, Rupert, 185–86

Holy herb. *See* ganja

House, 88–89

Howell, Leonard P.: arrest of, 59, 104; commune of, 43; ganja and, 61; Garveyism and, 60–61; Hill on, 1–2; Hinds and, 65; leadership and influence of, 62–63; preaching of, 2; Ras Tafari and, 40; Selassie and, 2, 41–42, 44; on taxes, 104; teachings of, 41–42, 61. *See also* Pinnacle commune

Hutchins, Edward, 25

Hylton, Edward, 14

I and I consciousness: Babylon and, 128–29; basis for, 90–91; black liberation theology and, 120–21; dreadlocks and, 105; interpretation of, 190; as key to identity and ethos, 88, 190–92; liberation, repatriation, and, 128

Identity, Rasta: Bobo community and, 73; early Rastafari and, 103; hermeneutic of return and, 152; history and, 181; I and I consciousness and, 88, 190–92; whites and, 82

"Identity and Subversion in Babylon" (Middleton), 178, 180–81

I-language, 83

Imitation, 167–68

Incarnational theology, 126–27
Independent Methodists, 23
Individualism, 89–90, 129, 190
Industry in Jamaica, 134–35
Integration, 150–51
International force, Rastafarianism as, xiii–xiv
International Monetary Fund, 135, 163
Intersubjectivity, 88, 90, 129. *See also* I and I consciousness
Isaiah 43:3, 47
Israelites, Rastas as, 67, 72, 75. *See also* Twelve Tribes of Israel
Ital living: food and, 94–96; ganja and, 96–102; herbal healing and, 96; as principle, 48–49, 93–94

Jah, Rastas as taking on form of, 84. *See also* Blackness of God; God
Jamaica. *See* Babylon
Jamaica Advocate (newspaper), 117
Jamaica Broadcast Corporation, 80
Jamaican history, 159–61
Jamaican Times, 43
Jamaican uprising of 1938, 40, 42–43
Jeremiah 46:9, 47
Johnson, William, 14
John the Baptist, 10–11
Jordan, Edward, 23
Journal of a West Indian Proprietor (Lewis), 6–7
Just society, creation of, 162–63

King, Martin Luther, Jr., 151, 174–75
King of King's Mission, 65–67
Kingston, Jamaica, 54–55
Knibb, William, 15, 22
Knowledge and salvation, 195–98

Labor, free, and economics, 17–18
Labor strike, 13–14
Lake, Obiagele: on head covering for women, 111; *Rastafari Women: Subordination in the Midst of Liberation Theology,* 50–51, 113–14; on women as polluted, 112
Land: attitude toward, 93; communalism and, 143–44; Love and, 117–18; religious

significance of, 19; respect for, 92–93; uprising of 1938 and, 40
Language, 83, 144–45, 165–67
Lawson, Winston, 8
Leader system, 10, 11–12, 86
Lewis, George, 9–10, 86
Lewis, M. G., *Journal of a West Indian Proprietor,* 6–7
Lewis, Rupert, 35–36, 121
Lewis, William, *Soul Rebels,* 39
Liberation: African history and, 153–54; music and, 184; religion and, 178; repatriation and, 127–28, 140, 197–98
Liberation theology: Garvey and, 124; Rastafari and, 4–5, 113–15
Liele, George: church of, 47; early life of, 86; life of, 9; religion and, 10
Lion symbol, 51, 106–8, 110
Liquor vs. ganja, 100–101
"Living holy," 29–30
Livingston (Wailer), Bunny, 171, 173, 187
Livity, 94
Love, Robert, 117–18
Love and black power, 151–52

Malcolm X, 150, 151
"Mammy," 12, 86
Manley, Michael, 182, 187
Manley, Norman, 42
Mansion, 89
Marley, Bob: Bobo community and, 72–73; career of, 184; *Children Playing in the Streets* album, 183–84; "Crazy Baldhead," 180; early life of, 169–70; "Exodus," 171, 178; *Exodus* album, 149–50, 172, 188; as father of reggae, 169; funeral of, 186–87; "No Woman No Cry," 160–61, 180, 184; "One love," 181–82; One Love Peace Concert and, 182, 183; Order of Distinction, xiii; Order of Merit, 186; Planno and, 170; "Redemption Song," 173, 178; *Redemption Song* album, 172, 188; Selassie and, 176; *Survival* album, 167, 183; "Them Belly Full But We Hungry," 188; Twelve Tribes and, 185–86; "War," 175
Marley, Rita, 184
Marley Museum, 106–7

prophet, 2, 45, 69, 122–23; Ital living, 48–49, 93–102; reasoning, 49–50. *See also* Repatriation

Prosperity gospel, 191–92

Protest, 152

Psalm 68:31, 2, 35, 47, 120

Psalm 72:9–11, 70

Quality of life, 136–37

Raboteau, Albert, 27

Race consciousness, 117

Racialism, 21–24

Racism, 146, 174–75

Ras Tafari. *See* Selassie, Haile

Rastafari and Other African-Caribbean Worldviews (Chevannes, ed.), xvi

Rastafari Global Reasoning conference, 193

Rastafari Women: Subordination in the Midst of Liberation Theology (Lake), 50–51

Ras Tafioritta, 106–7

Reasoning, 49–50, 98, 99

Rebellions: Coral Gardens, 101; maroon, of 1760, 7–8, 130; in Morant Bay, 17, 25–26; Myal and, 9; Native Baptists and, 12–13; uprising of 1938 and, 40, 42–43

Redemption Song album, 172, 188

"Redemption Song" (Marley), 173, 178

Red X tapes (Tosh), 171–72

Reggae music: community ethos of, 170–71; creation, doctrine of, 181–82; Dread Talk and, 166; embracing of, 185–86; liberation and, 184; poverty and, 188; power of, 187–88; repatriation and, 177–78; resistance, transformation, and, 179–80; themes of, 170, 180–81; women and, 114

Religion: in Africa, 5, 193; African expressions of, 20–21; blacks and, 17, 19–21, 35–36; as embodied, 130; land and, 19; liberation and, 178; Myal, 8–9, 11, 20; obeah, 6–8, 20, 95; social and political change and, 5–12. *See also* Church

Religious Cults of the Caribbean (Simpson), xv

Repatriation: criticism of, 76; emphasis on, 77–79; Garvey and, 30–31; Howell and, 2; liberation and, 127–28, 140, 197–98; as principle of Rastafari, 48; Rastas and,

124–25; reggae music and, 177–78; retrieval of past and, 131. *See also* Ethiopia

Resistance and reggae music, 179–80

Responsibility, mutual, 157–58

Revelation, 50

Revelation 5:5, 44, 70

Revelation 19:16, 70

Revival Church: Bedward and, 27, 29–30; description of, 26–28; Hinds and, 65–66; Rastafari and, 85–86; spirit and, 86–87; survival of, xiii; women in, 56

Rodney, Walter: banishment of, 154, 155; black power movement and, 152–53, 177; teachings of, 153–54, 156; youth culture and, 55

Rowe, Maureen, 51–53

Rude-boy culture, 54–55

Rules and games, 142, 143

Salt, 94

Salvation, knowledge and, 195–98

Scott, William R., 47–48

Scripture: questions in, 196; selective use of, 57. *See also* Bible; *specific verses*

Seaga, Edward, 182, 186–87

Selassie, Haile: belief in, 44, 70–71, 74–75, 104; as the Christ, 28–29; coronation of, 40, 59, 68–69; Garvey and, 36–37, 45, 119–21; Hinds and, 66; Howell and, 2, 41–42; speech by, 175–76; visit to Jamaica by, 78–79, 125; war with Italy and, 121

Shaming, 130–31

Sharp, Samuel "Daddy," 13, 14, 15, 16, 86

Simpson, George Eaton, xv, 52–53, 63

Slavery: Baptist War and, 13, 16; body, soul, and, 27–28, 129–30; emancipation of 1838, 17, 25; obeah and, 6; shaming and, 130–31; voice and, 187–88

Small businesses, 137–38

Smith, M. G., 76

Social change: Rastas and, 133–34, 177–78; reggae artists and, 175, 185; religion and, 5–12; self-distancing from, 192–93; spiritual approach to, 139–40

Social context of game, 142–43

Socioeconomic situation in Jamaica in 1930s, 59–60, 68–69

Noel Leo Erskine is associate professor of theology and ethics in the Candler School of Theology at Emory University. He is the author of *Decolonizing Theology: A Caribbean Perspective* and *King among the Theologians*.